TOEFL® TEST
模擬試験&
「レクチャー問題」
リスニング徹底練習
300問

SANSHUSHA

付属 MP3 ディスクについて

- 付属の MP3 ディスクには、本書の「模擬試験問題 Listening Section」「模擬試験問題 Speaking Section」「模擬試験問題 Writing Section」「リスニング・スペシャルトレーニング問題」「模擬試験解答の手引き Listening Section」「模擬試験解答の手引き Speaking Section」の各部分の音声が収録されています。

- MP3 ディスクの収録内容は以下の通りです。

トラック番号	内　容	ページ
001 - 040	模擬試験 Listening Section 問題	40 - 49
041 - 048	模擬試験 Speaking Section 問題	50 - 52
049	模擬試験 Writing Section 問題	54
050 - 409	リスニング・スペシャルトレーニング 問題	58 - 126
410 - 415	模擬試験 Speaking Section 解答例	66 - 77（別冊）

- 吹込者

    Howard Colefield

    Rachel Walzer

- 吹込時間

    415トラック

    3時間45分

- 本書付属 CD を権利者の許諾なく賃貸業に使用することや、収録されている音声データを複製、およびインターネット等電子メディアへ無断転載することを禁じます。
- ディスクに汚れが生じた場合は、市販の CD 用クリーナー剤をご使用ください。

> - MP3データ入りの CD です。パソコン、MP3対応 CD プレーヤーなどで再生できます。通常のオーディオ CD プレーヤーでは再生できませんので、ご注意ください。

はじめに

　本書は TOEFL iBT 初級者の方が、英語で講義を聞き、そこで得た情報を元に設問に答える、いわゆる「レクチャー問題」に慣れることを主眼に作成されており、短い講義から比較的長い講義まで全60講義300問題の演習が可能になっています。内容そのものは初級者の方にも使っていただけるよう配慮しておりますが、音声速度は本試験と同様になっており、レクチャー問題の入門書として最適だと思います。また、英文と和訳だけではなく、やや難易度の高い頻出英単語、熟語、慣用表現のリスト等も掲載し、受験者の皆様の効率的な英単語学習をサポートしたいと考えています。

　TOEFL iBT 120点満点中の65点がリスニングに関連する問題です。そのうちの45点はレクチャー問題ですので、特に講義聞き取りに特化した本書第2部の問題を作成しました。120点満点中の45点という配点の大きさからも、講義聞き取りのスキルはTOEFL iBT の最重要点であることがわかります。また、実際に TOEFL iBT 受験者の多くから「講義の聞き取りが難しい」という声があるにも関わらず、それに特化した書籍があまりない点も考慮しました。多くの受験者の、もっとリスニング練習用の教材が欲しいというご要望にもお応えできれば幸いです。

　本書には Reading, Listening, Speaking, Writing の TOEFL iBT の4セクション全てを収めた模擬試験が付いております。まだ TOEFL iBT を受験されたことがない方は、本番のテスト内容の把握のために一通り解いていただくことをお勧めします。初回は答え合わせのみで済ませて、日本語訳やスクリプトは極力読まないようにしましょう。リスニング問題を一通り演習してから、再度模擬試験を受け、どの程度聞き取り能力が上昇しているかを御確認ください。2度目からは Reading と Listening の内容を和訳、英文、音声の順番で確認しながら学習することをお勧めします。日本語に対応する英文をよく理解し、Listening では英文と音声が一致して聞けるようになるまで、何度でも練習をするようにしていただければと思います。

執筆編集　中野 正夫
イフ外語学院　学院長

目次

付属 MP3ディスクについて
2

はじめに
3

本書の使用法
5

TOEFL® iBT 攻略法
9

模擬試験（第1部）の採点方法
10

第1部
模擬試験
問題

Reading Section
22

Listening Section
40

Speaking Section
50

Writing Section
53

第2部
リスニング・スペシャルトレーニング
問題

58

本書の使用法

- 本書は 1 回分の TOEFL iBT 模擬試験と 60 パッセージ 300 問の英文の講義問題、和訳、英語リスニング音声によって成り立っている TOEFL iBT 対策問題集です。

- TOEFL iBT 試験の Listening Part の実力強化のため、本書をご活用ください。

- 全 60 パッセージの英語長文が和訳と共に掲載されておりますので、英文スクリプトを読み込んでいただくことで、英単語力と長文読解の基礎力養成にも効果があります。

- 初級者の方は、最初に和訳を読み、それから英文を読んで英単語力と読解力の養成から学習していただくと効果的です。「リスニング・スペシャルトレーニング」最初の 20 問の講義は、いきなり問題を解くのではなく、上記のような学習後の聞き取り問題として活用されるとよいでしょう。

- これらの講義問題は大学キャンパス内での講義を中心としたものとなっていますが、上記のような学習法をしていただくことで、中学生レベルの英語力からでも充分にリスニング演習が可能です。

- 単語帳の学習では忘れてしまうことも多い英単語ですが、長文のストーリーを読んでから聞くことにより、さらに高い記憶定着率を実現できます。

- TOEFL iBT の試験本番の Listening ではメモ取りが可能です。講義問題で、メモがなくては答えきれない問題も出題されます。中級者以上の方は最初から、初級者の方も中盤以降から、聞き取れた内容を書きとめる訓練をしてみてください。

- 「模擬試験」「リスニング・スペシャルトレーニング」の各リスニング問題には、会話や講義の音声を再度聞き、それについての質問に答えるタイプの問題があります。再度音声を聞く箇所には、問題文の後に♪マークを入れてあります。

  例) **Why does the woman say this?** ♪

模擬試験、リスニング・スペシャルトレーニングにおける
効果的な学習の仕方

　模擬試験はTOEFL iBTの全体像を理解するために解いてみてください。まず一度、模擬試験を解き、答え合わせをして自身の現在の実力を確かめ、その後、ある程度リスニングの訓練をしてから、更なる活用をされることをお勧めします。難易度は実際の試験よりも少し難しくなっています。復習の際にはReadingやListeningの和訳、英文を読み込んでください。

　Readingのポイントは、構文の難易度がTOEICよりも難しく長くなっており、時間配分が重要なことです。その点をまず理解できれば、最初の難関はクリアできます。全ての問題を時間内に解くことが大前提です。また出題傾向が決まっており、難易度の高い問題、時間がかかる問題も決まっていることを理解し、一つずつその対策を立ててください。また14問中の1～2問、和訳を読んでも一目では正解が理解できないような問題もあるかもしれません。このような難易度理解が時間配分を検討するための参考になると思います。

　Listening問題の英文スクリプトはReadingよりは易しいですが、聞き取り時間は本番の試験と同様の長さになっています。模擬テストとして何度か繰り返し演習して、ある程度問題の正解を覚えてしまった後でも、リスニングの集中力と持続力の養成のために何度も音声聞き取り教材、メモ取り教材として活用していただけます。

　Speaking、**Writing**はサンプルアンサーと採点表を参考にしていただくことになります。本書はあくまで読解、聞き取りを含むIntegrated問題への対応を主にしていますが、設問に対する自身の意見を述べる必要があるIndependent問題に関しても、採点基準を明示することで対策を示しています。以下の情報を参考にしてください。

▶ Speaking のカテゴリー

Familiar topics
1、2問目
Campus situations
3、5問目
Academic course content
4、6問目

の三種類があります。

Familiar topics には聞き取りが無く、設問の課題に対して自分がどう考えるかを答える問題です。

Campus situations は二人の生徒同士の会話から解答する問題ですが、1問は自分が彼らの会話に対してどう考えるのかを問う問題、そしてもう1問は聞き取った内容を正確に述べる問題です。

Academic course content は大学内での講義を聴き取り、その内容を正確に話すということが趣旨になっている問題です。

Familiar topics は、Independent 問題という、自身の考えを限られた時間の中でまとめて話すことができるかが問われるものです。初めて TOEFL iBT を受験される方に対するアドバイスとしては、全てのパターンに対応できるような意見を予め用意しておくのはとても難しいことですが、ある程度は対応できるよう、日常的に色々な選択に対する自身の考えを述べられるような練習をしてみてください。難しく考える必要はなく、様々な事柄に対して「私はこういった理由で、このように考えます」という意見を常に持つようにするだけです。日常的にそれができている方は、話をまとめて伝えやすくなります。

Campus situations 、**Academic course content** の2セクションでは読解、講義聞き取りの2点から正確に情報を抜き出すことが重要です。初級者の方は和文、英文、音声の識別、を反復して数をこなすことで読解、聞き取りの能力を高めて下さい。中級以上の方でも、Reading, Integrated 問題のパートで、Fair の評価を超えることができて

いない方にはこの学習方法をお勧めします。

　基本的なことではありますが、Speaking 試験の最大の敵は沈黙です。Independent では自身の意見を、Integrated では得られた情報を、可能な限り話し続けられるよう練習をしてください。

▶ Writing のカテゴリー

Independent

　基本的には二者択一問題、またはテーマに対して賛成か反対かを述べる問題となります。ですが、2014年の TOEFL iBT では「あなたにとって幸福とはなにか？」のような上記に分類できない問題も出題されています。サンプルアンサーから文章構造の作り方を学習してください。

Integrated

　限られた時間内に個々の段落の主題を理解する必要があります。講義聞き取りではこの主題に対しての教授の言及部分について、受験者が書くことになります。まずは主題を理解する読解力が必要ですので、模擬テストの Reading を学習し、聞き取りの内容がいかにそれらの主題に言及しているかを学習すれば、問題の本質を理解し効率的な解答をすることが可能です。

TOEFL iBT 攻略法

　TOEFL iBT の最大の特色は、聞き取り能力への配点が非常に大きいことです。120点満点のうち、Listening Section の配点が30点、英文を聞き取り、答える Speaking Section の Integrated（統合問題）への配点が20点、Writing Section の講義を聞き取り、その内容に関して解答する統合問題への配点が15点となり、合計では120点満点中の実に65点が聞き取り能力と直接関連した配点になっています。

　また TOEIC で950点程度得点できる人でも、TOEFL iBT の Listening Part では30点満点中の20点未満からスタートするケースも珍しくありません。本書で聞き取り能力を強化して、Listening Part を攻略していただければと思います。TOEFL iBT の聞き取りの難易度が高い理由は下記に起因しています。

　TOEFL iBT では formal な音声よりも casual な音声を重視しています。その結果、
- 発声されていない音が非常に多い。
- 複数の子音と母音がほぼ同時に発声されている。
　　例えば Flower では F 音、L 音、W 音、R 音がほぼ同時に発声され、個々の音声が時系列に沿って発声されない。同時に「フラワー」という単語の母音の内、「フ」の付属母音「ウ」、「ワー」の付属母音「ア」はほとんど発声されません。
- 1つの単語で発声された音が余韻としてその次の単語や、さらにその次の単語の音声にまで影響を与える。
　　例えば "For instance" というフレーズでは "For" の R 音が "instance" の S 音の箇所まで引っ張られることの方が普通です。

　このように複数の音が混じり合うと、個々の音声の発音が異なることに加え、これらが重合してさらに音声の聞き取り、識別の難易度が高くなります。イフ外語学院では、発音訓練により短期間で克服する「音声識別クラス」を開講することで対策をしていますが、本書の利用者は、これらの対策として和文確認、英文確認、音声確認、問題演習に加え、3～10単語ごとの音声チェックを自分で行い、聞き取りにくい箇所をチェックし、そこで発声されていない箇所を確認するという学習法をお勧めします。これを行うと発声されていない箇所が規則性を持つことが理解できるからです。学習効果が薄れますので、音声確認をする際には、最初は英文を見ずに行うようにしてく

ださい。

　本書の音声は、そのような発声されない箇所を多数含みます。講義内容そのものは初級者の方にも対応できるよう作成してありますが、音声識別の訓練としては実際のTOEFL iBTに対応したテキストになっています。

模擬試験（第1部）の採点方法

▶ 模擬試験 Reading Section 採点表

設問に配点を記載している問題以外の正解をそれぞれ1ポイントと計算し、その合計を素点とし、下の表を参考にスコアに換算してください。素点の最高点は47点となります。

素　点	スコア
46〜47	30
44〜45	29
42〜43	28
41	27
39〜40	26
38	25
36〜37	24
34〜35	23
32〜33	22
30〜31	21
29	20
27〜28	19
25〜26	18
23〜24	17
21〜22	16
20	15
18〜19	14
16〜17	13
14〜15	12
12〜13	11
10〜11	10
0〜9	0〜9

▶ 模擬試験 Listening Section 採点表

正解を複数選ぶ問題は全て正解で2ポイント、その他の問題を1ポイントで計算し、その合計を素点とし、下の表を参考にスコアに換算してください。素点の最高点は41点となります。

素　点	スコア
40〜41	30
39	29
37〜38	28
35〜36	27
34	26
32〜33	25
30〜31	24
29	23
28	22
26〜27	21
25	20
23〜24	19
22	18
20〜21	17
19	16
17〜18	15
16	14
14〜15	13
13	12
11〜12	11
0〜10	0〜10

▶ Speaking, Writing section の採点基準について

　Speaking, Writing Section は模擬試験の問題を解いても自己採点をすることがなかなか難しいセクションです。TOEFL iBT 採点官の採点基準をまとめてありますので参考にしてください。スコアの算出法は本来の方法と違いがありますので、実際の点数とは若干の差があります。

Speaking section では、TOEFL iBT の採点官の判断要素として次の3つが挙げられています。**Delivery**（話し方）、**Language Use**（言語の使用法、言葉の選択）、**Topic Development**（話の展開）。これらの要素を4段階で評価することになります。

基本的に評価の仕方は加点式ではなく、問題がある部分が見つかると低い評価になる減点式とされていますので、自分の Speaking 内容を録音して客観的に評価をしてみてください。また、録音した内容を他の人に聞いてもらい、下記の判断基準で評価してもらうこともお勧めします。

イフ外語学院の受講生の得点データを分析すると、Delivery（話し方）の要素の中でも、特に「発音」「話す速度」「空白の時間（沈黙）」での減点が著しいことが判明しています。

本来であれば、評価0というものもありますが、こちらは解答自体の放棄、設問とまったく関係ないことを話している等の評価ですので、ここでは割愛しています。
以降、各セクションの細かい採点基準について見ていきましょう。

▶ Speaking Independent Section の採点基準

評価4

情報が凝縮されており、発音が明朗なことが条件になる。些細な誤りを含むが非常に理解しやすく、問われた内容に即した意義のある解答ができている。
以下の3つのすべての条件と合致すればこの評価となる。

● **Delivery**
　採点者に判りやすい訛りが少ない発音で流暢に話すことができている。少々の言い間違いや沈黙、イントネーションの違和感はあっても、全体的にわかりやすく聞き取ることができる。

● **Language Use**
　文法や語彙を効果的に用いて、基本的な表現を自然に使いこなすことができている。些細な誤りがあっても、意味はしっかりと理解できる。

- **Topic Development**

　設問に沿った解答がされており、話の流れに違和感がない。具体的な因果関係が矛盾なく展開されている。

評価3

発音は上手くないが聞き取りにくいほどではない。課題に沿った解答をしているが、十分な論理展開がされていない。大体の部分は聞き取ることができて、理解も可能であるが話の途中で短い沈黙や躊躇がある。
以下の評価のうち2つ以上の条件に合致すればこの評価となる。

- **Delivery**

　流暢に話せているが、発音やイントネーション、速度といった部分に、聞き手が理解するための努力が必要な場面がある。おおよその話の内容は理解することができる。

- **Language Use**

　ある程度自然に文法や語彙を使用し、自身の考えを論理的に伝えることができる。時折、不正確な文法や単語を使ってしまい全体として見ると完成していないようにとれる。ただし、本人の伝えたい内容は理解できる。

- **Topic Development**

　ほとんどの部分で設問に沿った考えが展開されており、話の流れもまとまっている。ただ具体性、詳細な情報に欠ける点があり、自身の考えを述べている時、話が飛躍してしまってすぐには理解できない部分がある。

評価2

課題に沿って解答する努力は見られるが話の展開が乏しい。主題は適切だが内容が断片的なメモの羅列で、相互関係が意味不明になっている部分がある。
以下のうち2つ以上の条件が合致すればこの評価となる。

- **Delivery**

　多くの沈黙がある。大まかな内容は理解できるが、発音が悪く意味不明な箇所が多い。イントネーションも不自然で、言葉に詰まることも多い。理解するため

には聞き手の努力が必要となる。

● **Language Use**

　ほとんどの部分で単純な文章しか話せていないが、それらを止まりながら話すことはできている。文法や語彙が不足しているため、自身の考えを十分に表現できていない。文法、語彙力の弱さから、短く単純な文章や、一般的な主張がほとんどで、話のつながりのわかりにくさが見受けられる。

● **Topic Development**

　主題を間違えている。または解答は課題に即したものではあるが、自身の意見や話の発展性に欠ける。意思表示自体はしていても、何故自分がそう考えるのかという具体的な事例が無い。もしくは曖昧な例や同じ話の繰り返しが多く、話に脈絡がない。

評価1

音声空白や繰り返しだけで全体時間の3分の1以上になっている。結果として内容が非常に乏しく、一貫性に欠ける。設問主旨に合った解答になっていない。また、発言の大部分について、文法的に理解できないなどの問題点が挙げられる。

以下のうち2つ以上の条件が合致すればこの評価となる。

● **Delivery**

　発音やイントネーションの問題が常にあり、聞き取るのにかなりの努力が必要となる。頻繁に口ごもりや繰り返しがあり、話が中断してしまう。

● **Language Use**

　文法や語彙が不足しているため、自身の考えを表現できておらず、意見の伝達を阻んでいる。問題と関連のない事前に練習した文句を述べ続けている解答もこの評価に合致する。

● **Topic Development**

　主題が抜け落ちたり、全体の一部の情報しか述べられていない状態。全体として基本的な情報を繰り返している状態。

▶ Speaking Integrated Section の採点基準

評価 4

些細な誤りを含むものの話は非常に理解しやすく、問われた内容に即した意義のある解答ができている。
以下の3つの条件のすべてが合致すればこの評価となる。

- **Delivery**
  はっきりとした口調で流暢に話すことができている。少々の言い間違いや沈黙、イントネーションの違和感はあっても、全体的にわかりやすく聞き取ることができる。

- **Language Use**
  文法や語彙を効果的に用いて、基本的な文章や複雑な構造の文章も自然に使いこなすことができている。些細な誤りがあっても、意味はしっかりと理解できる。

- **Topic Development**
  設問の要求する情報を的確に伝えており、話の展開も明確である。多少の文法的な間違いや情報の洩れがあるものの、的確な解答をしている。

評価 3

課題に沿った解答をしているが、十分な論理展開がされていない。大体の部分は聞き取ることができて、理解も可能であるが、話の途中で沈黙や躊躇が目立つ。
以下の2つ以上の条件と合致すればこの評価となる。

- **Delivery**
  流暢に話せているが、発音やイントネーション、速度といった部分に、聞き手が理解するための努力が必要な場面がある。おおよその話の内容は理解することができる。

- **Language Use**
  法や語彙を使用し、自身の考えを論理的に伝えることができる。時折、不正確な文法や単語を使ってしまい、全体として見ると完成していないようにとれる。ただし、本人の伝えたい内容は理解できる。

- **Topic Development**

  大部分では首尾一貫しており、内容に沿った情報が述べられている。ただし、内容に不正確さ、情報の欠如などが見られる。

評価2

課題に沿って解答する努力は見られるが、話の展開が乏しい。何が言いたいのかは理解できるが、話が首尾一貫せず飛躍し、意味不明になっている部分がある。
以下の2つ以上の条件と合致すればこの評価となる。

- **Delivery**

  大まかな内容は理解できるが発音が悪く、イントネーションも不自然で言葉に詰まることも多い。理解するためには聞き手の努力が必要となる。また意味不明な部分もある。

- **Language Use**

  文法や語彙が不足しているため、自身の考えを十分に表現できていない。ほとんどの部分で単純な文章しか話せていないが、それらを流暢に喋ることはできている。文法、語彙力の弱さから、短く単純な文章や一般的な主張がほとんどで、文と文とのつながりのわかりにくさが見受けられる。

- **Topic Development**

  解答は設問に関連した情報を述べているが、明らかに重要な情報が述べられていない。もしくはあいまいな表現を使用している。Reading, Listeningで提供された情報を正確に理解しておらず、そのため解答に整合性がない。

評価1

内容が非常に乏しく一貫性に欠ける。設問に合った解答になっていない。また発言の大部分が理解できないなどの問題点が挙げられる。
以下のうち2つ以上の条件が合致すればこの評価となる。

- **Delivery**

  発音やイントネーションの問題が常にあり、聞き取るのにかなりの努力が必要となる。頻繁に口ごもり、話が中断してしまう。

● **Language Use**

　文法や語彙が非常に不足しているため、自身の考えを表現できておらず、意見の伝達を阻んでいる。事前に練習した文句を述べ続けている解答もこの評価に合致する。

● **Topic Development**

　限定的な情報しか述べられていない。全体としてとても基本的な情報の羅列となっており、設問に記載されている内容を繰り返している状態。

▶ Speaking Section のスコア算出方法

各6問を4段階で評価し、それらを足したスコアを1.25倍します。小数点を切り上げて出た整数が点数となります。

例)
1問目；評価4　　2問目；評価3　　3問目；評価3
4問目；評価4　　5問目：評価3　　6問目：評価2

合計19点×1.25＝23.75点　→　切り上げで24点

▶ Writing Integrated Section の採点基準

評価5

　リスニングから重要な情報をうまく選び出し、それを理路整然と的確にリーディング内の関連情報に結び付けて説明している。解答はリーディング及び講義内容に基づいてよく構成されていて、英単語スペルや文法に小さな間違いがあるものの、内容に不正確な部分はない。

評価4

　リスニングから重要な情報をうまく選び出し、それを理路整然と的確にリーディング内の関連情報に結び付けて説明しているが、講義に含まれない情報が見られる。文

法的なミスやタイプミスなどの些細な間違いが多い場合でも、情報の明確さや関連性がある程度理解できる範囲であればこの評価となる。

評価3

文章量が200ワード以上で、リスニングの重要情報とリーディングの関連情報をある程度伝えられてはいるが、以下のいずれかに合致すればこの評価となる。

- 解答は全体的に課題に沿って書かれているものの、リスニング、リーディングで得た情報の関連付けが不十分である。
- リスニング内の重要な情報が一つも正確に述べられていない。
- 言葉の選択や文法の間違いが頻繁にあり、情報を伝えることに大きな支障をきたしている。

評価2

文章量が200ワードよりも少なく、リスニング情報の一部を述べているが、重要な情報や、リスニングとリーディングの情報の関連性を伝えきれていない。文法、語彙にも問題があり、文意の不明箇所が多い。

以下のいずれか、または複数に合致すればこの評価となる。

- リスニングとリーディングの情報の関連性が完全に欠落している。または誤って記載している。
- リスニング内で述べられた重要情報が複数抜け落ちている。もしくは誤った情報を記載している
- 文法や語彙の誤用が多く文意を把握できない。

評価1

ワード数が100ワード以下になり、以下のいずれか、もしくは両方に合致すればこの評価となる。

- リスニング内の重要な情報についてほとんど、もしくは全く触れていない
- 言語レベルが低く、何について書いているのか理解が難しい。

▶ Writing Independent Section の採点基準

評価 5
以下のほぼ全ての条件と合致すればこの評価となる。

- 設問に沿って主題を捉え、客観的な論理構成で解答している。
- 具体的な事例が、適切なわかりやすい表現で書かれている。
- 話が首尾一貫しており、主題から逸脱する事例やコンセプトが現れない。
- 多種の構文や慣用表現、語彙を適切に用いており、言語能力の高さを示している。
- 些細な英単語や文法の誤りは許容される。

評価 4
以下のほぼ全ての条件と合致すればこの評価となる。

- 設問に沿った内容であるが、結論を導くための論理的、客観的な構成が単純である。
- 構成、論理展開は単純であっても、適切な説明や詳細を含んでいる。
- 個々の段落で重複表現がある。
- 個々の段落で設定した内容に、文全体の主題からの逸脱があり、段落そのものの内容は適切な表現で明確であるが、文章の目的が判わかりにくい。
- 多種の構文や慣用表現、語彙を適切に使用し、適切な説明や詳細を含んでいる。

評価 3
前述の減点に加え、以下の条件のいずれか、または複数と合致すればこの評価となる。

- ワード数が300ワードを大きく下回り、設問主題に対して適切な解答をしているが、具体性に欠ける。
- 文構成が論理的ではなく、主題に対する自分の意見の説明が不明瞭である。
- 語彙、文法で良い箇所もあるが、センテンスの表現が明確でなくなっている場面が多々ある。

評価 2
以下のいずれか、または複数の条件に合致すればこの評価となる。

- 課題に対して話の展開が短く、単純である。
- 構成や考えの脈絡、関連性に欠ける。
- 自身の論点を補足するための具体例が不適切、または不十分。
- 明らかに不適切な用語を文内で使用している。構文、語彙の誤用が多い。

評価 1

以下のいずれかもしくは双方の条件に合致すればこの評価となる。

- 解答が設問の意図に全く、またはほとんど沿っていない。
- 言語レベルが低く、何について書いているのか理解が難しい。

▶ Writing Section のスコア算出方法

それぞれの評価の合計を 3 倍します。

例)
Independent 評価 5、Integrated 評価 4
合計点 9 × 3 = 27 点

模擬試験
問題

Reading Section

22

....

Listening Section

40

....

Speaking Section

50

....

Writing Section

53

Reading Section

Questions 1 - 14

1 In addition to graphite and fullerite, there is one other form of naturally occurring carbon. It is the hardest, most concentrated form, and it is also widely considered to be the most beautiful: diamond. But unlike graphite, diamonds are rarely found in great quantity on the Earth's surface since they can only be formed hundreds of kilometers below the Earth's surface under severe geological pressure. The carbon must be under at least 435,000 psi (30 kilobars) of pressure at a temperature of at least 750 degrees Fahrenheit (400 degrees Celsius). If either the pressure or the heat drops below these points, graphite is formed.

2 From deep within the Earth diamonds are — or were — pushed to the surface in what we call *Kimberlite Pipes*, named after Kimberly, South Africa, where the pipes were first discovered. These are not really pipes at all, but eruptions of magma which force their way upward from deep cracks in the lower part of the Earth's crust, acting much like an elevator, pushed diamonds and many other rocks and minerals through the mantle very quickly. Such powerful eruptions occurred several hundred million years ago and the magma in these eruptions originated at depths up to three times deeper than the magma which is the source of modern volcanism.

3 When the magma in these pipes cooled, it left a vein of kimberlite rock which contained, among other things, diamonds. Kimberlite is the best indication that diamonds may be found nearby, so prospectors seek out deposits of the bluish rock. Kimberlite deposits are typically cone-shaped, with a smaller surface area of anywhere from two to 146 hectares. While this is not a small surface area, it is often difficult to locate such deposits since it has been many millions of years since the kimberlite first surfaced, and glaciers have scoured the surface of the Earth many times, altering the surface topography of every continent.

4 Although it's hard to create and locate diamonds on Earth, it's virtually raining diamonds on Neptune and Uranus. These planets contain 10-15 percent methane, and sufficient pressure and temperature to chemically convert the methane into diamonds and other complex hydrocarbons at relatively shallow depths. Geologists have recreated these conditions in a laboratory using something called a diamond anvil cell, which squeezes the methane to several thousand times atmospheric pressure. Geologists then focus a laser beam on the pressurized liquid, creating diamond dust.

5 However and wherever they are created, diamonds are the hardest mineral we know of, and are ranked 10th on the *Mohs Hardness Scale*. They can be anywhere from 10 to 100 times harder than minerals ranked 9th on the same scale — minerals such as corundum, including gems such as rubies and sapphires.

6 It is the molecular structure of diamonds that makes them so hard. Each carbon atom in a diamond shares electrons with four other carbon atoms, forming an incredibly strong, three-dimensional lattice-shaped molecule. In graphite, by contrast, each carbon atom is linked to only one other carbon atom in a two-dimensional ring-shaped structure. So even though graphite and diamonds share the same chemistry, their different structures gives them entirely different properties: whereas diamond is the hardest mineral known to man, graphite is one of the softest. Whereas diamond is an excellent electrical insulator, graphite is a good conductor of electricity. Whereas diamond is the ultimate abrasive, graphite is a very good lubricant. And whereas diamond is usually transparent, graphite is opaque.

7 [■ 1] Since diamonds are created under such severe conditions, at the earth's surface's temperatures and pressures they begin to degrade. [■ 2] Graphite is actually the most stable form of carbon, and in fact, all diamonds at or near the surface of the Earth is currently undergoing a transformation into graphite. [■3] But don't worry about that ring on your own or your beloved's finger; this reaction, fortunately, is extremely slow. [■4]

1 What can be inferred about graphite from paragraph 1?

(A) It is the most concentrated, but not the hardest form of carbon.
(B) It is derived from fullerite deep under the surface of the Earth.
(C) It does not need as much heat or pressure as diamonds to form.
(D) It is rarely found in great quantity on the Earth's surface.

2 Why does the author mention elevators in paragraph 2?

(A) To give an easy-to-understand metaphor for how diamonds came to the surface.
(B) To explain the geological force which pushed diamonds into the mantle.
(C) To contrast the *Kimberlite Pipes* with modern volcanic activity.
(D) To emphasize the speed at which the diamonds were forced to the surface.

3 The word vein in paragraph 3 is closest in meaning to:

(A) deposit.
(B) complex.
(C) trace.
(D) ditch.

4 What do scientists or prospectors do when they want to find diamonds?

(A) Search in areas which have a lot of volcanic activity.
(B) Carefully measure pressure and temperature.
(C) Look for kimberlite rock on the surface.
(D) Examine areas which were defaced by glaciers.

5 According to the passage, what is the usual shape of kimberlite deposits?

(A) They become wider as we dig deeper.
(B) They are shaped irregularly due to the glaciers.
(C) Like an elevator, they are shaped like tube.
(D) They become narrower as we dig deeper.

6 The word **topography** in paragraph 3 is closest in meaning to:

(A) mountains.
(B) mix.
(C) terrain.
(D) level.

7 Which of the sentences below best expresses the essential information in the highlighted sentence in the passage? *Incorrect* choices change the meaning in important ways or leave out essential information.

Although it's hard to create and locate diamonds on Earth, it's virtually raining diamonds on Neptune and Uranus.

(A) While humans have to dig for diamonds, they can be found on the surface of some other planets.
(B) While diamonds are created underground on Earth, there are some planets where they come from rain.
(C) Diamonds can be found in greater quantities on some planets other than Earth.
(D) Diamonds are easier to locate on Earth than on some other planets.

8 It can be inferred from the passage that rubies and sapphires are all of the following EXCEPT:

(A) softer than diamonds.
(B) often found in *kimberlite*.
(C) a kind of mineral.
(D) a kind of *corundum*.

9 According to paragraph 6, what is the essential structural difference between diamonds and graphite?

(A) Diamonds are structurally more complex.
(B) Graphite electrons are linked to fewer electrons.
(C) Diamonds have a ring-like structure.
(D) Graphite has a 3-dimensional structure.

10 The purpose of paragraph 6 is to:

(A) discuss reasons diamonds are harder than graphite.
(B) give examples of the structures of diamonds and graphite.
(C) contrast the structure and properties of diamonds and graphite.
(D) form a conclusion about the uses of diamonds and graphite.

11 The word transparent in paragraph 6 is closest in meaning to:

(A) unequivocal.
(B) arduous.
(C) unclouded.
(D) affluent.

12 The word degrade in the final paragraph is closest in meaning to:

(A) tear away.
(B) cut up.
(C) put out.
(D) break down.

13. Look at the 4 squares [■] in the final paragraph and indicate where the following sentence can best be added to the passage.

   Technically, they are described as unstable at the surface of the earth.

14. Complete the table by matching the phrases below.
   Directions: Select the best words or phrases from the answer choices and match them to either the Diamond column or the Graphite column. TWO of the answer choices will not be used.
   This question is worth 4 points.

Diamonds	Graphite
■	■
■	■
■	■

(A) abundant on Earth.
(B) one-dimensional structure.
(C) two-dimensional structure.
(D) three-dimensional structure.
(E) kimberlite rocks.
(F) electrical insulator.
(G) transparent luster.
(H) stable at the Earth's surface.

Questions 15 - 28

1 Tecumseh was a famous Shawnee American Indian leader who spent much of his life attempting to rally disparate North American Indian tribes in a mutual defense of their lands. He was greatly admired in his day, remains a respected icon for native Americans, and is a national hero in Canada. Even his longtime adversary, William Henry Harrison, considered Tecumseh to be "one of those uncommon geniuses which spring up occasionally to produce revolutions and overturn the established order of things."

2 Tecumseh was born in what is now Ohio around 1768. Shawnee children inherited a clan affiliation from their fathers, and Tecumseh belonged to the Panther clan, one of about a dozen exogamous Shawnee clans. In addition to clans, the Shawnee had five traditional divisions, membership of which was also inherited from the father. Tecumseh's father belonged to the Kispoko division, while his mother was a Shawnee of the Piqua division. There is some evidence to suggest that Tecumseh's paternal grandfather may have been a white British trader.

3 Warfare between whites and Indians loomed large in Tecumseh's youth. His father was killed in the Battle of Point Pleasant in 1774 prior to the American Revolutionary War, during which time many Shawnee villages were being destroyed by American frontiersmen. He left his boyhood home after the Battle of Piqua in 1780, and was raised in part by an older brother who was an important war leader. They fought together against whites in Kentucky and Ohio during the 1780s, then around 1790 Tecumseh traveled south to live among (and fight alongside) the Cherokees for two years. It was there that he met the famous leader Dragging Canoe, who led a resistance movement against U.S. expansion and encouraged him to return to Ohio.

4 Over the next two decades, he participated in nativist religious revivals with his younger brother, a religious teacher called "The Prophet", encouraging native Americans to reject the ways of the whites and to refuse to cede more lands to them. He attracted many American Indian followers from many different nations, emerging as the leader of this confederation, which was built upon a foundation established by the religious appeal of his younger brother. Relatively few of these followers were Shawnees; although Tecumseh is often portrayed as the leader of the Shawnees, most Shawnees in fact had little involvement with Tecumseh or the Prophet, and chose instead to move further west or to remain at peace with the United States.

5 [■1] Tecumseh's involvements with the future president William Henry Harrison began in August 1811, when Tecumseh met with then-Governor Harrison at Vincennes, assuring him that his Shawnee brothers meant to remain at peace with the United States. [■2] Harrison led more than a thousand men up the Wabash River, on an expedition to intimidate the Prophet and his followers. [■3] The native American warriors attacked the American encampment on the night of November 6, 1811, in what became known as the Battle of Tippecanoe, but Harrison's men held their ground; the Indians withdrew, and the victorious Americans burned the town. [■4]

6 Despite the failure of Tecumseh to halt the westward expansion of the whites, he remains an enigmatic figure in American history for the supposed curse he placed on the American presidents: that is, that every president elected in a year ending in zero would die in office. Indeed, the curse held true for 140 years, for all the presidents elected from 1840 to 1960. William Henry Harrison died of pneumonia in 1841, Abraham Lincoln was assassinated in 1865, James Garfield was assassinated in 1881, William McKinley was assassinated in 1901, Warren G. Harding died of a heart attack in 1923, Franklin D. Roosevelt died of a cerebral hemorrhage in 1945, and John F. Kennedy was assassinated in 1963. Some call this a coincidence, while others believe the curse has been lifted now that Ronald Reagan survived his presidency, which started in 1980.

15 The word **disparate** in paragraph 1 is closest in meaning to:
(A) dissenting.
(B) arrogant.
(C) flourishing.
(D) separated.

16 The quote by Harrison in the first paragraph emphasizes that Tecumseh was:
(A) an unrivaled prophet.
(B) a talented leader.
(C) a skillful negotiator.
(D) an unusual trader.

17 The word **inherited** in paragraph 2 is closest in meaning to:
(A) reproduced.
(B) refined.
(C) respected.
(D) received.

18 What is the purpose of the third paragraph?
(A) To provide a list of Tecumseh's youth activities.
(B) To show that Tecumseh was widely traveled.
(C) To describe how Tecumseh was influenced by war.
(D) To emphasize the importance of Tecumseh's father's death.

19 According to paragraph 3, Tecumseh fought in all of the following places *except* :
(A) Canada.
(B) Kentucky.
(C) the American south.
(D) Ohio.

20 The word **movement** in paragraph 3 is closest in meaning to:

(A) migration.
(B) transportation.
(C) campaign.
(D) motion.

21 It can be inferred from paragraph 4 that Tecumseh's younger brother:

(A) was a powerful warrior.
(B) was killed before Tecumseh.
(C) was a popular religious teacher.
(D) was not happy with other Shawnee.

22 Which of the sentences below best expresses the essential information in the highlighted sentence in the passage? Incorrect choices change the meaning in important ways or leave out essential information.

He attracted many American Indian followers from many different nations, emerging as the leader of this confederation, which was built upon a foundation established by the religious appeal of his younger brother.

(A) Tecumseh and his brother recruited the young religious Shawnee men for their war on the Americans.
(B) Tecumseh used his brother's popularity to recruit men to fight the Americans.
(C) Tecumseh's brother never could have been such a successful religious leader had it not been for Tecumseh's leadership.
(D) Tecumseh's warriors hailed from many different nations and had many different religions, but they were united in their desire to return to Canada.

23 According to paragraph 5, what can be inferred about the battle that Tecumseh and Harrison fought in Tippecanoe?

(A) Tecumseh won a brilliant overnight victory.
(B) Tecumseh was betrayed by his own warriors.
(C) Tecumseh was pushed out of his settlement.
(D) Tecumseh had a smaller force than Harrison.

24 Look at the 4 squares [■] in paragraph 5 and indicate where the following sentence can best be added to the passage.

Harrison, however, refused the olive branch.

25 The word **their** in the final sentence of paragraph 5 refers to:

(A) Shawnee.
(B) Americans.
(C) men.
(D) warriors.

26 The word **enigmatic** in paragraph 6 is closest in meaning to:

(A) hard to understand.
(B) hard to like.
(C) hard to describe.
(D) hard to depend.

27 Who did Tecumseh allegedly curse?

(A) The Shawnee.
(B) American presidents.
(C) William Henry Harrison.
(D) Governor Harrison's army.

28 An introductory sentence for a brief summary of the passage is provided below. Complete the summary by selecting the THREE answer choices that express the most important ideas in the passage. Some sentences do not belong in the summary because they express ideas that are not presented in the passage or are minor ideas in the passage. *This question is worth 2 points.*

Tecumseh was one of the most famous and influential American Indian leaders in history.

(A) With his brother, Tecumseh promoted a religion which encouraged native Americans to renounce the whites and their way of life.
(B) A brilliant warrior, his greatest accomplishment was to assist Dragging Canoe in fighting whites in the southern United States.
(C) Tecumseh gained fame and respect for his stance against the white Americans who were moving west.
(D) Tecumseh was ultimately unable to unite fellow American Indians, who fell, tribe by tribe, to the white man.
(E) Tecumseh's legend is based mostly on his stunning victory over Harrison at Tippecanoe.
(F) Tecumseh's curse is believed by some, but many think it is nothing more than a hoax or coincidence.

Questions 29 - 42

1 In contrast to cattle, for which the last wild ancestor — aurochs — died out in the 17th century, domesticated camels coexist happily with their wild cousins. Camelids originated in North America about 30 million years ago and split into two groups about 11 million years ago. One group eventually crossed the Bering Land Bridge to Asia, where it followed an evolutionary path that's only sketchily understood, resulting in the two-humped bactrian camel and the one-humped dromedary.

2 The other group migrated to South America, where it survives today as wild guanacos and vicunas and domesticated llamas and alpacas. [■ 1] For many years, historians and scientists assumed that the Incas had created both llamas and alpacas through selective breeding of the guanaco, which is larger and more widely distributed than the vicuna. [■ 2] But while the ancestor of the llama is indeed the guanaco, genetic studies show that the ancestor of the alpaca is actually the vicuna. [■ 3] But since speciation occurred thousands of years ago, it is certain that the Incas had no role in their breeding. [■ 4]

3 Of the many results of the Spanish conquest of South America, one was the mismanagement of camelid breeding and care. Within 100 years of conquest, up to 90 percent of South America's domesticated camelids had died off, mostly to be replaced by horses. Since then, Latin Americans have haphazardly crossbred the remaining alpacas and llamas, and today only about 20 percent of alpacas are genetically pure. This interbreeding among the alpacas and llamas has resulted in a significant increase in the thickness of alpaca fiber, making alpaca wool less valuable.

4 The Spaniards also began killing vicuna, which the Incan royalty had vigorously protected. Only Inca rulers could wear the revered vicuna wool, and the penalty for breaking the prohibition was death. New World settlers and their livestock also pushed the wild vicuna higher into the Andes grassland ranges, where hunters continued to stage organized kills for their pelts. Vicuna populations diminished and became fragmented.

5 Fortunately for the vicuna, its fiber — with a diameter of 12 micrometers — is the finest in the world. Vicuna garments are some of the most expensive luxury clothing items in the world, so in the 1970s, the species' native countries — Peru, Argentina, Bolivia, Chile, and Ecuador —signed a collective agreement to protect the animal. And in 1975, the Convention on International Trade in Endangered Species of Wild Fauna and Flora, or CITES, prohibited the commercial trade of vicuna products, from hides to wool. Today, approximately 220,000 vicuna — over half of which live in Peru — graze the high Andes. Remarkably, they have rebounded to the point where governments are permitting citizens to once again capture and shear the animals for their silky fibers, as South Americans had done for centuries.

6 In Asia, the Gobi's wild bactrian camels look quite distinct from their domestic counterparts. Wild camels are lithe and sleek, their humps small and conical, whereas the dromedaries are stocky and thick-wooled, with floppy, misshapen humps. The fate of these wild camelids in Asia has been less than kind. Living in isolated parts of Mongolia's and China's Gobi desert, bactrian camels are notoriously difficult to study. They are shy and live in an environment with extremely hot summers, bitterly cold winters, and little precipitation. They were discovered and first reported as recently as 1877. And although it is the largest grazer of central Asia's deserts, biologists don't even know if the bactrian is descended from the dromedary or vice versa. There isn't even any reliable data on population numbers, with estimates ranging from 1000 to 5000 head. Nor is there reliable data on breeding, though a Russian study in 1980 reported herds made up of 11% juveniles, while more recent studies report 5% juveniles. Our best guess why is that the persistence of drought conditions since the 1970s is to blame.

29 In paragraph 1, what does the author say about the origin of camelids?
(A) That their ancestors came from Asia.
(B) That the one-humped variety evolved earlier than the two-humped variety.
(C) That they came to Asia from North America.
(D) That they originated from ancient cattle species.

30 What can be inferred from paragraph 1 about the animals mentioned in paragraph 2?
(A) They share a common ancestor with camels.
(B) They were carefully bred by the South American Incas.
(C) There were great numbers of them.
(D) The smaller animals are descended from the larger animals.

31 The word distributed in paragraph 2 is closest in meaning to:
(A) compressed.
(B) disjointed.
(C) circumstantial.
(D) scattered.

32 According to paragraph 2 of the passage, the alpaca evolved from:
(A) aurochs.
(B) guanacos.
(C) vicunas.
(D) llamas.

33 Look at the 4 squares [■] in paragraph 2 and indicate where the following sentence can best be added to the passage.

It is believed that, about 6,000 years ago, alpacas were created through selective breeding which was heavily influenced by the vicuna.

34. The word **domesticated** in paragraph 3 is closest in meaning to:
   (A) soft.
   (B) popular.
   (C) sober.
   (D) tame.

35. Which of the sentences below best expresses the essential information in the highlighted sentence in the passage? Incorrect choices change the meaning in important ways or leave out essential information.

   Of the many results of the Spanish conquest of South America, one was the mismanagement of camelid breeding and care.

   (A) The Spanish made many errors in managing their South American colonies, including camelid breeding and care.
   (B) The Spanish mismanaged many of South America's natural resources, especially its native animal species.
   (C) Under Spanish rule, the various species of camelids in its colonies were cross-bred and poorly cared for.
   (D) The skillful management of South American camelids by the Spanish has helped their numbers grow in recent years.

36. Which of the following can be inferred from the passage about the wool of South American camelids?
   (A) The wool of pure alpacas is the most expensive in the world.
   (B) The Inca rulers preferred the wool of vicunas.
   (C) Less than a quarter of the remaining vicunas have pure vicuna blood.
   (D) It is a serious crime in Peru to capture and shear vicunas and alpacas.

37 The word they in the final sentence of paragraph 5 refers to:
(A) Peruvians.
(B) vicunas.
(C) CITES.
(D) alpacas.

38 Why does the author use the word remarkably in paragraph 5?
(A) It is very important for CITES to continue to protect the remaining vicunas.
(B) Alpacas and vicunas share a surprising resemblance.
(C) The wool from vicunas has become an incredible success.
(D) The numbers of vicuna in South America have grown significantly.

39 The word isolated in the final paragraph is closest in meaning to:
(A) barren.
(B) heavily populated.
(C) mountainous.
(D) remote.

40 According to the final paragraph, what seems to be happening to wild Asian camel populations?
(A) They are in fierce competition with the dromedaries.
(B) They have been well studied by Russian scientists.
(C) They are shrinking due to lack of food.
(D) Their numbers have rapidly rebounded.

41 The word drought in paragraph 6 is closest in meaning to:
(A) dehydrated.
(B) depicted.
(C) denounced.
(D) decarbonized.

42 Three of the answer choices below provide the correct sequence of events in the history of the vicuna. Put those THREE answers in order. The other three sentences do not belong in this sequence because they express ideas that are not presented in the passage or are minor ideas in the passage. *This question is worth 2 points.*

The vicuna were highly prized by the Incan rulers before the Spanish arrived in South America.

(A) The vicuna evolved from the alpaca.
(B) Trade of vicuna products was outlawed.
(C) Vicuna populations were forced to move to remote locations.
(D) Vicunas migrated to South America.
(E) The vicuna were widely slaughtered.
(F) Vicuna wool and fiber began to lose value

Listening Section

Questions 1 - 5

Conversation 001.mp3 | 002.mp3

1 What is the man's problem?

(A) He has no idea how to prepare for the placement test for Spanish class.
(B) He thinks his Spanish class is much too easy for him.
(C) He is unsure whether or not he should take Spanish class this semester.
(D) He is unhappy about the level of the class he has been assigned to.

2 What does the woman say about her Spanish class? 003.mp3

(A) It involved a lot of homework.
(B) It was difficult but useful for her.
(C) The tests were very challenging.
(D) The level was much too high for her.

3 Why does the woman think placement tests were introduced? 004.mp3

(A) Many students' high school records didn't reflect their ability accurately.
(B) Too many students were choosing to study in the high level classes.
(C) The department didn't have time to check every student's level.
(D) Many students had never had their language skills tested before.

4 Why does the woman say this? 🎵 005.mp3

(A) To imply it is not the man's fault that his ability is poor.
(B) To show that she is not criticizing the man personally.
(C) To apologize for asking personal questions about the man's high school record.
(D) To imply that the man has only himself to blame for his current situation.

5. **What does the woman mean when she says this?**
   - (A) She has no idea what her score was on the placement test.
   - (B) Her good score on the test was due to luck more than hard study.
   - (C) She would probably have been placed in a lower level class if she had taken the test.
   - (D) She doesn't enjoy studying on courses that give students lots of tests.

Questions 6 - 11

Lecture

6. **Which of the following does the professor NOT mention as a reason for the existence of public goods?**
   - (A) The good or service would be a market failure.
   - (B) Too many people could use the good or service without paying.
   - (C) Governments have to use tax funds for something.
   - (D) The good or service is necessary.

7. **According to the lecture, what are the basic problems which prevent public goods from being provided as profitable commercial services?**

   (Choose 2 answers.)
   - (A) There is no effective way of collecting a fee from each and every person who uses the good.
   - (B) Public goods can only be funded through taxation.
   - (C) Many people can use the good without decreasing or reducing its availability to other users.
   - (D) Public goods are generally services which people don't want to pay for.

8. **According to the professor, what is a free rider?**
   - (A) A person who avoids paying for public transportation.
   - (B) A person who can easily use a good without paying for it.
   - (C) A person who is excluded from using public goods.

(D) A person who collects fees for use of public goods.

9 Why does the professor mention public service radio? [011.mp3]
(A) To illustrate why public goods can not use commercial advertising.
(B) As an example of how public goods can sometimes be commercially funded.
(C) As an additional example of a non-excludable public good.
(D) To demonstrate that people will pay a fee to hear important information.

10 What does the professor mean when he says this? 🎵 [012.mp3]
(A) The discussion will focus on other subjects, so there is no need for more information.
(B) A more detailed explanation is likely to confuse the students.
(C) This basic explanation provides sufficient background information for today's discussion.
(D) It is now time to start the discussion.

11 Why does the professor say this? 🎵 [013.mp3]
(A) He doesn't know whether the students have ever seen a lighthouse.
(B) He hopes the students can understand the example for themselves before she explains it.
(C) He is asking for one of the students to volunteer to explain.
(D) He is checking whether the students are paying attention.

Questions 12 - 17

Lecture [014.mp3] [015.mp3]

12 What is the talk mainly about?
(A) Introducing a theory about why some businesses are successful.
(B) Introducing a theory that explains how systems change and grow.
(C) Explaining why George's Land's book, "Grow or Die", was very influential.

(D) Explaining the rules for success and survival in business.

[016. mp3]

13 **The professor describes several stages in the process of growth. Indicate whether each of the following is a step in the process. Check the correct box for each answer.**

(A) The system repeats its formula for success.
　　　　　　　　　　　　　　　　　　　　--Yes ☐ No ☐
(B) The system searches for a breakpoint.
　　　　　　　　　　　　　　　　　　　　--Yes ☐ No ☐
(C) The system experiments with its resources.
　　　　　　　　　　　　　　　　　　　　--Yes ☐ No ☐
(D) The system searches for a connection with its environment.
　　　　　　　　　　　　　　　　　　　　--Yes ☐ No ☐
(E) The system innovates and reinvents itself.
　　　　　　　　　　　　　　　　　　　　--Yes ☐ No ☐

[017. mp3]

14 **How does the professor explain the significance of Land's statement that "nothing fails like success"?**

(A) Too much easy success always results in failure.
(B) A system must not fail to consume all its resources if it wants to succeed.
(C) A system will fail unless it finds ideal conditions for success.
(D) Continued success will ultimately lead to failure unless changes are made.

[018. mp3]

15 **According to the professor, what two things does a successful system do simultaneously at the second breakpoint?**

(Choose 2 answers.)
(A) It consumes all the resources needed for success.
(B) It begins to innovate in order to find other methods of success.
(C) It introduces a new S-shaped curve and changes the rules for success.
(D) It diversifies and reinvents itself to start a new process of growth.

16. **Why does the professor say this?** 🔊   019. mp3
   (A) She wants the students to know how vital this theory is.
   (B) She wants to talk about a different, more important topic.
   (C) She wants to summarize the theory quickly before moving onto the main explanation.
   (D) She wants the students to understand that they must read the book.

17. **What does the professor mean when she says this?** 🔊   020. mp3
   (A) Using the theory will change some of the familiar ideas about running a business.
   (B) The practical applications of the theory will be easier for students to understand.
   (C) Students will not need the theory if they plan to run their own business.
   (D) The students are unlikely to be able to understand the theory.

Questions 18 - 22

Conversation   021. mp3   022. mp3

18. **Why is the student unsure about the assignment?**
   (A) He lost his notes for the professor's explanation.
   (B) He misunderstood the previous assignment so wants to be sure this time.
   (C) He was late for class and so didn't hear the full explanation.
   (D) It is different from all the previous class assignments.

023. mp3

19. **What does the student think is the professor's aim with this assignment?**
   (A) To challenge the students' conventional views of history.
   (B) To encourage students to consult a variety of sources.
   (C) To challenge students to imagine an opposite point of view.
   (D) To encourage the students to think more positively about history.

20 Which of the following best describes the assignment? [024. mp3]

(A) A study of changing perspectives on a single historical person or event.
(B) A review of all the available historical sources for a famous event.
(C) A summary of the main events, both good and bad, in an historical figure's life.
(D) An analysis of contrasting modern opinions of historical events.

21 What does the professor mean when she says this? ♪ [025. mp3]

(A) She doesn't have time to explain it all again so the student just do what he thinks is best.
(B) The student needs to complete the assignment first so that she can check it.
(C) She will listen to the student's explanation and correct it if necessary.
(D) She will have to end the discussion soon, as it is time for class.

22 What does the professor imply when she says this? ♪ [026. mp3]

(A) The student has probably studied or read about this topic before.
(B) The student is always too passive and waits for an explanation to be given.
(C) The student should speak more formally and politely.
(D) The student should be able to work out the answer by himself.

Questions 23 - 28

Lecture [027. mp3] [028. mp3]

23 What is the talk mainly about?

(A) Explaining the particle and wave theories of light.
(B) Describing Isaac Newton's major scientific achievements.
(C) Tracing the development and acceptance of two theories.
(D) Summarizing the science and philosophy of the 18th century.

[029. mp3]

24 Why does the professor say that René Descartes was very influential at this time?

(A) He had discovered that white light can be separated into a spectrum of colors.
(B) He had developed the exact science of mechanics.
(C) He had developed a new branch of mathematics.
(D) He had introduced the idea that the universe is a mechanical system.

[030. mp3]

25 According to the lecture, what were the main factors in the particle theory of light gaining wide acceptance at first?

(Choose 3 answers.)

(A) Newton was the first to get his theory published and widely read.
(B) There was no data to enable an objective comparison between the two theories.
(C) Isaac Newton was the most famous scientist of the time.
(D) Huygens focused on promoting his mechanical clock rather than his wave theory of light.
(E) The particle theory equated with the science and philosophy of mechanics.

26 Why does the professor say this? 🎵 [031. mp3]

(A) To emphasize the relative weakness of Huygens' theory.
(B) To introduce the next section of the talk.
(C) To emphasize the dominant influence of Isaac Newton.
(D) To illustrate that Huygens' theory was already outdated.

27 What does the professor mean when he says this? 🎵 [032. mp3]

(A) People believed Newton's opinions because of his reputation and past record.
(B) Newton's reputation was undeserved and based only on his early discoveries.

(C) Scientific questions were always directed at Newton because of his leading status.

(D) Newton's theories were never questioned or tested objectively.

28 According to the lecture, why did the wave theory eventually become the dominant theory of the nature of light in the 19th century?

(A) Newton's reputation and influence started to fade at that time.

(B) The development of better technology allowed wave patterns to be observed.

(C) Electromagnetic theory proved all of Newton's ideas to be wrong.

(D) The results of experiments conducted then could only be explained by the wave theory.

Questions 29 - 34

29 What is the main purpose of the lecture?

(A) To introduce the life and ideas of Robert Malthus.

(B) To introduce Malthus's ideas and compare them with the reality of population growth and resources.

(C) To compare Malthus's theories with the ideas of modern economists.

(D) To investigate the social, political, and historical background of Malthus's ideas and their impact.

30 According to the lecture, when does a Malthusian catastrophe occur?

(A) When population growth increases geometrically.

(B) When agricultural production can no longer meet the needs of a rapidly growing population.

(C) When the working poor have to struggle too much to survive.

(D) When the growth of the population is limited by the amount of land available for housing.

[037. mp3]

31 According to the lecture, why were Malthus's ideas unpopular at the time?

(Choose 2 answers.)

(A) He proposed pessimistic theories during an era of generally optimistic thinking.
(B) The government was already struggling to help the poor, so they didn't welcome Malthus's criticism.
(C) Agricultural and political leaders didn't agree with Malthus's ideas for improving production.
(D) Rapid population growth was believed to be beneficial for the economy, but Malthus disagreed.

[038. mp3]

32 The professor describes the impact of Malthus's ideas. Indicate whether each of the following events was influenced in some way by Malthus. Check the correct box for each answer.

(A) Charles Darwin's theories on evolution.
　　　　　　　　　　　　　　　　　　　　-------Yes ☐ No ☐
(B) Massive population growth in the 20th century.
　　　　　　　　　　　　　　　　　　　　-------Yes ☐ No ☐
(C) Political reform on poverty and welfare issues.
　　　　　　　　　　　　　　　　　　　　-------Yes ☐ No ☐
(D) The first British population census.
　　　　　　　　　　　　　　　　　　　　-------Yes ☐ No ☐
(E) Increased agricultural production in 19th century England.
　　　　　　　　　　　　　　　　　　　　-------Yes ☐ No ☐

[039. mp3]

33 According to the lecture, what modern factors have given humankind greater control over population growth?

(Choose 3 answers.)

(A) War and disaster.
(B) Improved contraception.
(C) Moral restraint and late marriage.

(D) Better education.

(E) Lower infant mortality.

34 **What can be inferred about the professor?** [040. mp3]

(A) He believes modern economic ideas have many advantages over Malthus's ideas.

(B) He thinks Malthus's ideas are weakened by Malthus's failure to foresee many changes.

(C) He thinks it is unreasonable to criticize Malthus's 200-year-old ideas based on modern knowledge.

(D) He thinks Malthus's ideas have critical advantages over many modern economic theories.

Speaking Section

Question 1
041.mp3

It is generally considered that the young learn from the old. Describe something that you think young people can teach older people. Include details and examples to support your explanation.

Preparation time : 15 seconds   Response time : 45 seconds

Question 2
042.mp3

Do you think attending classes should only be an option for students at university, or should it be required? Include details and examples in your explanation.

Preparation time : 15 seconds   Response time : 45 seconds

Question 3 《 Reading 》
043.mp3

Reading time : 45 seconds

University to Increase Campus Security

The university has decided to hire two new part-time campus police officers and increase its numbers of patrols beginning March 1. We have had to take these measures due to an increase in thefts in our dormitories and in vehicles parked in back lots A through F. Anderson and Woodward Halls are of particular concern to campus security. In order to pay for the added expenses a portion of the student entertainment fund will be used for this purpose.

《 Listening 》 044.mp3

> The man expresses his opinion about the university's plan to increase security. State his opinion and explain why he holds that opinion.

Preparation time : 30 seconds   *Response time : 60 seconds*

Question 4 《 Reading 》 045.mp3

Reading time : 45 seconds

Agriculture in Louisiana

Subtropical in the south and temperate in the north, Louisiana's climate, low lying land, and rich alluvial soil make the state one of the United States' leading agricultural producers. Water defines the state: Louisiana has 5,000 miles of waterways, and contains over 40% of the nation's wetlands. The Mississippi dominates the many waterways, but there are other rivers, most notably the Red River, and the coast is threaded by many slow-moving bayous. The rainy coast country on the Gulf coastal plain and the Mississippi alluvial plain contains marshes and fertile delta lands ideal for rice, sweet potatoes, and sugarcane. Inland are low rolling pine hills and prairies where cotton predominates. Other major commodities include soybeans and dairy products, while, statewide, forestry is the leading agricultural industry.

《 Listening 》 046.mp3

> The professor describes the development of sugarcane and rice production in southern Louisiana. Summarize and explain the reasons the region's agriculture developed in this way.

Preparation time : 30 seconds   *Response time : 60 seconds*

Question 5

[047.mp3]

The students discuss two possible solutions to the man's problem. Describe the problem. Then state which of the two solutions you prefer and explain why.

Preparation time : 20 seconds   Response time : 60 seconds

Question 6

[048.mp3]

Using points and examples from the talk, summarize and explain the differences between accounting profit and economic profit.

Preparation time : 20 seconds   Response time : 60 seconds

Writing Section

Question 1 《 Reading 》

Now read the passage about the phenomenon called Will-o'-the-wisp. You have 3 minutes to read the passage. Begin reading now.

"Will-o'-the-wisp" is one of several names given to a curious, but rarely seen, phenomenon typically observed over marshy ground at night. Numerous legends have grown up around this phenomenon, involving spirits of the dead and malicious supernatural entities intent on luring lonely travellers to their deaths. Meanwhile, a number of attempts have been made to find a rational, scientific explanation, and scientists have provided at least a couple of possible explanations for the phenomenon of Will-o'-the-wisp.

The most common explanation put forth is that Will-o'-the-wisp is generated by the oxidation of methane gases and hydrogen phosphide produced by the decay of organic material in bogs. Both methane gases and hydrogen phosphide are highly flammable and will ignite under normal atmospheric conditions. These chemicals have been shown to provide light when combined under laboratory conditions. In fact, in 2008, the Italian chemists Luigi Garlaschelli and Paolo Boschetti attempted to replicate ignis fatuus under laboratory conditions. They successfully created a faint cool light by mixing phosphine with air and nitrogen.

Some scientists have postulated about the possibility of a piezoelectric effect. Piezoelectricity is generated by materials, such as certain ceramics and crystals, which generate electricity and sparks when bent or squeezed. A very similar phenomenon called triboluminescence, in which electricity and light are created when a material is broken rather than bent similarly to piezoelectricity, can be seen in the sparks of Wint O Green Lifesavers.* This would partially explain the occasionally erratic movement of Will-o'-the-wisp.

Bioluminescence, the production of light by living organisms, has also been proposed as a possible explanation. Certain microorganisms, such as fungi, are capable of producing chemical reactions that create light without any significant heat. And, this kind of luminescence has been reportedly observed in barn owls. One of the possible causes for this account could be that the owls have rubbed up against luminescent fungi (several species of which exist) in their nest or roosting holes. Then, the owls carry the luminescent material on their feathers, and, from time to time, it can reflect enough light from sources such as the moon to appear as the Will-'o-the wisp.

* Wint O Green Life Savers is an American brand of ring-shaped hard candy. The candy is known to produce visible light when you crunch on it, the effect called triboluminescence as above.

《 Listening 》 [049. mp3]

Now listen to part of a lecture on the topic you just read about.

Question: Summarize the points made in the lecture you just heard, explaining how they challenge points made in the reading.

Response time : 20 minutes

【解答欄】

Question 2

Question: Students at universities often have a choice of places to live. They may choose to live in university dormitories, or they may choose to live in apartments in the community. Compare the advantages of living in university housing with the advantages of living in an apartment in the community. Where would you prefer to live? Give reasons for your preference.

【解答欄】

第2部

リスニング・スペシャルトレーニング

問題

リスニング・スペシャルトレーニング 問題

Questions 1 - 5

Lecture 050.mp3 051.mp3

1 What is the audience listening to?

(A) A radio broadcast.
(B) A political discussion.
(C) A sales promotion.
(D) A health documentary.

2 What is the source of the ethylene described in the talk? 052.mp3

(A) The fruit itself.
(B) The air surrounding the fruit.
(C) The spray applied by farmers.
(D) The tree or vines to which the fruit is attached.

3 According to the speaker, what does ethylene do? 053.mp3

(A) Makes fruit greener in color.
(B) Increases fruit production.
(C) Causes fruit to ripen.
(D) Discourages attacks by fruit flies.

054.mp3

4 According to the speaker, when fruit "breathes" oxygen, what begins to happen?

(A) The fruit loses its sweetness.
(B) The fruit falls off the tree.
(C) Bees begin to pollinate the fruit.
(D) The temperature inside the fruit increases.

5 Listen again to 🎵

Why does the speaker say this? *"in short, delicious."*

(A) To mention that she likes fruit.
(B) To indicate that some fruits taste better than others.
(C) To summarize the result of ripening.
(D) To note that fruit ripens quickly.

Questions 6 - 10

6 Why does the speaker talk about pulsars?

(A) To answer a question.
(B) To settle a debate.
(C) To suggest future research projects.
(D) To describe a newly discovered planet.

7 What does the speaker say about the electromagnetic signal?

(A) It comes from a great distance.
(B) It's produced by a group of stars.
(C) It comes from a nearby planet.
(D) It's about to disappear.

8 According to the speaker, in what way is the pulsar's rate of spin changing?

(A) It's becoming more like that of the Earth.
(B) It's growing erratic.
(C) It's becoming more regular.
(D) It's slowing down.

9 Listen again to 🎵   060. mp3

Why does the professor say this? *"One astronomer, I forget his name right now, thinks the pulsar's spin is more regular, in fact, than the vibrations of atomic clocks."*

(A) To ask students to recall the name of an astronomer.
(B) To emphasize the regularity of the pulsar's spin.
(C) To explain how atomic clocks work.
(D) To name the astronomer who found the pulsar..

061. mp3

10 According to the speaker, what may scientists use some day to keep precise time?

(A) A solar clock.
(B) A magnet.
(C) An atomic calendar.
(D) A pulsar.

Questions 11 - 15

Lecture 062. mp3 063. mp3

11 In the type of settlements described by the speaker, which building was probably the oldest?

(A) The grocery store.
(B) The gristmill.
(C) The church.
(D) The school.

12 What did farmers trade for the supplies they needed?   064. mp3

(A) Cash.
(B) Credit.
(C) Grain.
(D) Gold.

13 What usually happened after a grist mill was built in an area? [065. mp3]

(A) Local stores lost business.
(B) A new town was established.
(C) Less farmland was used to produce grain.
(D) Farmers built gristmills on their own property.

14 At the end of the talk, what will the listeners most likely do? [066. mp3]

(A) Unpack for the night.
(B) Take photographs.
(C) Sit down to dinner.
(D) Grind flour.

15 Listen again to 🎵 [067. mp3]

Why does the speaker say this? *"Have your cameras ready,"*

(A) To prevent students from failing to take pictures.
(B) To highlight the historical importance of a building.
(C) To emphasize the beauty of a town.
(D) To warn students not to leave their cameras behind.

Questions 16 - 20

Lecture [068. mp3] [069. mp3]

16 What is the main topic of the talk?

(A) The burning of different types of fossil fuels.
(B) An unexpected effect of changes in the atmosphere.
(C) Warnings by scientists not to use fertilizers.
(D) Recently discovered tree species.

070. mp3

17 What does the speaker say about the carbon dioxide level of the atmosphere?

(A) It has decreased steadily.
(B) It has been stable.
(C) It has fluctuated.
(D) It has increased noticeably.

071. mp3

18 According to the speaker, what has been most affected by the carbon dioxide level?

(A) Record-keeping.
(B) Rainfall.
(C) Tree growth.
(D) Fertilizers.

072. mp3

19 According to the speaker, what have researchers found to be one unusual result of certain climatic changes?

(A) The increased fertilization of trees.
(B) The increased oxidation of coal.
(C) The reduced burning of fuels.
(D) The reduced layering of fossils.

20 Listen again to 🔊

073. mp3

Why does the speaker say this? *"Namely a fertilization effect."*

(A) To show how much carbon dioxide level has increased.
(B) To specify the point of his discussion.
(C) To introduce a new topic.
(D) To support the ideas proposed by the researchers.

Questions 21 - 25

Lecture 074.mp3 075.mp3

21 Who first brought the ancestors of wild burros to North America?

(A) Early miners.
(B) Spanish explorers.
(C) African naturalists.
(D) Early industrialists.

22 What were the prospectors looking for? 076.mp3

(A) Gold.
(B) Settlements.
(C) New routes for the railroads.
(D) New sources of water.

23 What was done with many of the burros when the prospectors no longer needed them? 077.mp3

(A) They were sent to zoos.
(B) They were given to miners.
(C) They were raised commercially in herds.
(D) They were set free.

24 What is the main reason that the speaker wants the students to study the burro? 078.mp3

(A) Burros are relatives of the horse.
(B) Burros can adapt easily.
(C) Burros are common farm animals.
(D) There are many burros in the United States.

25 Listen again to 🎵 079. mp3

What does the professor imply when she says this? *"and these pack burros were, in turn, the descendants of wild African asses."*

(A) That Spanish explorers took pack burros back to Africa.
(B) That burros can't live long.
(C) That African asses are already extinct.
(D) That burros are highly adaptive.

Questions 26 - 30

Lecture 080. mp3 081. mp3

26 Which group of students is the speaker addressing?
(A) Those who will be on campus during a vacation period.
(B) Those who work part-time in the administration offices.
(C) Those who normally live in Butler Hall.
(D) Those who will be moving on campus in a few months.

27 For how long will the dormitories remain closed? 082. mp3
(A) One weekend.
(B) Five days.
(C) Ten days.
(D) Two weeks.

083. mp3
28 Which statement is true about college facilities during the vacation period?
(A) Most facilities will be closed.
(B) Only a few facilities will be closed.
(C) Most facilities will operate on a reduced schedule.
(D) All facilities will be open.

29 Which topic is not discussed by the speaker?   　084.mp3

(A) Which dormitory will be open.
(B) Where students will eat.
(C) Whether any forms need to be filled out.
(D) Whether the computer center will be open.

30 Listen again to 🎵   　085.mp3

What does the speaker imply when he says this? *"Please move all the belongings you will need to your temporary accommodations by the 7th,"*

(A) That students can return to their current rooms after the winter break.
(B) That students should vacate their current rooms completely.
(C) That the earlier a student moves his or her belongings, the better room he or she will be assigned.
(D) That students will not be assigned rooms if they fail to move their belongings by the 7th.

Questions 31 - 35

Lecture 086.mp3　087.mp3

31 How long should each paper be?

(A) No more than one page.
(B) At least one page but no more than eight pages.
(C) At least eight pages but no more than twelve pages.
(D) At least twelve pages.

32 What is the format of this course?   　088.mp3

(A) Lecture only.
(B) Discussion and laboratory.
(C) Lecture and laboratory.
(D) Lecture and discussion.

[089. mp3]

33 What must a student do with a paper that is returned on Thursday?

(A) Rewrite it.
(B) Present it to the class.
(C) Use it to study for the final exam.
(D) Incorporate it into a longer paper.

34 When will the speaker be available to discuss papers? [090. mp3]

(A) Before class on Tuesdays.
(B) After class on Thursdays.
(C) Over the weekend.
(D) On Tuesday and Friday afternoons.

35 Listen again to 🎵 [091. mp3]

Why does the professor say this? *"I might talk about justice, for example."*

(A) To specify her topic for the next Monday.
(B) To help students get a better idea of their assignment.
(C) To suggest that she is not sure what to talk about.
(D) To name an especially important political concept.

Questions 36 - 40

Lecture [092. mp3] [093. mp3]

36 What is the speaker's profession?

(A) Anthropologist.
(B) Nutritionist.
(C) Historian.
(D) Geochemist.

37 The speaker is primarily concerned with what group? [094. mp3]

(A) Nonhuman primates.
(B) Existing hunting and gathering societies.

(C) Contemporary city dwellers.
(D) Prehistoric humans.

38 According to the speaker, the amount of strancheum in a fossil bone depends on what factor?

(A) Where the bone was found.
(B) How deeply the home was buried.
(C) How long ago the animal lived.
(D) What the animal ate.

39 What does the speaker think about the diet of prehistoric humans?

(A) It was identical to that of nonhuman primates.
(B) It contained only insignificant traces of strontium.
(C) It is not possible to generalize about the diet of prehistoric humans.
(D) Prehistoric humans were not exclusively herbivorous or carnivorous.

40 Listen again to 🎵

What does the professor mean when he says this? *"As you may or may not be aware,"*

(A) That the topic is very exciting.
(B) That students should already be familiar with the topic.
(C) That he assumes that the topic could be new to some students.
(D) That the topic is not the focus of his lecture.

Questions 41 - 45

41 What was the woman doing when the accident occurred?

(A) Watching sailboats.
(B) Competing in a race.
(C) Working for the Coast Guard.
(D) Repairing a boat.

42 What were the weather conditions at the time of the accident?

(A) There was no wind.
(B) It was clear and sunny.
(C) It was stormy.
(D) There was heavy fog.

43 What happened to the woman?

(A) She was thrown overboard.
(B) She hurt her hand.
(C) She was blown off course.
(D) She ran aground.

44 How was the woman rescued?

(A) By a companion.
(B) By a fisherman.
(C) By another sailboat.
(D) By a patrol boat.

45 Listen again to 🎵

Why does the speaker say this? *"Their job lasted only 50 minutes."*

(A) To indicate that the rescue team failed in the mission.
(B) To emphasize the difficulty of the search.
(C) To criticize the rescue team for giving up too early.
(D) To note that the search was successful.

Questions 46 - 50

46 What is the purpose of the meeting?

(A) To determine who will graduate this year.
(B) To discuss the seating arrangement.
(C) To choose the chairperson of the ceremonies.
(D) To begin planning the graduation ceremonies.

47 What should the students write on the paper?

(A) Their names, phone numbers, and job preference.
(B) The names and addresses of their guests.
(C) The names of the committees they worked on last year.
(D) Their dormitory name, address, and phone number.

48 Who should sign up?

(A) Only students who have time for the work.
(B) All the students who are at the meeting.
(C) Only students who have a telephone.
(D) All the students who worked on the project last year.

49 When is the next meeting?

(A) In an hour.
(B) Next week.
(C) In one month.
(D) Next year.

50 Listen again to 🎵 [109. mp3]

What does the speaker imply when he says this? *"Remember, as a representative, you will have a lot of responsibilities, so only sign up if you feel you have the time to participate."*

(A) That participation requires commitment.
(B) That the ceremonies will take long time.
(C) That he wants everyone to participate.
(D) That he wants to discourage people from signing up.

Questions 51 - 55

[Lecture] [110. mp3] [111. mp3]

51 What did children need to learn how to do in the earliest times mentioned by the speaker?
(A) Count money.
(B) Read and write.
(C) Draw moving objects.
(D) Hunt and farm.

[112. mp3]

52 Why was formal education in schools not necessary for a long time?
(A) Teachers came to children's homes.
(B) Children acquired the information they needed by direct experience.
(C) Children taught one another in small supervised groups.
(D) Parents instructed their children in the "three R's."

[113. mp3]

53 What changes in society first made it important to teach children the "Three R's"?
(A) A new dependence on people far away and the use of money.
(B) The introduction of a new alphabet and numerical system.
(C) Outmoded methods of farming and ineffective means of transportation.
(D) Larger family units and greater financial hardships.

54 What is the topic the speaker will most likely discuss next? [114.mp3]

(A) The various means of survival taught by parents in contemporary society.
(B) The importance of history instruction in the first schools.
(C) The increasingly complex skills subsequently taught in schools.
(D) The problems involved in the construction of new schools.

55 Listen again to ♪ [115.mp3]

Why does the professor say this? *"They had to learn to be careful around moving objects, to draw back when they got too close to something dangerous."*

(A) To tell students about her own experience in childhood.
(B) To describe what children are most interested in.
(C) To give examples of what children had to learn in their early days.
(D) To emphasize the carelessness of children.

Questions 56 - 60

Lecture [116.mp3] [117.mp3]

56 Capital punishment was usually utilized in what sort of cases?

(A) Theft.
(B) Murder.
(C) Fraud.
(D) Rape.

57 What sort of punishment often replaced capital punishment? [118.mp3]

(A) Life imprisonment.
(B) Public beatings.
(C) Forced labor.
(D) Jury duty.

58 When was capital punishment most common in America? [119. mp3]
(A) In the early 1980s.
(B) In the early 1990s.
(C) In the mid 1800s.
(D) In the early 1800s.

59 What is the main idea of this lecture? [120. mp3]
(A) The decline of the popularity of capital punishment.
(B) The ability of one landmark case to change American law.
(C) The growth of the American legal system.
(D) The increasing popularity of capital punishment.

60 Listen again to 🔊 [121. mp3]

What does the professor imply when he says this? *"along with the fact that it had never been an effective deterrent to crime,"*

(A) That a particular case made capital punishment less effective.
(B) That the movement failed although it was popular.
(C) That capital punishment had never been implemented.
(D) That multiple reasons justified the abolition of capital punishment by many states.

Questions 61 - 65

Lecture [122. mp3] [123. mp3]

61 When does the talk take place?
(A) On course-registration day.
(B) During the first week of classes.
(C) A short time before the end of the semester.
(D) During the graduation ceremony.

62 What will having the pink form signed in the maintenance office indicate?

(A) All furniture repairs have been listed.
(B) Room charges have been refunded.
(C) The room is in good condition.
(D) Students are permitted to pay by check.

63 What must students do before the librarian will sign the yellow form?

(A) Register for graduate courses and pay tuition.
(B) Sign their library cards.
(C) Show copies of their final grades.
(D) Return all library books and pay any fines.

64 Why is it important for the students to turn in all of the signed forms before graduation?

(A) So that the administration can issue guest invitations.
(B) So they can have their rooms cleaned free of charge.
(C) So they can prove they are outstanding students.
(D) So they'll be allowed to graduate on time.

65 Listen again to

What does the speaker imply when she says this?
"I'll try to make this as quick as possible since I know how much you have to do in these last two weeks before graduation."

(A) That students tend to confuse the forms.
(B) That she wants students to work harder so that they can graduate.
(C) That it will take two weeks for students to complete the forms.
(D) That she does not want to make students feel more stress.

Questions 66 - 70

Lecture 128. mp3 129. mp3

66 In what type of climate is the saguaro plant found?
(A) Cold and dry.
(B) Warm and humid.
(C) Cool and rainy.
(D) Hot and dry.

67 Why is the saguaro plant unusual?   130. mp3
(A) It can store water.
(B) It has many roots.
(C) It is more than 10 feet tall.
(C) It bears small white flowers.

68 What happens to the plant when it rains?   131. mp3
(A) It loses its flowers.
(B) It expands to hold water.
(C) It bends down to the ground.
(D) It grows more leaves.

69 Why does water enter the saguaro plant quickly?   132. mp3
(A) Its roots are not deep.
(B) It is very tall.
(C) Its leaves absorb water.
(D) It has many branches.

70 Listen again to ♪   [133. mp3]

What does the professor imply when he says this?
"It may stand more than fifty feet tall and weigh as much as ten tons."

(A) That the saguaro has never been accurately measured nor weighed.
(B) That some saguaros grow very large.
(C) That most saguaros are small.
(D) That the saguaro grows quickly.

Questions 71 - 75

Lecture [134. mp3] [135. mp3]

71 Where was Andre born?

(A) In Atlantic City.
(B) In Marblehead, Massachusetts.
(C) In Rockport, Maine.
(D) In Boston, Massachusetts.

72 What does Andre do each year that is so unusual?   [136. mp3]

(A) Returns to his birthplace.
(B) Communicates with humans.
(C) Abandons his parents.
(D) Calls long distance.

73 How was Andre recently honored?   [137. mp3]

(A) A granite statue was dedicated to him.
(B) He was allowed to spend winters in an aquarium.
(C) He was set free in the ocean.
(D) He was fed well.

74 Who unveiled the town's monument? 138. mp3

(A) Mr. Goodridge.
(B) A dentist.
(C) The aquarium director.
(D) Andre.

75 Listen again to 🎵 139. mp3

Why does the speaker say this?
"Andre himself unveiled it, using his teeth to pull off the cloth."

(A) To explain why Andre became famous.
(B) To note that the statue was an accurate copy of the seal.
(C) To indicate that Andre broke the gift by accident.
(D) To show how impressive the ceremony was.

Questions 76 - 80

Lecture 140. mp3 141. mp3

76 Who is the speaker?

(A) An artist.
(B) A professor of library science.
(C) A doctor specializing in vision.
(D) A professor of art history.

77 What is the main topic of the talk? 142. mp3

(A) The history of the slide library.
(B) The use of slides in the course.
(C) The material to be tested that day.
(D) The outline of the course.

78 At what point during the semester would this talk be given? [143. mp3]

(A) The beginning.
(B) Just before the first weekly exam.
(C) Halfway through the course.
(D) Just before the final exam.

79 The course is designed with what kind of people in mind? [144. mp3]

(A) Those who have visual disabilities.
(B) Those who intend to become artists.
(C) Those who have no interest in painting.
(D) Those who have never taken art history before.

80 Listen again to 🎵 [145. mp3]

Why does the professor say this?
"experience has shown me that this is the best way"

(A) To encourage students to follow the professor's instruction.
(B) To note that there is no other means to attain the goals of the course.
(C) To remind students of the fun of studying art history.
(D) To convince students that identifying 2,000 slides is actually easy.

Questions 81 - 85

Lecture [146. mp3] [147. mp3]

81 When did the Spanish first begin to use quinine?

(A) In A.D. 600.
(B) During the third century.
(C) More than three hundred years ago.
(D) In the 1940's.

82 What is quinine used for?   148. mp3

(A) Curing leather.
(B) Treating deep cuts.
(C) Curing a disease.
(D) Preserving food supplies.

83 What happened while quinine was being exported to Europe?   149. mp3

(A) Quinine dropped in value.
(B) Cinchona trees almost disappeared.
(C) Quinine was often mixed with other substances.
(D) Cinchona supplies were cut off by the Peruvians.

84 Why were Cinchona trees cut down?   150. mp3

(A) To make room for settlements.
(B) To provide a fuel supply.
(C) To make a road through Peru.
(D) To get all the bark off.

85 Listen again to 🎵   151. mp3

Why does the professor say this?
"It was the only medicine effective in treating a disease called malaria."

(A) To show how threatening malaria is.
(B) To provide a fuel supply.
(C) To show how valuable quinine is.
(D) To identify the cause of malaria.

Questions 86 - 90

Lecture 152.mp3 153.mp3

86 What is the speaker's main topic?
(A) Sanitation in American cities of the nineteenth century.
(B) Sanitary conditions in early American farm houses.
(C) The care and feeding of pigs in the early United States.
(D) A comparison of urban and rural living conditions.

154.mp3

87 According to the speaker, what was true of American farmyards of the early nineteenth century?
(A) They were full of garbage.
(B) They were cleaner than cities of the time.
(C) They were extremely crowded.
(D) They had no pigs.

155.mp3

88 According to the speaker, what was the primary function of pigs in American cities?
(A) They provided food.
(B) They clean city streets.
(C) They chased uninvited guests from homes.
(D) They consumed much of the street garbage.

89 What does the speaker imply about the meat of the city pigs? 156.mp3
(A) It was sold cheaply.
(B) It was not fit for consumption.
(C) It was considered a rare delicacy.
(D) It was difficult to obtain.

90 Listen again to 🎵   157. mp3

Why does the professor say this?
"New York City's accumulation of garbage was so great that it was generally believed that the actual surface of many streets had not been seen for decades."

(A) To illustrate how fast the city's economy was growing.
(B) To explain how bad the sanitation of the city was.
(C) To criticize the exaggerated story about the overpopulated city.
(D) To praise the effort of the city's residents to preserve traditional landscapes.

Questions 91 - 95

Lecture 158. mp3 159. mp3

91 What is the main idea of this lecture?
(A) Soybeans are known in China.
(B) Soybeans have many uses.
(C) Soybeans are easy to grow.
(D) Some people like soybeans.

92 What soybean product can be used to enrich baked goods?   160. mp3
(A) Soy flour.
(B) Soybean leaves.
(C) Soybean oil.
(D) Soy sauce.

93 What is one important attribute of the soybean?   161. mp3
(A) It is a meat substitute.
(B) It is often used for backyard decoration.
(C) It is a complete milk substitute.
(D) It is easily processed into flour at home.

94 In the past, what was the main reason soybeans were grown in the United States?

(A) As an expensive food item.
(B) As a commercial agricultural crop.
(C) As an ingredient in Chinese cooking.
(D) As a vegetable in most backyard gardens.

95 Listen again to ♪

What does the speaker imply when she says this?
"Now, however, the soybean is being raised in backyard gardens."

(A) That raising soybeans has become common.
(B) That soybeans grow better in the shade.
(C) That the professor raises soybeans.
(D) That the United States does not export soybeans anymore.

Questions 96 - 99

96 What is the main topic of the lecture?

(A) Laboratory methods in psychology.
(B) How to make psychology respectable.
(C) A critique of behaviorist psychology.
(D) Recent advances in theoretical psychology.

97 What does the speaker think is the best way to study human psychology?

(A) Use experimental data only.
(B) Ask people's opinions on various matters.
(C) Use statistical data based on scientific models.
(D) Observe people in real-life situations.

98 What does the next part of the lecture most probably deal with?

(A) Further criticisms of behaviorist psychology.
(B) Criticism of other theories of psychology.
(C) Methods of studying human behavior in natural settings.
(D) New designs in equipment for psychology laboratories.

99 Listen again to 🎵

What does the speaker imply when he says this?
"Behaviorism seems to want the respectability of the natural sciences but it uses the methods of 50 years ago."

(A) That the history of behaviorism is old.
(B) That psychology owes much to natural sciences.
(C) That psychologists are generally more respected than natural scientists.
(D) That behaviorism has not attained its goal.

Questions 100 - 105

100 According to the speaker, why have many animals and birds lost their homes?

(A) Because of the enforcement of laws regarding wildlife.
(B) Because of ancient Cherokee Indian.
(C) Because of lack of water.
(D) Because of the excavation of archaeological sites.

101 What kinds of projects does the 1934 law deal with?

(A) Wildlife.
(B) Archaeological.
(C) Water.
(D) Soil.

102 According to the speaker, how many southern states have lost land because of dams?

(A) Two.
(B) Three.
(C) Four.
(D) Five.

103 Why have people fought a plan to build a dam in Tennessee?

(A) Because it would flood farm land and destroy homes.
(B) Because many people would lose their jobs.
(C) Because valuable topsoil would be washed away.
(D) Because it would endanger fish and destroy archaeological sites.

104 According to the speaker, who can prevent further destruction?

(A) The Cherokee Indians.
(B) The federal government.
(C) Lawyers.
(D) An informed public.

105 Listen again to 🎵

What does the speaker imply when she says this?
"The proposed dam would also destroy several important archaeological sites, including the ancestral capital of the ancient Cherokee Indian nation."

(A) That Cherokee Indians have proposed the construction of a dam in Tennessee.
(B) That the damage caused by the proposed dam would be extensive.
(C) That the proposed dam would not cause damage to wildlife.
(D) That constructing a dam is more beneficial than preserving cultural heritage.

Questions 106 - 110

Lecture 176.mp3 | 177.mp3

106 What special kind of services is the airline advertising?

(A) Quick service.
(B) Economical service.
(C) Luxury service.
(D) Individual service.

107 What is said about departure? 178.mp3

(A) It's always prompt.
(B) It's during business hours.
(C) It's in the evening.
(D) It's first thing in the morning.

108 What is the plane's destination? 179.mp3

(A) Luxembourg.
(B) London.
(C) Ireland.
(D) Chicago.

109 What kind of traveler does the airline want to attract? 180.mp3

(A) Wealthy businessmen.
(B) Vacationing families.
(C) Airline employees.
(D) Tourist groups.

110 What can be assumed about the arrival time? 181.mp3

(A) There are various arrival times.
(B) Early in the morning.
(C) Late at night.
(D) Approximately 6:45am.

Questions 111 - 115

Lecture

111 Where is the talk probably taking place?

(A) In a harbor.
(B) At an aquarium.
(C) On a bus.
(D) In a classroom.

112 Why was the animal given the name jellyfish?

(A) Because of its transparent body.
(B) Due to its odd shape.
(C) Because of their sweet taste.
(D) Due to the way it attacks enemies.

113 How does the jellyfish swim?

(A) By altering the shape of its body.
(B) By lowering and raising its "clapper."
(C) By spitting out its needles.
(D) By shedding its buds.

114 What part of the jellyfish sometimes injures people?

(A) Its "clapper."
(B) Its stomach.
(C) Its needle-shaped organs.
(D) Its teeth.

115 What kind of sea creature is the jellyfish?

(A) Bell fish.
(B) Water fish.
(C) Not a fish.
(D) Sweet fish.

Questions 116 - 120

Lecture 188.mp3 189.mp3

116 What was usually transported from west to east?

(A) Agricultural products.
(B) Manufactured goods.
(C) Settlers.
(D) Farm animals.

117 What new system soon replaced inland waterways?   190.mp3

(A) Railroads.
(B) Highways.
(C) Wagon trails.
(D) Sea routes.

118 When was inland waterway travel most popular?   191.mp3

(A) In the early 1800's.
(B) In the mid-1800's.
(C) In the late 1800's.
(D) In the early 1900's.

119 What is the main idea of this lecture?   192.mp3

(A) The role of inland waterways in the nation's growth.
(B) The development of New York City as a seaport.
(C) The growth of the railroads.
(D) The disappearance of the canal system.

193.mp3

120 What was the initial main result of the completion of the Erie Canal?

(A) It connected the Great Lakes region with New York City.
(B) It connected Detroit with New York.
(C) It connected Chicago with New York.
(D) It connected the Great Lakes with the Mississippi River.

Questions 121 - 125

Lecture 194.mp3 | 195.mp3

121 What information about cicadas does the speaker emphasize?

(A) The length of their life cycle.
(B) The damage they do to crops.
(C) Their time of emergence.
(D) Their ability to make noises.

122 Where do cicadas lay their eggs? 196.mp3

(A) Under the ground.
(B) On the surface of the ground.
(C) On twigs.
(D) In muddy puddles.

123 What do cicada nymphs eat? 197.mp3

(A) Bacteria.
(B) Small insects.
(C) Root sap.
(D) Young plants.

124 What kind of class is the speaker most probably addressing? 198.mp3

(A) Geography.
(B) Forestry.
(C) Biology.
(D) Engineering.

125 What can be said about the cicada's metamorphosis? 199.mp3

(A) They change their body by 20%.
(B) Changes usually occur in winter.
(C) The longest.
(D) Like that of locusts.

Questions 126 - 130

Lecture 200.mp3 201.mp3

126 What is the main point of the talk?

(A) How to benefit more from various practice techniques.
(B) How silver-plating and lacquer can make an instrument heavier.
(C) How to test whether instruments have been well-cared for.
(D) How the tone quality of an instrument is affected by its surface.

127 What is the speaker comparing?   202.mp3

(A) The differences among kinds of lacquer.
(B) The differences in plating techniques.
(C) Three horns with different finishes.
(D) Three different types of musical instruments.

203.mp3

128 What have French Horn players complained about over the years?

(A) The necessity of polishing unlacquered instruments.
(B) The way the prices of instruments keep going up.
(C) The difficulty of removing corrosion from their horns.
(D) The way lacquered horns produce a weaker sound.

129 What is the speaker going to do at the end of his talk?   204.mp3

(A) Remove lacquer from all the instruments.
(B) Play each of the instruments he has described.
(C) Show the listeners how to polish the horns.
(D) Repeat the sounds until they are clearer.

205.mp3

130 What is the main reason for using lacquer on the instruments?

(A) To polish them and make them look shiny.
(B) To increase their sound quality.
(C) So one doesn't need to use silver plating.
(D) To protect them from damage.

Questions 131 - 135

Lecture 206.mp3 207.mp3

131 Where was the carp originally found?

(A) Asia.
(B) Germany.
(C) Poland.
(D) The United States.

132 Why did the immigrants want to import carp? 208.mp3

(A) They would eat nothing else.
(B) They had no food.
(C) They wanted a reminder of home.
(D) They wanted to eat and to sell them.

209.mp3

133 What problem was encountered in raising carp in the United States?

(A) Most people didn't like to eat them.
(B) The number of carp increased too rapidly.
(C) There were too many import regulations.
(D) It was too expensive to feed them.

134 What do carp eat? 210.mp3

(A) Small wild animals.
(B) Other fish.
(C) Water plants.
(D) Pond decorations.

211.mp3

135 Why was the importing of carp to North America "too successful"?

(A) Farmers couldn't make any money for selling carp.
(B) They disappeared.
(C) There wasn't enough food for them.
(D) People wanted to eat water plants, native fish and wildlife.

Questions 136 - 140

Lecture 212.mp3 | 213.mp3

136 What development greatly contributed to the popularity and affordability of cotton fabric?

(A) The discovery of cotton in North America.
(B) The development of a seedless variety.
(C) Improved agricultural methods.
(D) Improvement of the method of processing cotton.

214.mp3

137 How much more efficient was the new machine than hand labor?

(A) Twice.
(B) Ten times.
(C) Five times.
(D) Fifty times.

215.mp3

138 According to the speaker, how much credit did the inventor actually receive?

(A) Enough to make him extremely wealthy.
(B) Enough to help him establish an empire.
(C) Almost none at all.
(D) None at all.

139 What did Eli Whitney invent?   216.mp3

(A) A machine that separated cotton seeds and fibers.
(B) An apparatus that planted cotton efficiently.
(C) A device that harvested cotton efficiently.
(D) A chemical that dissolved cotton fibers.

140 Why were the cotton seeds troublesome?   217.mp3

(A) They required a great deal of water.
(B) They were difficult to separate from the cotton plants.
(C) They were easy to copy.
(D) They were cool and lightweight.

Questions 141 - 145

Lecture 218. mp3 219. mp3

141 What is the topic of this talk?

(A) The salinity of the ocean.
(B) Pollutants found at sea.
(C) The composition of coral reefs.
(D) The weather patterns of coastal areas.

220. mp3

142 What does the speaker say about the ocean's level of saltiness?

(A) It is measured annually.
(B) It is highest at the ocean's surface.
(C) It has increased over time.
(D) It has decreased over time.

221. mp3

143 What is one of the sources of oceanic salinity mentioned in the talk?

(A) Seaweed found in kelp beds.
(B) Industrial waste.
(C) Meteorites.
(D) Underwater volcanoes.

144 Why does the speaker mention oysters and clams?

222. mp3

(A) They are more nutritious than freshwater shellfish.
(B) They contribute to the salinity of the ocean.
(C) They use salt to build their shells.
(D) They inhabit coral reefs.

145 What does the speaker mention about the rocky mantle?

223. mp3

(A) It contains traces of salt.
(B) It produces evaporation and thus rain.
(C) It erupts at the mid-ocean ridge.
(D) Its erosion produces minerals such as salt.

Questions 146 - 150

Lecture 224. mp3 225. mp3

146 What class might the speaker be teaching?
(A) Statistics.
(B) Cultural Anthoropology.
(C) Micro Economics.
(D) Meteorology.

147 What is the main subject of this talk?   226. mp3
(A) The history and traditions of early corn farmers.
(B) The growing cycle of Indian corn.
(C) Differences between the two corn harvests.
(D) Various ways to prepare corn.

227. mp3

148 According to the speaker, how was most of the corn prepared?
(A) It was first boiled and then dried.
(B) It was braided in bundles and steamed.
(C) It was dried and then ground into flour.
(D) It was roasted and wrapped in husks.

228. mp3

149 After the farmers ate the corn from the second corn harvest, what did they do with the husks?
(A) They braided them with animal hair for clothing.
(B) They bundled them together for fuel.
(C) They used them to insulate their homes.
(D) They made various items from them.

229. mp3

150 Which of the following correctly describes the Indians' corn harvests?
(A) First harvest: Yellow corn; Second harvest: Five months later.
(B) First harvest: Green corn; Second harvest: Yellow corn.
(C) First harvest: Ripe corn; Second harvest: Thanksgiving corn.
(D) First harvest: Sweet corn; Second harvest: Six months later.

Questions 151 - 156

151 Who is the speaker addressing?

(A) Engineers.
(B) Photographers.
(C) Fashion designers.
(D) College students.

152 What is the class called?

(A) Color and Design.
(B) Black and White.
(C) Materials and Techniques.
(D) First Design Principles.

153 What will the class work on during the first semester?

(A) The blending of colors.
(B) The checking of color cards.
(C) Black and white design.
(D) Basic slidemaking.

154 What is a critique?

(A) A shape.
(B) A design technique.
(C) A way to hang pictures.
(D) A discussion of a person's work.

155 What should the first design be composed of?

(A) Colored circles.
(B) White squares.
(C) Eleven triangles.
(D) Black rectangles.

156 What will happen at the beginning of each class? 236. mp3
(A) The teacher will show slides related to current projects.
(B) The students will only work with black and white.
(C) They will spend time critiquing their work.
(D) Discussion of good/bad points, Q & A, and current work.

Questions **157** - **161**

Lecture 237. mp3 238. mp3

157 What is the speaker's main point about urban vegetable gardens?
(A) They rarely produce enough crops to be worth the trouble.
(B) They are so contaminated with lead that they shouldn't be used.
(C) The lead concentration in them can be reduced by taking precautions.
(D) The produce grown in them must be washed before being eaten.

239. mp3

158 According to the speaker why should urban gardens be located away from roads?
(A) To decrease exposure to exhaust fumes.
(B) To lower contamination from roadside salt.
(C) To improve plants' ability to form fruit.
(D) To limit the amount of bacteria in the soil.

240. mp3

159 What is the effect of adding lime and organic material to the soil?
(A) The amount of lead in the soil can then be measured.
(B) Bacteria in the soil are destroyed.
(C) The fruit of the plants is protected.
(D) Less lead is absorbed by plants.

[241. mp3]

160 According to the speaker, which vegetable probably contains the most lead?

   (A) Lettuce.
   (B) Tomatoes.
   (C) Cucumbers.
   (D) Squash.

[242. mp3]

161 What may be the best way to determine lead concentration?

   (A) Expand proximity to exhaust fumes and paint chips.
   (B) Test children under six years-old regularly.
   (C) The soil should be tested regularly.
   (D) Test the plants regularly.

Questions 162 - 165

[Lecture] [243. mp3] [244. mp3]

162 When did the class start studying the Civil War?

   (A) Today.
   (B) Last Monday.
   (C) Three weeks ago.
   (D) At the start of the semester.

[245. mp3]

163 What feature of the Civil War will probably be emphasized in this unit?

   (A) Its battles.
   (B) Its causes.
   (C) Its conclusion.
   (D) Its journalists.

164 What will the class do on Monday? 246. mp3
(A) Answer questions in the textbook.
(B) Review an important battle.
(C) Write an essay about the Civil War.
(D) Discuss an article from a historical journal.

247. mp3

165 Why might the class spend a lot of time discussing the Civil War?
(A) It's one of the most important events in US history.
(B) The professor wrote her thesis paper on the Civil War.
(C) There are so many important generals and battles.
(D) There are so many essays and journals on two-hour reserve in the library.

Questions 166 - 170

Lecture 248. mp3 249. mp3

166 To whom is this announcement directed?
(A) Young students.
(B) College professors.
(C) Adults who want to finish college.
(D) Technicians who are training for jobs.

167 Why are older students welcomed?

(A) They discuss their problems openly.
(B) They talk more in class.
(C) They discipline others.
(D) They are very reliable.

168 What are returning students advised to do first?

(A) Try one course.
(B) Consult a counselor.
(C) Define a full program.
(D) Decide on a professional goal.

169 How does the announcer suggest that one get further information?

(A) By returning to college and asking.
(B) By calling a nearby college.
(C) By talking to another student.
(D) By checking a college catalog.

170 Why does the announcement suggest trying a single, non-credit course first?

(A) To get motivated to take classes again and a better idea of career plan.
(B) The cost can be a bit expensive for some students.
(C) The homework workload may be a bit too difficult for some students.
(D) It may be difficult to fit with older students' work schedule.

Questions 171 - 175

Lecture 254. mp3 255. mp3

171 Who is the speaker?
(A) A school administrator.
(B) A member of the student government.
(C) A company representative.
(D) A graduate student.

172 Why are the students at the meeting? 256. mp3
(A) They plan to take a trip.
(B) They are interested in summer jobs.
(C) They want to become travel agents.
(D) They have to write papers about the class trip.

173 What does the speaker ask the students to do? 257. mp3
(A) Return the yellow sheet to her.
(B) Write questions on their papers as she speaks.
(C) Make a list of the items she covers.
(D) Read along as she reviews the sheet.

258. mp3

174 How should the students indicate that they want to ask a question?
(A) By writing on a piece of paper.
(B) By raising their hands.
(C) By interrupting the speaker.
(D) By following the speaker when she leaves.

175 How are the students expected to sign up? 259. mp3
(A) By asking questions.
(B) By contacting Jane Murphy at Travel-Ease.
(C) Individually.
(D) By checking the information sheet.

Questions 176 - 180

Lecture 260.mp3 | 261.mp3

176 What is the main topic of the speaker's talk?
- (A) Conferences.
- (B) Index cards.
- (C) Examinations.
- (D) Research papers.

177 When will conferences be held?   262.mp3
- (A) Immediately.
- (B) The following week.
- (C) In two weeks.
- (D) At the end of the semester.

178 What is the purpose of the conference?   263.mp3
- (A) To narrow down the research topic.
- (B) To give a model of outline style.
- (C) To discuss the preliminary outline.
- (D) To prepare a thesis statement.

179 What term does the speaker define?   264.mp3
- (A) Thesis statement.
- (B) Research paper.
- (C) Final outline.
- (D) Conclusion.

265.mp3

180 What was the most frequent error by students in proposing their topics?
- (A) They chose irrelevant topics.
- (B) They chose too broad a topic.
- (C) They only submitted a preliminary outline.
- (D) They didn't include a clear thesis statement.

Questions 181 - 185

Lecture 266.mp3 267.mp3

181 What is the main subject of the lecture?

(A) The history of educational philosophy in the United States.
(B) How education in the United States has improved.
(C) Education in the United States before 1900.
(D) Different types of schools in the United States.

182 What was the role of education in the colonial period? 268.mp3

(A) To train philosophers.
(B) To help fight against England.
(C) To educate all students.
(D) To improve moral behavior.

183 What is Horace Mann known for? 269.mp3

(A) He was the first trained teacher.
(B) He wanted education for all.
(C) He wanted to use non-professional teachers.
(D) He was in favor of private schools.

270.mp3

184 What has characterized education in the United States in this century?

(A) It has been anti-religious.
(B) It has changed many times.
(C) It has been socially oriented.
(D) It has been concerned with rural problems.

185 What is John Dewey known for? 271.mp3

(A) Education without religion.
(B) His belief of the importance of school in our lives.
(C) His concern for social problems.
(D) He wanted education for all.

Questions 186 - 190

Lecture 272. mp3 | 273. mp3

186 Who is the speaker?

(A) A history teacher.
(B) A geology professor.
(C) An explorer.
(D) An astronomer.

187 Why did the speaker change his scheduled lecture? 274. mp3

(A) To report on an article about oceans he had read.
(B) To give a new assignment about mineral deposits.
(C) To discuss pressure cookers.
(D) To review the numerous formulas for salt.

188 What information is provided by this discovery? 275. mp3

(A) The location of large salt deposits.
(B) A new understanding of the chemistry and history of oceans.
(C) A new system of manufacturing pressure cookers.
(D) The latest theory about the age of the earth.

189 What does the speaker want his listeners to do? 276. mp3

(A) To attend his next lecture.
(B) To read the article themselves.
(C) To take a chemistry course.
(D) To copy the article.

190 Which of the following best describes this new discovery? 277. mp3

(A) A dynamic new system of recycling earth's plant life.
(B) A new understanding of the way the earth is changing.
(C) A different perspective on the history of chemistry.
(D) A manner in which balance is maintained in our seas.

Questions 191 - 195

Lecture 278. mp3 279. mp3

191 To whom is this report directed?

(A) Newspaper writers.
(B) Retiring teachers.
(C) Third-year graduate students.
(D) Graduating seniors.

192 How is job hunting different today? 280. mp3

(A) Recommendations aren't necessary.
(B) Filling out forms is usually adequate.
(C) Placement offices locate most jobs for you.
(D) A few recommendations won't get you a job.

193 What kind of course would be helpful to college students? 281. mp3

(A) A letter-writing course.
(B) A reading course.
(C) A course on job hunting.
(D) A course on newspapers.

282. mp3

194 How can newspaper reports about job hunting be best described?

(A) Optimistic.
(B) Impractical.
(C) Discouraging.
(D) Helpful.

283. mp3

195 What statistics does the professor give to demonstrate the difficulty in finding a job?

(A) 500 teachers applied for 4 openings and only 1/3 of new graduates found jobs.
(B) 5,000 teachers applied for 400 openings and only 1 in 3 new graduates found jobs.
(C) 500 teachers applied for 400 openings and only 103 new graduates found jobs.
(D) 5,000 teachers applied for 40 openings and only 1 in 3 new graduates found jobs.

Questions 196 - 199

Lecture 284. mp3 285. mp3

196 What happens to most meteors?

(A) They are collected by scientists.
(B) They are buried in craters.
(C) They leave the Earth's atmosphere.
(D) They burn up in the air.

197 Why does the speaker mention Arizona?

286. mp3

(A) A very large meteorite struck there.
(B) An important observatory is located there.
(C) Its desert is a good source of cosmic dust.
(D) An unusual number of meteorites land there.

198 What will the speaker probably discuss next?

287. mp3

(A) The effects of friction on satellites.
(B) The inner solar system.
(C) What meteorites reveal about the history of the Earth.
(D) Famous meteorites in recorded history.

199 Why is studying meteorites so important to scientists?   [288. mp3]

(A) They can learn how to destroy dangerous meteorites.
(B) They can learn more about the Arizona meteorite.
(C) Meteors could contain important evidence about our planet.
(D) They can learn more about shooting stars.

Questions 200 - 205

[Lecture] [289. mp3] [290. mp3]

200 When did the first battle of ironclads take place?

(A) During the Civil War.
(B) In colonial times.
(C) In the early twentieth century.
(D) In the 1960s.

201 What did the South use to construct its ironclad?   [291. mp3]

(A) The Monitor.
(B) Metal from many guns.
(C) A damaged wooden ship.
(D) Pieces of various ships.

[292. mp3]

202 What was the original name of the ship that the South used for its ironclad?

(A) The Merrimack.
(B) The Virginia.
(C) The Monitor.
(D) The Ironclad.

203 What advantage did the Merrimack enjoy in the battle?   [293. mp3]

(A) Its size.
(B) Its speed.
(C) Its trained crew.
(D) Its metal plating.

204 According to the speaker, what was proved by the battle?

(A) Southern engineering was superior.
(B) Ironclad ships were impractical.
(C) Wooden ships were out of date.
(D) Speed is more important than size.

205 Why was the battle indecisive?

(A) The North's Merrimack ship was slow; the South's Monitor ship was small.
(B) Both sides needed more preparation, and their ships had weaknesses.
(C) Wooden ships were out of date.
(D) Speed is more important than size.

Questions 206 - 210

206 What kind of motion picture camera shots were generally used in early films?

(A) Close-up shots.
(B) Full shots.
(C) Long shots.
(D) Action shots.

207 What occupation did Edwin S. Porter probably have?

(A) Film producer.
(B) Movie critic.
(C) Stuntman.
(D) Actor.

208 When was *After Many Years* produced? [299.mp3]
  (A) 1898.
  (B) 1903.
  (C) 1905.
  (D) 1908.

[300.mp3]

209 Why was the close-up of Annie Lee followed by a shot of Annie's husband?
  (A) To shock Griffith's contemporaries.
  (B) To show who Annie Lee was thinking about.
  (C) To indicate when Annie Lee's husband would return.
  (D) To avoid criticism of the close-up shot.

[301.mp3]

210 Which of the following were innovations by Griffith? (Choose 2 answers.)
  (A) Slow motion.
  (B) Close-up.
  (C) Cutting from one scene to another.
  (D) Long shot.

Questions 211 - 215

Lecture [302.mp3] [303.mp3]

211 What is the purpose of this talk?
  (A) To explain the high drop-out rate in the sport of competitive swimming.
  (B) To enlist support from parents for scholarship contributions.
  (C) To recruit swimmers from other sports.
  (D) To raise funds for a swimming competition.

212 What group is the speaker addressing?

(A) Parents of swimmers.
(B) Tennis coaches.
(C) Candidates for the swim team.
(D) Competitive runners.

213 The speaker compares competitive swimming with what sport, in terms of the athletes' age?

(A) Golfing.
(B) Tennis.
(C) Football.
(D) Running.

214 What does the speaker say about competitive swimming?

(A) It is a lifelong sport.
(B) It may interfere with academic studies.
(C) It does not offer many financial rewards.
(D) It is less demanding than other sports.

215 Why do most swimmers stop competing after college?

(A) There's not much pleasure or glory in winning.
(B) Swimming can be very expensive - they have to pay a heavy price.
(C) There are not enough athletic scholarships these days.
(D) They have to sacrifice most of their life for winning competition.

Questions 216 - 220

216 What is the main topic of the talk?

(A) The development of cement.
(B) The uses for cement.
(C) Various construction materials.
(D) Cement-producing countries.

217 Who developed the kind of cement that is used today? [310. mp3]
  (A) An Egyptian.
  (B) An ancient Roman.
  (C) A bricklayer.
  (D) An architect.

218 What was significant about the new kind of cement? [311. mp3]
  (A) It was very strong.
  (B) It looked like stone.
  (C) It resisted heat.
  (D) It cooled quickly.

219 How was cement stored? [312. mp3]
  (A) As a water-based paste.
  (B) As a liquid.
  (C) In stone-sized blocks.
  (D) In powdered form.

220 Which of the following best describes cement? [313. mp3]
  (A) Hard, solid stone mixture used for buildings and roads.
  (B) A powder comprised mainly of clay and limestone.
  (C) A watery, stone-lined chunk of material.
  (D) A mixture heated and cooled and often used in kitchen floors.

Questions 221 - 225

Lecture [314. mp3] [315. mp3]

221 Where does this talk take place?
  (A) In a department store.
  (B) In a mechanic's workshop.
  (C) At a newsstand.
  (D) In a newspaper pressroom.

222 What is the main topic of the talk?

(A) Recent developments in news photography.
(B) A new process to print newspaper.
(C) The advisability of frequent changes in dry-cleaning methods.
(D) Experimental printing with oil-based inks.

223 In what way is the "flexo" process considered better than standard printing?

(A) The newspapers remain thin and flexible.
(B) The presses can print larger sheets of paper.
(C) The ink is fast-drying and clean.
(D) The ink can be changed and retested.

224 According to the speaker, what advantage is there for people who read newspapers printed by flexography?

(A) Large print.
(B) Smooth pages.
(C) Pleasant smell.
(D) Clean hands.

225 What is a possible negative point of "flexography"?

(A) It can be quite expensive.
(B) It can only be used with special paper.
(C) The ink may dry too rapidly.
(D) They might have to change and retest the machines.

Questions 226 - 230

Lecture 320.mp3 321.mp3

226 What is the main topic of the talk?
(A) How quartz sand is formed.
(B) How underground waters differ.
(C) How rain is formed.
(D) How water tables change over time.

227 What was discussed in class last week?   322.mp3
(A) The formation of sand dunes.
(B) The purification of water.
(C) The formation of limestone.
(D) The weathering of rocks.

323.mp3

228 What characteristic of hard-water does the speaker mention?
(A) It is undrinkable.
(B) It has minerals in it.
(C) It is slightly colored.
(D) It feels slightly oily.

229 What does the speaker say about quartz?   324.mp3
(A) It usually absorbs mineral impurities.
(B) It is rarely found in sand dunes.
(C) It does not dissolve in water.
(D) It wears away other rocks.

230 What characteristic of soft water does the speaker mention?   325.mp3
(A) It contains a few impurities.
(B) A lot of minerals are dissolved in it.
(C) It contains few impurities.
(D) It contains many dissolved ions and other materials.

Questions 231 - 235

Lecture 326.mp3 327.mp3

231 Where is the talk taking place?
(A) In Texas.
(B) In Idaho.
(C) In Mexico.
(D) In Canada.

232 What does the speaker say is true of whooping cranes? 328.mp3
(A) They usually lay two eggs every season.
(B) They seldom lay more than one egg every two years.
(C) They have often been known to hide their eggs.
(D) They have recently increased their rate of egg production.

233 Why has research on whooping cranes been done recently? 329.mp3
(A) They protect smaller birds.
(B) They will soon be exported to other countries.
(C) They are in danger of dying out.
(D) They have been laying extra eggs.

234 What have scientists done to help improve the survival rate of whooping cranes? 330.mp3
(A) Placed their eggs in the care of other types of cranes.
(B) Cross-bred the cranes with stronger varieties of birds.
(C) Combined several small flocks into one large flock.
(D) Encouraged the cranes to nest in warmer regions.

235 How many birds that the speaker mentioned arrive early and how long is their journey? 331.mp3
(A) 760 birds; 25 miles.
(B) 1,706 birds; 25,000 miles.
(C) 76 birds; 2,500 miles.
(D) 706 birds; 205 miles.

Questions 236 - 240

Lecture 332. mp3 333. mp3

236 What is the main topic of this talk?
(A) Hungry people of the world.
(B) A good source of food.
(C) New varieties of fruits.
(D) The processing of food.

334. mp3

237 According to the speaker, what new food source are scientists studying now?
(A) Olive oil.
(B) Human mothers' milk.
(C) A kind of palm tree.
(D) A rare type of grain.

238 What is an essential quality of a good food source?   335. mp3
(A) Attractive foliage and fruit.
(B) The ability to yield oil.
(C) A similarity to mothers' milk.
(D) A high caloric content.

239 What can be inferred about a human mother's milk?   336. mp3
(A) Nothing equivalent to it occurs elsewhere in nature.
(B) It is relatively low in calories, but high in protein.
(C) Only babies can benefit from it.
(D) It is considered a high-quality food.

240 What areas would benefit most from the new tree?   337. mp3
(A) Regions which grow products such as wheat and barley.
(B) South America.
(C) Southern U.S.
(D) Regions which produce olive oil.

Questions 241 - 245

Lecture 338. mp3 339. mp3

241 What is the intended purpose of the new product?

(A) To stop air from drying out the fruit.
(B) To keep the fruit's skin clean.
(C) To slow down the fruit's breathing.
(D) To prevent the fruit from being bruised.

242 How is the new product applied? 340. mp3

(A) By spraying it on the trees.
(B) By putting it into the soil.
(C) By dipping the fruit into it.
(D) By wrapping it around the fruit.

243 From the talk, what can be inferred about the use of the new product? 341. mp3

(A) It's difficult to apply.
(B) It's only for certain types of fruit.
(C) It won't be effective in warm climates.
(D) It won't change the taste of the fruit.

244 According to the talk, what often happens when fruit is shipped? 342. mp3

(A) It's badly damaged.
(B) It ripens too quickly.
(C) It acquires a new flavor.
(D) It turns an unusual color.

245 What is one of the benefits of the new process from a business point of view? 343. mp3

(A) It will decrease the number and length of delays in shipping.
(B) It will allow the company to send the fruit to places farther away.
(C) It will help to decrease the fruit's price on the commodities market.
(D) It will help scientists to focus on testing other products.

Questions 246 - 250

Lecture 344.mp3 345.mp3

246. According to the speaker, where do insect eating birds usually fly?

(A) Above the clouds.
(B) Below the insects.
(C) Near the ground.
(D) Quite high in the air.

346.mp3

247. What does increased atmospheric pressure and humidity cause insects to do?

(A) Cease flying.
(B) Fly lower.
(C) Fly faster.
(D) Fly higher.

347.mp3

248. What weather conditions would cause swallows to fly the highest?

(A) Dry and clear.
(B) Cool and damp.
(C) Heavy rain.
(D) Fog.

348.mp3

249. What can be inferred from the speaker's comments about the flight of swallows in clear, fair weather?

(A) They probably fly high in the air.
(B) They probably fly in small groups.
(C) They probably fly quite slowly.
(D) They fly faster than other birds.

[349. mp3]

250 What can be inferred about the professor's explanation that insects are more affected by this phenomenon than the actual birds themselves?

(A) Increased atmospheric pressure and humidity make the insects fly more slowly and closer to the ground.
(B) The insects are part of the birds' food supply and the birds are forced to fly at the same altitude as the insects.
(C) In clear fair weather, the insects fly further from the ground.
(D) They fly considerably lower just before a storm or other changes in the weather.

Questions 251 - 255

Lecture [350. mp3] [351. mp3]

251 What does the speaker mainly discuss?

(A) A theory of population growth.
(B) The latest theory of social development.
(C) Results of global economic progress.
(D) The importance of demography.

252 What does the speaker use to help the students understand? [352. mp3]

(A) A three-dimensional model.
(B) An illustration in the textbook.
(C) A graph on the board.
(D) A large cardboard poster.

[353. mp3]

253 According to the speaker, what do the first and third stages have in common?

(A) High death rates.
(B) Food production difficulties.
(C) Rapid economic development.
(D) Slow population growth.

254 What problem concerning Notstein's model does the speaker mention?

(A) Accurate statistics are lacking.
(B) The model is too complex to be applied in practice.
(C) It fails to account for wars and natural disasters.
(D) It does not weigh equally the experiences of all countries.

255 What does the professor mention about the second stage?

(A) Social and economic development reduces the people's desire to have large families.
(B) Both birth and death rates are high, and as a result of this, population grows slowly.
(C) The birthrate and the death rate are in equilibrium.
(D) The population grows more rapidly because of improved living conditions through public health measures and increased food production.

Questions 256 - 260

256 Why did people first wear objects of adornment?

(A) To keep themselves warm.
(B) To become magicians.
(C) To protect themselves.
(D) To fasten their clothing.

257 Who was Henry Walters?

(A) A medical doctor.
(B) A railroad owner.
(C) A history professor.
(D) A clothing manufacturer.

258 What did Henry Walters collect?

(A) Coins.
(B) Magnets.
(C) Badges.
(D) Jewelry.

259 Where is this talk probably being given?

(A) In a temple.
(B) In a jewelry store.
(C) In a bank.
(D) In a classroom.

260 According to the professor, how many pieces of jewelry were involved in traveling exhibits, and in how many cities were they displayed at museums?

(A) Less than 200 pieces in more than 10 cities.
(B) Around 200 pieces in approximately 10 cities.
(C) 200 pieces in 10 cities.
(D) More than 200 pieces in 10 cities.

Questions 261 - 265

261 What is the main subject of the talk?

(A) Nineteenth-century political activists.
(B) The work of Clara Barton.
(C) A comparison of Clara Barton and Florence Nightingale.
(D) The ratification of the Geneva Treaty.

262 What was Clara Barton's original profession? 364. mp3
(A) School teacher.
(B) Hospital nurse.
(C) Military advisor.
(D) Zoologist.

263 How did military authorities react to Clara Barton's work on the battlefields? 365. mp3
(A) They recognized her medical expertise.
(B) They proclaimed her a heroine.
(C) They gave her administrative tasks.
(D) They opposed her presence there.

264 What does the speaker mean by referring to Clara Barton as a "living legend"? 366. mp3
(A) She became famous in her own lifetime.
(B) She lived according to her beliefs.
(C) She was a talented storyteller.
(D) She was a fictional character.

265 Why did Clara Barton feel that it was important for female nurses to serve on the battlefield regardless of their gender? 367. mp3
(A) Because the injured soldiers needed food, clothing and bandages to stay alive.
(B) Because nurses were vital to help maintain a positive morale in combat.
(C) Because that nurses provided a different perspective than regular doctors.
(D) Because that she was convinced they needed an organization to extend relief efforts.

Questions 266 - 270

Lecture 368.mp3 | 369.mp3

266 What is the speaker's main topic?
(A) How changes in architectural styles can make peoples' lives easier.
(B) What kinds of heating systems are least wasteful of energy.
(C) What homeowners can do to prevent energy waste.
(D) How energy used inside buildings can be cut down.

370.mp3

267 According to the speaker, what is true concerning the energy used in buildings?
(A) The sources of the energy used will disappear.
(B) The kinds of energy used can be changed.
(C) The cost of energy used must remain unchanged.
(D) The amount of energy used can be cut.

371.mp3

268 What energy-saving procedure does the speaker suggest for buildings in cool climates?
(A) Blow the cold air outside.
(B) Increase the amount of glass on the south side.
(C) Make the north-facing walls thick and dark.
(D) Use low-cost materials in their construction.

372.mp3

269 According to the speaker, where are the brightest lights needed in office buildings?
(A) In stairwells.
(B) In working areas.
(C) In elevators.
(D) In halls and lobbies.

[373. mp3]

270 According to the speaker, why were ecologically-inefficient architectural styles used in the past?

(A) The most important thing to focus was cheap material to build.
(B) They ignored the operating costs for the life of the building.
(C) They wanted to use heat in the winter and cool air in the summer.
(D) The glass-box office building was so popular.

Questions 271 - 275

[Lecture] [374. mp3] [375. mp3]

271 What is the purpose of the talk?

(A) To tell campers where to buy inexpensive equipment.
(B) To discuss necessary camping supplies.
(C) To tell campers about new products on the market.
(D) To warn campers about dangerous campsites.

272 What audience is the speaker addressing? [376. mp3]

(A) Veteran campers.
(B) Sales representatives.
(C) Students in summer camp.
(D) First-time campers.

[377. mp3]

273 What comment does the speaker make regarding the price of equipment?

(A) Quality is worth the extra cost.
(B) A good bargain is easy to find.
(C) Money can't buy safety.
(D) Lighter equipment is generally cheaper.

274 What does the speaker imply that campers should have in their backpacks?

(A) A guide to campgrounds.
(B) A tent frame.
(C) A folding chair.
(D) A first-aid kit.

275 According to the speaker, what are some of the features of the best equipment?

(A) Cool, stylish, fashionable, trendy.
(B) Practical, rugged, strong, waterproof.
(C) Lightweight, comfortable, convenient.
(D) Colorful, good design, long-lasting.

Questions 276 - 280

276 What is the main topic of this lecture?

(A) Bicycles and cars.
(B) Building codes.
(C) Energy conservation.
(D) New housing construction.

277 Why is insulation required in new houses?

(A) To limit discussion on heating bills.
(B) To prevent heat loss.
(C) To determine the temperature in homes.
(D) To convert homes to electric heat.

278 What is the purpose of building new houses facing north or south? [383. mp3]
(A) To avoid direct sunlight.
(B) To limit space used.
(C) To keep out the cold.
(D) To conform to other houses.

279 What has the city of Davis provided for bicycle riders? [384. mp3]
(A) Special paths.
(B) Resurfaced highways.
(C) More parking space.
(D) Better street lighting.

280 What was the first energy-saving action taken by the city of Davis? [385. mp3]
(A) Banning large, inefficient automobiles.
(B) Enacting more energy-conserving construction laws.
(C) Utilizing more fuel-efficient public transportation.
(D) Reducing the number of parking spaces.

Questions 281 - 285

Lecture 386. mp3 387. mp3

281 Who is the speaker?
(A) A poet.
(B) A teacher.
(C) A student.
(D) An artist.

282 What is the main topic? [388. mp3]
(A) The life of Emily Dickinson.
(B) The poetry of Walt Whitman.
(C) The poem "I Heard a Fly Buzz."
(D) The poem "I'm Nobody."

[283] **Approximately how old was Emily Dickinson when she died?**

(A) In her twenties.
(B) In her thirties.
(C) In her fifties.
(D) In her eighties.

[284] **What will the class do now?**

(A) Hear another report.
(B) Discuss one of Emily Dickinson's poems.
(C) Hear a lecture by the teacher.
(D) Discuss poems they have written themselves.

[285] **What happened to Emily Dickinson starting in her 20s?**

(A) She began to write her most famous poetry.
(B) She began to write many mystery poems.
(C) She became a very unsociable isolated person.
(D) She began to love the great outdoors.

Questions [286] - [290]

[286] **What will be the subject of the lectures to be presented on campus?**

(A) Police departments.
(B) European universities.
(C) Political changes in Europe.
(D) A new system of economics.

[287] **What is the purpose of the lectures?**

(A) To raise money for a new political movement.
(B) To explain why change occurs slowly in Europe.
(C) To increase aid to needy nations.
(D) To explain what is currently happening in Europe.

288 Why does the man recommend the lectures? 　395. mp3
(A) Because they are required for all majors.
(B) Because they were very expensive to fund.
(C) Because they are a good opportunity to get the most recent information.
(D) Because all of the lecturers are famous.

289 Why should the lectures be interesting? 　396. mp3
(A) Because they are sweeping across Europe.
(B) Because the speakers are all well-known.
(C) Because the speakers are all experts in their field.
(D) Because the man highly recommends them.

290 Who is required to go to all of the lectures? 　397. mp3
(A) Science majors.
(B) Physical Science majors.
(C) International Politics majors.
(D) Political Science majors.

Questions 291 - 295

Lecture　398. mp3　399. mp3

291 When did American figureheads start to have a distinct national style?
(A) In the Colonial period.
(B) Soon after the American Revolution.
(C) Around 1880.
(D) Around 1930.

400. mp3

292 According to the speaker, what determined the type of figurehead used on a ship?
(A) The kind of wood it was carved from.
(B) The kinds of models the carver used.
(C) The kinds of tools that were available.
(D) The kind of ship it was made for.

293. What did the figurehead on a whaling boat most often portray?

(A) A woman.
(B) An animal.
(C) A national hero.
(D) A captain.

294. What caused the disappearance of figureheads?

(A) The deaths of the leading carvers.
(B) Changes in the types of ships used.
(C) Lack of interest in folk art.
(D) The decline of the whaling industry.

295. Which models did American figureheads originally follow?

(A) British models.
(B) American Revolution models.
(C) Folk Sculpture models.
(D) Folk Art models.

Questions 296 - 300

296. What period of time is discussed in the lecture?

(A) 1970-1980.
(B) 1980-1985.
(C) 1985-1990.
(D) 1985-the present.

297. How does the speaker describe the economic conditions of that period?

(A) They were dreary.
(B) They were mixed.
(C) They were upbeat.

(D) They were hopeful.

407. mp3

298 According to the speaker, what caused the rise in unemployment?
(A) The lack of dedication among workers.
(B) The workers' desire to move to other regions.
(C) The closing of work places.
(D) The increase in the population.

408. mp3

299 What can be said about the majority of the displaced workers?
(A) They soon went on to other jobs.
(B) They were male.
(C) They had a great deal of working experience.
(D) They lived in the North Central states.

409. mp3

300 When they looked for new jobs, how many workers found a new job and in how long of a time period did it take them to do so?
(A) More than half found a new job within two years.
(B) A few more than half found a job after two years.
(C) About half found a job in under two years.
(D) Less than half found a job in two years or less.

編著者

イフ外語学院(いふ がいごがくいん)/ 中野 正夫(なかの まさお)

著者

山下 譲(やました ゆずる)　　　　丸井 亜紀子(まるい あきこ)
Shawn Wilenken(ショーン・ウィレンケン)　　皆川 祐太(みながわ ゆうた)
中野 文斗(なかの ふみと)

MP3付　TOEFL®TEST模擬試験&「レクチャー問題」リスニング徹底練習300問

2014年6月10日　第1刷発行

編著者　イフ外語学院/中野 正夫
著　者　山下 譲/丸井 亜紀子/Shawn Wilenken/皆川 祐太/中野 文斗
発行者　前田 俊秀
発行所　株式会社 三修社
　　　　〒150-0001 東京都渋谷区神宮前2-2-22
　　　　TEL03-3405-4511　FAX03-3405-4522
　　　　振替 00190-9-72758
　　　　http://www.sanshusha.co.jp
　　　　編集担当　山本 拓

印刷・製本　広研印刷株式会社

©Institute of Foreign Study, Masao NAKANO 2014 Printed in Japan　ISBN978-4-384-05772-0 C2082

カバーデザイン：CCK
本文DTP：CCK
付属MP3録音：財団法人 英語教育協議会(ELEC)
付属MP3制作：高速録音株式会社

®〈日本複製権センター委託出版物〉

本書を無断で複写複製(コピー)することは、著作権法上の例外を除き、禁じられています。
本書をコピーされる場合は、事前に日本複製権センター(JRRC)の許諾を受けてください。
JRRC〈http://www.jrrc.or.jp/　e-mail：info@jrrc.or.jp　tel：03-3401-2382〉

TOEFL® TEST
模擬試験＆「レクチャー問題」リスニング徹底練習300問

別冊解答集

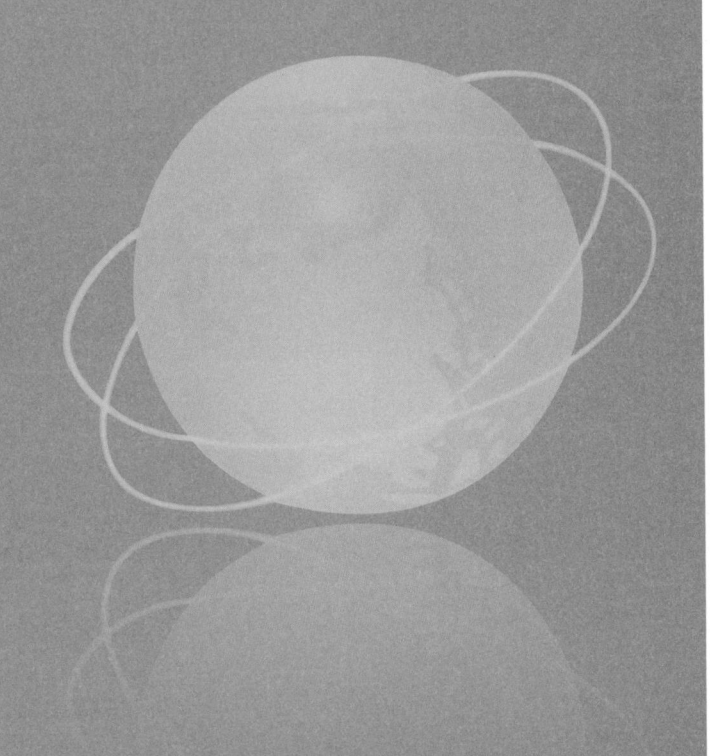

SANSHUSHA

TOEFL® TEST
模擬試験＆「レクチャー問題」リスニング徹底練習300問

別冊解答集

SANSHUSHA

別冊解答集
目次

第1部

模擬試験
解答の手引き

Reading Section
6

Listening Section
40

Speaking Section
66

Writing Section
78

第2部

リスニング・スペシャルトレーニング
解答の手引き

86

「解答の手引き」の活用法

▶ 模擬試験 Reading Section

　模擬試験 Reading Section の「解答の手引き」は、「解答」「解答のポイント」で構成されています。問題を解いた後、まず「解答」を確認しましょう。「解答のポイント」には、最初に各問題の選択肢があり、正答の選択肢が太字で示してあります。次に、解答に必要なパラグラフを示し、ヒントとなる部分に下線を施し、下線の最後に問題番号を付しています。

▶ 模擬試験 Listening Section

　模擬試験 Listening Section の「解答の手引き」は、「解答」「解答のポイント」で構成されています。問題を解いた後、まず解答をここで確認しましょう。「解答のポイント」には「スクリプト」と「スクリプト和訳」が付いていますので、解答の確認と復習の際に役立ててください。

▶ 模擬試験 Speaking Section

　模擬試験 Speaking Section の「解答の手引き」は、「スクリプト」「スクリプト和訳（会話、講義問題のみ）」「解答例」で構成されています。模擬試験の問題に解答した後、これらを参照して、復習してみましょう。

▶ 模擬試験 Writing Section

　模擬試験 Writing Section の「解答の手引き」は、「スクリプト」「和訳」「解答例」で構成されています。問題を解いた後、これらを参照して復習してみましょう。Question 2の解答例は、標準的な解答例（Standard Model）と、より簡易な解答例（Simple Model）の2つの解答例を載せています。ご自身のレベルに合わせて、参考にしてみましょう。

▶ リスニング・スペシャルトレーニング

　リスニング・スペシャルトレーニングの「解答の手引き」は、「解答」「スクリプト／解答のポイント」「スクリプト和訳」「重要単語」で構成されています。まず「解答」を確認しましょう。「スクリプト／解答のポイント」には、最初に各問題のスクリプトがあります。ヒントとなる部分に下線を施し、下線の最後に問題番号を付しています。次に正答の選択肢が太字で示してあります。答え合わせをした後、わからなかった部分を「スクリプト和訳」「重要単語」で確認して復習してみましょう。

第1部

模擬試験
解答の手引き

Reading Section

6

Listening Section

40

Speaking Section

66

Writing Section

78

Reading Section

解答 Questions 1 - 14

1. C 2. A 3. A 4. C 5. A 6. C 7. C 8. B 9. A
10. C 11. C 12. D 13. ■2 14. Diamonds: D, F, G Graphite: A, C, H

解答のポイント Questions 1 - 14

1 What can be inferred about graphite from paragraph 1?

(A) It is the most concentrated, but not the hardest form of carbon.
(B) It is derived from fullerite deep under the surface of the Earth.
(C) It does not need as much heat or pressure as diamonds to form.
(D) It is rarely found in great quantity on the Earth's surface.

Paragraph 1　　In addition to graphite and fullerite, there is one other form of naturally occurring carbon. It is the hardest, most concentrated form, and it is also widely considered to be the most beautiful: diamond. But unlike graphite, diamonds are rarely found in great quantity on the Earth's surface since they can only be formed hundreds of kilometers below the Earth's surface under severe geological pressure. The carbon must be under at least 435,000 psi (30 kilobars) of pressure at a temperature of at least 750 degrees Fahrenheit (400 degrees Celsius). If either the pressure or the heat drops below these points, graphite is formed. (1)

2 Why does the author mention elevators in paragraph 2?

(A) To give an easy-to-understand metaphor for how diamonds came to the surface.
(B) To explain the geological force which pushed diamonds into the mantle.
(C) To contrast the *Kimberlite Pipes* with modern volcanic activity.

(D) To emphasize the speed at which the diamonds were forced to the surface.

Paragraph 2   From deep within the Earth diamonds are — or were — pushed to the surface in what we call *Kimberlite Pipes*, named after Kimberly, South Africa, where the pipes were first discovered. These are not really pipes at all, but eruptions of magma which force their way upward from deep cracks in the lower part of the Earth's crust, acting much like an elevator, pushed diamonds and many other rocks and minerals through the mantle very quickly. (2) Such powerful eruptions occurred several hundred million years ago and the magma in these eruptions originated at depths up to three times deeper than the magma which is the source of modern volcanism.

3 The word **vein** in paragraph 3 is closest in meaning to:
 (A) **deposit.**   鉱床、鉱脈
 (B) complex.   複合体
 (C) trace.   跡
 (D) ditch.   水路

Paragraph 3   When the magma in these pipes cooled, it left a vein of kimberlite rock which contained, among other things, diamonds. Kimberlite is the best indication that diamonds may be found nearby, so prospectors seek out *deposits* of the bluish rock. (3) Kimberlite deposits are typically cone-shaped, with a smaller surface area of anywhere from two to 146 hectares. While this is not a small surface area, it is often difficult to locate such deposits since it has been many millions of years since the kimberlite first surfaced, and glaciers have scoured the surface of the Earth many times, altering the surface topography of every continent.

4 What do scientists or prospectors do when they want to find diamonds?
 (A) Search in areas which have a lot of volcanic activity.
 (B) Carefully measure pressure and temperature.

(C) Look for kimberlite rock on the surface.
(D) Examine areas which were defaced by glaciers.

Paragraph 3　　When the magma in these pipes cooled, it left a vein of kimberlite rock which contained, among other things, diamonds. Kimberlite is the best indication that diamonds may be found nearby, so *prospectors* seek out deposits of the bluish rock. (4) Kimberlite deposits are typically cone-shaped, with a smaller surface area of anywhere from two to 146 hectares. While this is not a small surface area, it is often difficult to locate such deposits since it has been many millions of years since the kimberlite first surfaced, and glaciers have scoured the surface of the Earth many times, altering the surface topography of every continent.

5 According to the passage, what is the usual shape of kimberlite deposits?
(A) They become wider as we dig deeper.
(B) They are shaped irregularly due to the glaciers.
(C) Like an elevator, they are shaped like tube.
(D) They become narrower as we dig deeper.

Paragraph 3　　When the magma in these pipes cooled, it left a vein of kimberlite rock which contained, among other things, diamonds. Kimberlite is the best indication that diamonds may be found nearby, so prospectors seek out deposits of the bluish rock. Kimberlite deposits are typically cone-shaped, with a smaller surface area (5) of anywhere from two to 146 hectares. While this is not a small surface area, it is often difficult to locate such deposits since it has been many millions of years since the kimberlite first surfaced, and glaciers have scoured the surface of the Earth many times, altering the surface topography of every continent.

6 The word **topography** in paragraph 3 is closest in meaning to:
(A) mountains.　山地の
(B) mix.　混合

(C) terrain. 地形
(D) level. 高さ、基準位置

Paragraph 3 When the magma in these pipes cooled, it left a vein of kimberlite rock which contained, among other things, diamonds. Kimberlite is the best indication that diamonds may be found nearby, so prospectors seek out deposits of the bluish rock. Kimberlite deposits are typically cone-shaped, with a smaller surface area of anywhere from two to 146 hectares. While this is not a small surface area, it is often difficult to locate such deposits since it has been many millions of years since the kimberlite first surfaced, and glaciers have scoured the surface of the Earth many times, altering the surface topography of every continent. (6)

[7] Which of the sentences below best expresses the essential information in the highlighted sentence in the passage? *Incorrect* choices change the meaning in important ways or leave out essential information.

Although it's hard to create and locate diamonds on Earth, it's virtually raining diamonds on Neptune and Uranus.

(A) While humans have to dig for diamonds, they can be found on the surface of some other planets.
(B) While diamonds are created underground on Earth, there are some planets where they come from rain.
(C) **Diamonds can be found in greater quantities on some planets other than Earth.**
(D) Diamonds are easier to locate on Earth than on some other planets.

Paragraph 4 Although it's hard to create and locate diamonds on Earth, it's virtually raining diamonds on Neptune and Uranus. (7) These planets contain 10-15 percent methane, and sufficient pressure and temperature to chemically convert the methane into diamonds and other complex hydrocarbons at relatively shallow depths. (7) Geologists have recreated these conditions in a laboratory using something called a diamond anvil cell, which squeezes the methane to several thousand times atmospheric pressure. Geologists then focus a laser beam on the pressurized liquid, creating diamond dust. (7)

8 It can be inferred from the passage that rubies and sapphires are all of the following EXCEPT:

(A) softer than diamonds.
(B) often found in *kimberlite*.
(C) a kind of mineral.
(D) a kind of *corundum*.

Paragraph 5 However and wherever they are created, diamonds are the hardest (8) mineral we know of, and are ranked 10 on the *Mohs Hardness Scale*. They can be anywhere from 10 to 100 times harder than minerals ranked 9 on the same scale; minerals such as corundum, including gems such as rubies and sapphires. (8)

9 According to paragraph 6, what is the essential structural difference between diamonds and graphite?

(A) **Diamonds are structurally more complex.**
(B) Graphite electrons are linked to fewer electrons.
(C) Diamonds have a ring-like structure.
(D) Graphite has a 3-dimensional structure.

Paragraph 6 It is the molecular structure of diamonds that makes them so hard. Each carbon atom in a diamond shares electrons with four other carbon atoms, forming an incredibly strong, three-dimensional lattice-shaped molecule. In graphite, by contrast, each carbon atom is linked to only one other carbon atom in a two-dimensional ring-shaped structure. (9) So even though graphite and diamonds share the same chemistry, their different structures gives them entirely different properties: whereas diamond is the hardest mineral known to man, graphite is one of the softest. Whereas diamond is an excellent electrical insulator, graphite is a good conductor of electricity. Whereas diamond is the ultimate abrasive, graphite is a very good lubricant. And whereas diamond is usually transparent, graphite is opaque.

10 The purpose of paragraph 6 is to:

(A) discuss reasons diamonds are harder than graphite.
(B) give examples of the structures of diamonds and graphite.
(C) contrast the structure and properties of diamonds and graphite.
(D) form a conclusion about the uses of diamonds and graphite.

Paragraph 6　　It is the molecular structure of diamonds that makes them so hard. Each carbon atom in a diamond shares electrons with four other carbon atoms, forming an incredibly strong, three-dimensional lattice-shaped molecule. In graphite, by contrast, (10) each carbon atom is linked to only one other carbon atom in a two-dimensional ring-shaped structure. So even though graphite and diamonds share the same chemistry, their different structures gives them entirely different properties: whereas (10) diamond is the hardest mineral known to man, graphite is one of the softest. Whereas (10) diamond is an excellent electrical insulator, graphite is a good conductor of electricity. Whereas diamond is the ultimate abrasive, graphite is a very good lubricant. And whereas diamond is usually transparent, graphite is opaque.

11 The word transparent in paragraph 6 is closest in meaning to:

(A) unequivocal.　曖昧でない
(B) arduous.　努力を要する
(C) unclouded.　澄んだ
(D) affluent.　裕福な

Paragraph 6　　It is the molecular structure of diamonds that makes them so hard. Each carbon atom in a diamond shares electrons with four other carbon atoms, forming an incredibly strong, three-dimensional lattice-shaped molecule. In graphite, by contrast, each carbon atom is linked to only one other carbon atom in a two-dimensional ring-shaped structure. So even though graphite and diamonds share the same chemistry, their different structures gives them entirely different properties: whereas diamond is the hardest mineral known to man, graphite is one of the softest. Whereas diamond is an excellent electrical insulator, graphite is a good conductor of electricity. Whereas diamond is the ultimate abrasive, graphite is a very good lubricant. And whereas diamond is usually transparent, graphite is opaque. (11)

12. The word **degrade** in the final paragraph is closest in meaning to:
(A) tear away.
(B) cut up.
(C) put out.
(D) **break down.**

7 [■ 1] Since diamonds are created under such severe conditions, at the earth's surface's temperatures and pressures they begin to degrade. [■ 2] Graphite is actually the most stable form of carbon, and in fact, all diamonds at or near the surface of the Earth are currently undergoing a transformation into graphite. (12) [■ 3] But don't worry about that ring on your own or your beloved's finger; this reaction, fortunately, is extremely slow. [■ 4]

13. Look at the 4 squares [■] in the final paragraph and indicate where the following sentence can best be added to the passage.

Technically, they are described as unstable at the surface of the earth.

7 [■ 1] Since *diamonds* are created under such severe conditions, at the earth's surface's temperatures and pressures they begin to degrade. [■ 2] *Graphite is actually the most stable* form of carbon, and in fact, all diamonds at or near the surface of the Earth are currently undergoing a transformation into graphite. (13) [■ 3] But don't worry about that ring on your own or your beloved's finger; this reaction, fortunately, is extremely slow. [■ 4]

14 Complete the table by matching the phrases below.
Directions: Select the best words or phrases from the answer choices and match them to either the Diamond column or the Graphite column. TWO of the answer choices will not be used.
This question is worth 4 points.

Diamonds	Graphite
· (D) three-dimensional structure	· (A) abundant on Earth
· (F) electrical insulator	· (C) two-dimensional structure
· (G) transparent luster	· (H) stable at the Earth's surface

Paragraph 1 In addition to graphite and fullerite, there is one other form of naturally occurring carbon. It is the hardest, most concentrated form, and it is also widely considered to be the most beautiful: diamond. But unlike graphite, diamonds are rarely found in great quantity on the Earth's surface (14-A) since they can only be formed hundreds of kilometers below the Earth's surface under severe geological pressure. The carbon must be under at least 435,000 psi (30 kilobars) of pressure at a temperature of at least 750 degrees Fahrenheit (400 degrees Celsius). If either the pressure or the heat drops below these points, graphite is formed.

Paragraph 6 It is the molecular structure of diamonds that makes them so hard. Each carbon atom in a diamond shares electrons with four other carbon atoms, forming an incredibly strong, three-dimensional (14-D) lattice-shaped molecule. In graphite, by contrast, each carbon atom is linked to only one other carbon atom in a two-dimensional (14-C) ring-shaped structure. So even though graphite and diamonds share the same chemistry, their different structures gives them entirely different properties: whereas diamond is the hardest mineral known to man, graphite is one of the softest. Whereas diamond is an excellent electrical insulator, (14-F) graphite is a good conductor of electricity. Whereas diamond is the ultimate abrasive, graphite is a very good lubricant. And whereas diamond is usually transparent(14-G), graphite is opaque.

Paragraph 7

[■1] Since diamonds are created under such severe conditions, at the earth's surface's temperatures and pressures they begin to degrade. [■2] Graphite is actually the most stable form of carbon,(14-H) and in fact, all diamonds at or near the surface of the Earth are currently undergoing a transformation into graphite. [■3] But don't worry about that ring on your own or your beloved's finger; this reaction, fortunately, is extremely slow. [■4]

和訳

Paragraph 1

　グラファイトとフラライトに加えて、別にもう一つ自然発生の炭素の形態がある。それは最も硬く、最も凝縮された形であり、また最も美しい物として広く知られている。それはダイアモンドである。しかし、グラファイトと違いダイアモンドは地球の表面ではあまり多くは発見されない。なぜなら、それら（ダイヤモンド）は地表の数百キロ下で強烈な地質の圧力のもとでのみ形成されるからである。炭素は少なくとも435,000psiの圧力で華氏750度の状況の下に置かれていなければならない。もし圧力か熱のいずれかでもこれらのポイントから下がると、グラファイトができてしまうのである。

Paragraph 2

　地球の奥深くから、ダイアモンドはいわゆる"Kimberlite Pipes"と呼ばれる鉱脈を通って地上へと押し出される（もしくは、押し出された）が、"Kimberlite Pipes"は鉱脈が最初に見つかった南アフリカのKimberlyにちなんで名づけられた。これらは実はまったく鉱脈ではなくマグマの噴出である。そのマグマの噴出は、地殻下部の割れ目深くからまるでエレベーターのように上方へと押し上がってきて、急激な速さでマントルを通ってダイアモンドと他の岩と鉱物を押し上げた。そのような激しい噴出は数億年前に起こり、これらの噴出のマグマは現代の火山活動の源のマグマより最大では３倍ほど深いところから発生し

たものである。

Paragraph 3

　これらの鉱脈のマグマが冷えると、他のさまざまな物に混じってダイヤモンドを含む kimberlite 石の鉱脈を残す。Kimberlite はダイヤモンドが近くに見つかるかもしれないという最良の目印である。従って、山師たちは、その青みがかった岩の鉱床を探す。Kimberlite の鉱床は一般的に円錐形で、小さいほうの表面積は、2～146ヘクタールの間である。これは小さい表面積ではないのだが、しばしばそのような鉱床を見つけるのが困難である。なぜなら、Kimberlite が最初に地表に現れてから、もう何百万年も過ぎてしまっているし、氷河が地球の表面を何度も削ってすべての大陸の表面地形を変えてしまっているからである。

Paragraph 4

　地球でダイアモンドを造り、見つけ出すのは困難だが、海王星や天王星では「ダイアモンドが浴びるほどある。」といってもいいくらいである。これらの惑星は10～15％のメタンを含み、比較的浅いところで、化学的にメタンをダイアモンドや他の複雑な炭化水素に転化させる十分な圧力と温度を備えている。地質学者はこれらの状態を実験室で"diamond anvil cell"と呼ばれる物を使って再現した。この"diamond anvil cell"は、メタンを大気圧の数千倍に圧縮して作る。地質学者たちは、その後レーザー光線を圧縮された液体に当て、ダイアモンドの粉末を造りだした。

Paragraph 5

　どのようにして、また、どこで形成されたにしろ、ダイアモンドは私たちの知っている最も固い鉱物であり、"Mohs Hardness Scale（モースの硬度計）"で10位をしめている。ダイアモンドは同じ計りで9位をしめた鉱物、ルビーやサファイヤなどの宝石を含む鋼玉などの鉱物、の10倍から100倍硬い。

Paragraph 6

　ダイアモンドをそれほど硬くしているのはその分子構造である。ダイアモンドの炭素原子ひとつひとつは、4つの別の炭素原子と電子を共有し、驚くほど強力な立体の格子状の分子を造る。反対にグラファイトの炭素原子のおのおのは、平面的な環状構造の中で、たった1つの炭素原子と結びついている。だか

ら、たとえグラファイトとダイアモンドが同じ化学物質を含んでいても、異なった構造がまったく違った特性をあたえている。ダイアモンドが人間に知られている最も硬い鉱物であるのに対し、グラファイトは最もやわらかい鉱物の一つである。ダイアモンドが優れた電気断熱体であるのに対し、グラファイトは有効な電気伝導体である。ダイアモンドが最高の研磨剤であるのに対し、グラファイトは大変よい潤滑剤である。そしてダイアモンドがたいてい透明なのに対し、グラファイトは不透明である。

Paragraph 7

ダイアモンドは、こういう厳しい状況で造られるので、地球の上面での温度や圧力のもとでは劣化し始める。

グラファイトは、実際最も安定した炭素の形態である。事実、地表や、地表近くののすべてのダイアモンドは今グラファイトへと変化している最中である。しかし、あなたの指、若しくはあなたの愛する人の指の指輪について心配する必要はない。この反応は、幸いなことに、極めてゆっくり進むのである。

解答 Questions 15 - 28

15 D　16 B　17 D　18 C　19 A　20 C　21 C　22 B　23 C　24 ■2
25 C　26 A　27 B　28 A, C, F

解答のポイント Questions 15 - 28

15 The word **disparate** in paragraph 1 is closest in meaning to:

(A) dissenting.　異議を唱える

(B) arrogant.　傲慢な

(C) flourishing.　繁栄している

(D) **separated.**　拡散した

Paragraph 1

Tecumseh was a famous Shawnee American Indian leader (16) who spent much of his life attempting to rally(15) disparate North American Indian tribes(15) in a mutual defense(15) of their lands. He was greatly admired in his day, remains a respected icon for Native Americans, and is a national hero in Canada. Even his longtime adversary, William Henry Harrison, considered Tecumseh to be "one of those uncommon geniuses which spring up occasionally to produce revolutions and overturn the established order of things."

16 The quote by Harrison in the first paragraph emphasizes that Tecumseh was:

(A) an unrivaled prophet.
(B) a talented leader.
(C) a skillful negotiator.
(D) an unusual trader.

Paragraph 1　　Tecumseh was a famous Shawnee American Indian leader (16) who spent much of his life attempting to rally disparate North American Indian tribes in a mutual defense of their lands. He was greatly admired in his day, remains a respected icon (16) for Native Americans, and is a national hero (16) in Canada. Even his longtime adversary, William Henry Harrison, considered Tecumseh to be "one of those uncommon geniuses (16) which spring up occasionally to produce revolutions and overturn the established order of things."

17 The word inherited in paragraph 2 is closest in meaning to:

(A) reproduced.　再生する、繁殖させる
(B) refined.　洗練する、精製する
(C) respected.　尊敬する
(D) received.　受け取る、受理する

Paragraph 2　　Tecumseh was born in what is now Ohio around 1768. Shawnee children inherited a clan affiliation from their fathers, (17) and Tecumseh belonged to the Panther clan, one of about a dozen exogamous Shawnee clans. In addition to clans, the Shawnee had five traditional divisions, membership of which was also inherited from the father.

Tecumseh's father belonged to the Kispoko division, while his mother was a Shawnee of the Piqua division. There is some evidence to suggest that Tecumseh's paternal grandfather may have been a white British trader.

18 What is the purpose of the third paragraph?
(A) To provide a list of Tecumseh's youth activities.
(B) To show that Tecumseh was widely traveled.
(C) **To describe how Tecumseh was influenced by war.**
(D) To emphasize the importance of Tecumseh's father's death.

Paragraph 3 Warfare(18)between whites and Indians loomed large in Tecumseh's youth. His father was killed in the Battle of Point Pleasant(18)in 1774 prior to the American Revolutionary War, (18)during which time many Shawnee villages were being destroyed by American frontiersmen. He left his boyhood home after the Battle of Piqua(18)in 1780, and was raised in part by an older brother who was an important war leader. (18)They fought together against whites in Kentucky and Ohio(18)during the 1780s, then around 1790 Tecumseh traveled south to live among(and fight alongside)(18) the Cherokees for two years. It was there that he met the famous leader Dragging Canoe, who led a resistance movement(18)against U.S. expansion and encouraged him to return to Ohio.

19 According to paragraph 3, Tecumseh fought in all of the following places *except* :
(A) **Canada.**
(B) Kentucky.
(C) the American south.
(D) Ohio.

Paragraph 3 Warfare between whites and Indians loomed large in Tecumseh's youth. His father was killed in the Battle of Point Pleasant in 1774 prior to the American Revolutionary War, during which time many Shawnee villages were being destroyed by American frontiersmen. He left his boyhood home after the Battle of Piqua in 1780, and was raised in part by an older brother who was an important war leader. They fought together against whites in Kentucky and Ohio(19)during the 1780s, then around 1790 Tecumseh traveled south to live among(and fight alongside(19)the Cherokees for two years. It was there that he met the famous leader Dragging Canoe, who led a resistance movement against U.S. expansion and encouraged him to return to Ohio.

20 The word movement in paragraph 3 is closest in meaning to:
 (A) migration.
 (B) transportation.
 (C) campaign.
 (D) motion.

Paragraph 3　(Warfare between whites and Indians loomed large in Tecumseh's youth. His father was killed in the Battle of Point Pleasant in 1774 prior to the American Revolutionary War, during which time many Shawnee villages were being destroyed by American frontiersmen. He left his boyhood home after the Battle of Piqua in 1780, and was raised in part by an older brother who was an important war leader. They fought together against whites in Kentucky and Ohio during the 1780s, then around 1790 Tecumseh traveled south to live among(and fight alongside the Cherokees for two years. It was there that he met the famous leader Dragging Canoe, who led a resistance movement against U.S. expansion(20)and encouraged him to return to Ohio.

21 It can be inferred from paragraph 4 that Tecumseh's younger brother:
 (A) was a powerful warrior.
 (B) was killed before Tecumseh.
 (C) was a popular religious teacher.
 (D) was not happy with other Shawnee.

Paragraph 4　Over the next two decades, he participated in nativist religious revivals with his younger brother, a religious teacher (21) called "The Prophet", encouraging Native Americans to reject the ways of the whites and to refuse to cede more lands to them. He attracted many American Indian followers from many different nations, emerging as the leader of this confederation, which was built upon a foundation established by the religious appeal of his younger brother. (21) Relatively few of these followers were Shawnees; although Tecumseh is often portrayed as the leader of the Shawnees, most Shawnees in fact had little involvement with Tecumseh or the Prophet, and chose instead to move further west or to remain at peace with the United States.

22 Which of the sentences below best expresses the essential information in the highlighted sentence in the passage? *Incorrect* choices change the meaning in important ways or leave out essential information.

He attracted many American Indian followers from many different nations, emerging as the leader of this confederation, which was built upon a foundation established by the religious appeal of his younger brother.

(A) Tecumseh and his brother recruited the young religious Shawnee men for their war on the Americans.

(B) **Tecumseh used his brother's popularity to recruit men to fight the Americans.**

(C) Tecumseh's brother never could have been such a successful religious leader had it not been for Tecumseh's leadership.

(D) Tecumseh's warriors hailed from many different nations and had many different religions, but they were united in their desire to return to Canada.

Paragraph 4 Over the next two decades, he participated in nativist religious revivals with his younger brother, a religious teacher called "The Prophet", encouraging Native Americans to reject the ways of the whites and to refuse to cede more lands to them. He attracted many American Indian followers from many different nations, emerging as the leader of this confederation, which was built upon a foundation established by the religious appeal of his younger brother. (22) Relatively few of these followers were Shawnees; although Tecumseh is often portrayed as the leader of the Shawnees, most Shawnees in fact had little involvement with Tecumseh or the Prophet, and chose instead to move further west or to remain at peace with the United States.

23 According to paragraph 5, what can be inferred about the battle that Tecumseh and Harrison fought in Tippecanoe?

(A) Tecumseh won a brilliant overnight victory.
(B) Tecumseh was betrayed by his own warriors.
(C) Tecumseh was pushed out of his settlement.
(D) Tecumseh had a smaller force than Harrison.

Paragraph 5

[■1] Tecumseh's involvement with the future president William Henry Harrison began in August 1811, when Tecumseh met with then-Governor Harrison at Vincennes, assuring him that his Shawnee brothers meant to remain at peace with the United States. [■2] Harrison led more than a thousand men up the Wabash River, on an expedition to intimidate the Prophet and his followers. [■3] The Native American warriors attacked the American encampment on the night of November 6, 1811, in what became known as the Battle of Tippecanoe, but Harrison's men held their ground; (23) the Indians withdrew, (23) and the victorious Americans burned the town. [■4]

24 Look at the 4 squares [■] in paragraph 5 and indicate where the following sentence can best be added to the passage.

Harrison, however, refused the olive branch.

Paragraph 5

[■1] Tecumseh's involvement with the future president William Henry Harrison began in August 1811, when Tecumseh met with

21

then-Governor Harrison at Vincennes, assuring him that his Shawnee brothers meant to remain at peace with the United States. (24) [■ 2] Harrison led more than a thousand men up the Wabash River, on an expedition to intimidate the Prophet and his followers. (24) [■ 3] The Native American warriors attacked the American encampment on the night of November 6, 1811, in what became known as the Battle of Tippecanoe, but Harrison's men held their ground; the Indians withdrew, and the victorious Americans burned the town. [■ 4]

25 The word **their** in the final sentence of paragraph 5 refers to:
(A) Shawnee.
(B) Americans.
(C) **men.**
(D) warriors.

Paragraph 5 [■ 1] Tecumseh's involvement with the future president William Henry Harrison began in August 1811, when Tecumseh met with then-Governor Harrison at Vincennes, assuring him that his Shawnee brothers meant to remain at peace with the United States. [■ 2] Harrison led more than a thousand men up the Wabash River, on an expedition to intimidate the Prophet and his followers. [■ 3] The Native American warriors attacked the American encampment on the night of November 6, 1811, in what became known as the Battle of Tippecanoe, but Harrison's men held their ground;(25)the Indians withdrew, and the victorious Americans burned the town. [■ 4]

26 The word **enigmatic** in paragraph 6 is closest in meaning to:
(A) **hard to understand.** 理解しがたい
(B) hard to like. 好きになりがたい
(C) hard to describe. （言葉で）説明しがたい
(D) hard to depend. 信頼しがたい

Paragraph 6 Despite the failure of Tecumseh to halt the westward expansion of the whites, he remains an enigmatic figure in American history for the supposed curse he placed on the American presidents: that is, that every president elected in a year ending in zero would die in office. (26) Indeed, the curse held true for 140 years, for all the presidents elected from 1840 to 1960. William Henry Harrison died of pneumonia in 1841, Abraham Lincoln was assassinated in 1865, James Garfield was assassinated in 1881, William McKinley was assassinated in 1901, Warren G. Harding died of a heart attack in 1923, Franklin D. Roosevelt died of a cerebral hemorrhage in 1945, and John F. Kennedy was assassinated in 1963. Some call this a coincidence, while others believe the curse has been lifted now that Ronald Reagan survived his presidency, which started in 1980.

27 Who did Tecumseh allegedly curse?

(A) The Shawnee.

(B) **American presidents.**

(C) William Henry Harrison.

(D) Governor Harrison's army.

Paragraph 6   Despite the failure of Tecumseh to halt the westward expansion of the whites, he remains an enigmatic figure in American history for the supposed curse he placed on the American presidents): (27) that is, that every president elected in a year ending in zero would die in office. Indeed, the curse held true for 140 years, for all the presidents elected from 1840 to 1960. William Henry Harrison died of pneumonia in 1841, Abraham Lincoln was assassinated in 1865, James Garfield was assassinated in 1881, William McKinley was assassinated in 1901, Warren G. Harding died of a heart attack in 1923, Franklin D. Roosevelt died of a cerebral hemorrhage in 1945, and John F. Kennedy was assassinated in 1963. Some call this a coincidence, while others believe the curse has been lifted now that Ronald Reagan survived his presidency, which started in 1980.

28 An introductory sentence for a brief summary of the passage is provided below. Complete the summary by selecting the THREE answer choices that express the most important ideas in the passage. Some sentences do not belong in the summary because they express ideas that are not presented in the passage or are minor ideas in the passage. *This question is worth 2 points.*

Tecumseh was one of the most famous and influential American Indian leaders in history.

(A) With his brother, Tecumseh promoted a religion which encouraged native Americans to renounce the whites and their way of life.
(B) A brilliant warrior, his greatest accomplishment was to assist Dragging Canoe in fighting whites in the southern United States.
(C) Tecumseh gained fame and respect for his stance against the white Americans who were moving west.
(D) Tecumseh was ultimately unable to unite fellow American Indians, who fell, tribe by tribe, to the white man.
(E) Tecumseh's legend is based mostly on his stunning victory over Harrison at Tippecanoe.
(F) Tecumseh's curse is believed by some, but many think it is nothing more than a hoax or coincidence.

Paragraph 4 Over the next two decades, he participated in nativist religious revivals with his younger brother, a religious teacher called "The Prophet", encouraging Native Americans to reject the ways of the whites and to refuse to cede more lands to them. He attracted many American Indian followers from many different nations, emerging as the leader of this confederation, which was built upon a foundation established by the religious appeal of his younger brother. (28-A) Relatively few of these followers were Shawnees; although Tecumseh is often portrayed as the leader of the Shawnees, most Shawnees in fact had little involvement with Tecumseh or the Prophet, and chose instead to move further west or to remain at peace with the United States.

Paragraph 6　　Despite the failure of Tecumseh to halt the westward expansion of the whites), (28-C) he remains an enigmatic figure in American history for the supposed curse he placed on the American presidents: that is, that every president elected in a year ending in zero would die in office. Indeed, the curse held true for 140 years, for all the presidents elected from 1840 to 1960. William Henry Harrison died of pneumonia in 1841, Abraham Lincoln was assassinated in 1865, James Garfield was assassinated in 1881, William McKinley was assassinated in 1901, Warren G. Harding died of a heart attack in 1923, Franklin D. Roosevelt died of a cerebral hemorrhage in 1945, and John F. Kennedy was assassinated in 1963. Some call this a coincidence, while others believe the curse has been lifted now that Ronald Reagan survived his presidency, which started in 1980. (28-F)

和訳

Paragraph 1

　　テカムセは、異なる北アメリカ・インディアンの部族が、自分たちの土地を共同で守ることにおいて団結させることに人生の多くを費やした有名なアメリカ・インディアンの Shawnees（ショーニー族）のリーダーであった。彼は若き日の全盛期には非常に敬服され、今でもアメリカ原住民にとって敬意を払われている偶像的存在であり続け、カナダでは国民的英雄である。彼の長年の敵対者である William Henry Harrison（ウィリアム・ヘンリー・ハリソン）でさえも、テカムセを、「革命を起こし、確立された秩序をくつがえすために時折出現する、稀に見る天才の一人」と見なしていた。

Paragraph 2

　　テカムセは1768年頃、現在のオハイオ州にあたるところで生まれた。ショーニー族の子どもたちは父親から一族への所属を受け継いだ。テカムセはパンサー族に属していたが、パンサー族は、約12族あった、異族婚からなるショーニー族のひとつである。部族に加えて、ショーニーには５つの伝統的な区分があり、それらへの加入もまた父親から受け継がれた。テカムセの父親は Kispoko 部に、母親は Piqua 部に属していた。テカムセの父方の祖父が白系英国人の貿易

商だったということを示唆する証拠もある。

Paragraph 3

　白人とインディアンの間の戦いは、テカムセの青年時代に大きく立ちはだかった。彼の父親は、多くのショーニー族の村がアメリカ人開拓者によって破壊された時期であるアメリカ革命戦争前の、ポイント・プレザントの戦いで1774年に亡くなった。彼は1780年のピクアの戦いの後、幼少時代の家を離れ、重要な戦争指導者であった兄にも多少は育てられた。彼らは共に、1780年代に、ケンタッキー州とオハイオ州で白人たちに立ち向かった。その後1780年頃、2年間Cherokees（チェロキ族）とともに暮らし、（そしてチェロキ族とともに闘うために）テカムセは、南部に移動した。合衆国拡大への抵抗運動を導き、テカムセにオハイオへ戻るように勧めた有名なリーダーであるドラッギング・カヌーに出会ったのはそこであった。

Paragraph 4

　その後20年以上の間、彼は先住民保護主義宗教復活に、"Prophet（預言者）"と呼ばれた宗教的リーダーであった弟とともに加わり、白人たちのやり方を拒み、彼らに土地を譲渡することを拒否するようアメリカ原住民たちに促した。彼は多くの異なる部族から、アメリカ・インディアン信者を集め、その同盟のリーダーとなったが、その同盟は彼の弟の宗教家としての人気を基盤として設立されたものだった。これらの信者のうち、ショーニー族の数は比較的少なかった。つまり、テカムセはよくショーニー族のリーダーとして描写されるが、実はほとんどのショーニー族はテカムセやProphetには関わっていなかった。それよりも、彼らは西部へ移動することを選択したり、合衆国と平和を保つことを選んだ。

Paragraph 5

　テカムセと、未来の大統領であるウィリアム・ヘンリー・ハリソンの関わりは1811年の8月に始まったが、それは、テカムセがVincennes（ビンセンズ）で当時知事であったハリソンと会見し、ショーニー族の彼の同志たちは合衆国と平和を保つつもりだと断言した時であった。（Q9: しかし、ハリソンはその親善の申し出を拒否した。）ハリソンは千人以上の兵士をWabash Riverへと率いたが、これは、Prophetと彼の信者たちを威嚇する遠征であった。インディアン

の戦士たちは1811年11月6日の夜、ティッペカヌーの戦いとして知られるようになった戦闘で、アメリカ軍の野営地を襲った。しかしハリソンの部下たちは陣地を守った。インディアンたちは撤退して、勝利を収めたアメリカ人たちは街を焼き払った。

Paragraph 6

テカムセが、白人の西方への領土拡大の停止に失敗したにもかかわらず、彼が合衆国大統領にかけたと思われる呪いのために、謎めいた存在としてアメリカの歴史に残っている。その呪いは「0」で終わる年に選出された大統領は皆、在任期間中に死ぬというものである。実際、その呪いは1840年～1960年の140年間にわたり、任期を務めた大統領たちにとって事実となってしまった。ウィリアム・ヘンリー・ハリソンは1841年に肺炎で亡くなり、Abraham Lincoln（エイブラハム・リンカーン）は1865年に、James Garfield（ジェームス・ガーフィルド）は1881年に、William McKinley（ウィリアム・マッキンリー）は1901年に暗殺された。Warren G. Harding（ウォレン・G・ハーディング）は1923年に心臓発作で亡くなり、Franklin D. Roosevelt（フランクリン・D・ルーズベルト）は脳溢血で1945年に亡くなり、John F. Kennedy（ジョン・F・ケネディ）は1963年に暗殺された。ある者はこれを偶然と呼び、また Ronald Reagan（ロナルド・レーガン）が1980年に始まった大統領任期を生き残ったので、呪いは解かれたと信じる者もいる。

解答 Questions 29 - 42

29 C　30 A　31 D　32 C　33 ■3　34 D　35 C　36 B　37 B　38 D
39 D　40 C　41 A　42 E・C・B in that order

解答のポイント Questions 29 - 42

29 In paragraph 1, what does the author say about the origin of camelids?

(A) That their ancestors came from Asia.
(B) That the one-humped variety evolved earlier than the two-humped variety.

(C) That they came to Asia from North America.
(D) That they originated from ancient cattle species.

Paragraph 1   In contrast to cattle, for which the last wild ancestor — aurochs — died out in the 17th century, domesticated camels coexist happily with their wild cousins. Camelids originated in North America about 30 million years ago and split into two groups about 11 million years ago. One group eventually crossed the Bering Land Bridge to Asia, (29)where it followed an evolutionary path that's only sketchily understood, resulting in the two-humped bactrian camel and the one-humped dromedary.

30 What can be inferred from paragraph 1 about the animals mentioned in paragraph 2?
(A) They share a common ancestor with camels.
(B) They were carefully bred by the South American Incas.
(C) There were great numbers of them.
(D) The smaller animals are descended from the larger animals.

Paragraph 1   In contrast to cattle, for which the last wild ancestor — aurochs — died out in the 17th century, domesticated camels coexist happily with their wild cousins. Camelids originated in North America about 30 million years ago and split into two groups about 11 million years ago. (30) One group eventually crossed the Bering Land Bridge to Asia, where it followed an evolutionary path that's only sketchily understood, resulting in the two-humped bactrian camel and the one-humped dromedary.

Paragraph 2   The other group migrated to South America, where it survives today as wild guanacos and vicunas and domesticated llamas and alpacas. (30) [■1] For many years, historians and scientists assumed that the Incas had created both llamas and alpacas through selective breeding of the guanaco, which is larger and more widely distribute than the vicuna. [■2] But while the ancestor of the llama is indeed the guanaco, genetic studies show that the ancestor of the alpaca is actually the vicuna. [■3] But since speciation occurred thousands of years ago, it is certain that the Incas had no role in their breeding. [■ 4]

31 The word **distributed** in paragraph 2 is closest in meaning to:

(A) compressed.　圧縮された

(B) disjointed.　支離滅裂な

(C) circumstantial.　状況的な

(D) **scattered.**　散在した

Paragraph 2　The other group migrated to South America, where it survives today as wild guanacos and vicunas and domesticated llamas and alpacas. [■ 1] For many years, historians and scientists assumed that the Incas had created both llamas and alpacas through selective breeding of the guanaco, which is larger and more widely distributed (31) than the vicuna. [■ 2] But while the ancestor of the llama is indeed the guanaco, genetic studies show that the ancestor of the alpaca is actually the vicuna. [■ 3] But since speciation occurred thousands of years ago, it is certain that the Incas had no role in their breeding. [■ 4]

32 According to paragraph 2 of the passage, the alpaca evolved from:

(A) aurochs.

(B) guanacos.

(C) **vicunas.**

(D) llamas.

Paragraph 2　The other group migrated to South America, where it survives today as wild guanacos and vicunas and domesticated llamas and alpacas. [■ 1] For many years, historians and scientists assumed that the Incas had created both llamas and alpacas through selective breeding of the guanaco, which is larger and more widely distributed than the vicuna. [■ 2] But while the ancestor of the llama is indeed the guanaco, genetic studies show that the ancestor of the alpaca is actually the vicuna. (32) [■ 3] But since speciation occurred thousands of years ago, it is certain that the Incas had no role in their breeding. [■ 4]

33 Look at the 4 squares [■] in paragraph 2 and indicate where the following sentence can best be added to the passage.

It is believed that, about 6,000 years ago, alpacas were created through selective breeding which was heavily influenced by the vicuna.

Paragraph 2 The other group migrated to South America, where it survives today as wild guanacos and vicunas and domesticated llamas and alpacas. [■ 1] For many years, historians and scientists assumed that the Incas had created both llamas and alpacas through selective breeding of the guanaco, which is larger and more widely distributed than the vicuna. [■ 2] **But while the ancestor of the llama is indeed the guanaco, genetic studies show that the ancestor of the alpaca is actually the vicuna.** (33) [■ 3] But since speciation occurred thousands of years ago, it is certain that the Incas had no role in their breeding. [■ 4]

34 The word domesticated in paragraph 3 is closest in meaning to:
(A) soft.　柔らかい
(B) popular.　人気のある
(C) sober.　しらふの
(D) **tame.**　飼いならされた

Paragraph 3 Of the many results of the Spanish conquest of South America, one was the mismanagement of camelid breeding and care. Within 100 years of conquest, up to 90 percent of South America's domesticated (34) camelids had died off, mostly to be replaced by horses. Since then, Latin Americans have haphazardly crossbred the remaining alpacas and llamas, and today only about 20 percent of alpacas are genetically pure. This interbreeding among the alpacas and llamas has resulted in a significant increase in the thickness of alpaca fiber, making alpaca wool less valuable.

35 Which of the sentences below best expresses the essential information in the highlighted sentence in the passage? *Incorrect* choices change the meaning in important ways or leave out essential information.

Of the many results of the Spanish conquest of South America, one was the mismanagement of camelid breeding and care.

(A) The Spanish made many errors in managing their South American colonies, including camelid breeding and care.
(B) The Spanish mismanaged many of South America's natural resources, especially its native animal species.
(C) **Under Spanish rule, the various species of camelids in its colonies were cross-bred and poorly cared for.**
(D) The skillful management of South American camelids by the Spanish has helped their numbers grow in recent years.

Paragraph 3   Of the many results of the Spanish conquest of South America, one was the mismanagement of camelid breeding and care. (35) Within 100 years of conquest, up to 90 percent of South America's domesticated camelids had died off, (35)mostly to be replaced by horses. Since then, Latin Americans have haphazardly crossbred the remaining alpacas and llamas, and today only about 20 percent of alpacas are genetically pure. This interbreeding among the alpacas and llamas has resulted in a significant increase in the thickness of alpaca fiber, making alpaca wool less valuable.

36 Which of the following can be inferred from the passage about the wool of South American camelids?
(A) The wool of pure alpacas is the most expensive in the world.
(B) The Inca rulers preferred the wool of vicunas.
(C) Less than a quarter of the remaining vicunas have pure vicuna blood.
(D) It is a serious crime in Peru to capture and shear vicunas and

alpacas.

Paragraph 3 Of the many results of the Spanish conquest of South America, one was the mismanagement of camelid breeding and care. Within 100 years of conquest, up to 90 percent of South America's domesticated camelids had died off, mostly to be replaced by horses. Since then, Latin Americans have haphazardly crossbred the remaining alpacas and llamas, and today only about 20 percent of alpacas are genetically pure. This interbreeding among the alpacas and llamas has resulted in a significant increase in the thickness of alpaca fiber, making alpaca wool less valuable. (36)

Paragraph 5 Fortunately for the vicuna, its fiber — with a diameter of 12 micrometers — is the finest in the world. Vicuna garments are some of the most expensive luxury clothing items in the world, so in the 1970s, the species' native countries — Peru, (36) Argentina, Bolivia, Chile, and Ecuador —(36) signed a collective agreement to protect the animal. (36) And in 1975, the Convention on International Trade in Endangered Species of Wild Fauna and Flora, or CITES, prohibited the commercial trade of vicuna products, from hides to wool. (42-B) Today, approximately 220,000 vicuna — over half of which live in Peru — graze the high Andes. (36) Remarkably, they have rebounded to the point where governments are permitting citizens to once again capture and shear the animals for their silky fibers, as South Americans had done for centuries.

37 The word **they** in the final sentence of paragraph 5 refers to:
(A) Peruvians.
(B) vicunas.
(C) CITES.
(D) alpacas.

Paragraph 5 Fortunately for the vicuna, its fiber — with a diameter of 12 micrometers — is the finest in the world. Vicuna garments are some of the most expensive luxury clothing items in the world, so in the 1970s, the species' native countries — Peru, Argentina, Bolivia, Chile, and Ecuador —signed a collective agreement to protect the animal. And in 1975, the Convention on International Trade in Endangered Species of Wild Fauna and Flora, or CITES, prohibited the commercial trade of vicuna products, from hides to wool. Today, approximately 220,000 vicuna — over half of which live in Peru — graze the high Andes. Remarkably, they have rebounded to the point where governments are permitting citizens to once again capture and shear the animals for their silky fibers, as South Americans had done for centuries. (37)

38 Why does the author use the word remarkably in paragraph 5?

(A) It is very important for CITES to continue to protect the remaining vicunas.
(B) Alpacas and vicunas share a surprising resemblance.
(C) The wool from vicunas has become an incredible success.
(D) The numbers of vicuna in South America have grown significantly.

Paragraph 5   Fortunately for the vicuna, its fiber — with a diameter of 12 micrometers — is the finest in the world. Vicuna garments are some of the most expensive luxury clothing items in the world, so in the 1970s, the species' native countries — Peru, Argentina, Bolivia, Chile, and Ecuador — signed a collective agreement to protect the animal. And in 1975, the Convention on International Trade in Endangered Species of Wild Fauna and Flora, or CITES, prohibited the commercial trade of vicuna products, from hides to wool. Today, approximately 220,000 vicuna — over half of which live in Peru — graze the high Andes. Remarkably, they have rebounded to the point where governments are permitting citizens to once again capture and shear the animals for their silky fibers, as South Americans had done for centuries. (38)

39 The word isolated in the final paragraph is closest in meaning to:

(A) barren.　不毛の地

(B) heavily populated.　人口の多い
(C) mountainous.　山地の
(D) **remote.**　人里離れた

Paragraph 6　In Asia, the Gobi's wild bactrian camels look quite distinct from their domestic counterparts. Wild camels are lithe and sleek, their humps small and conical, whereas the dromedaries are stocky and thick-wooled, with floppy, misshapen humps. The fate of these wild camelids in Asia has been less than kind. Living in isolated parts of Mongolia's and China's Gobi desert, bactrian camels are notoriously difficult to study. (39) They are shy and live in an environment with extremely hot summers, bitterly cold winters, and little precipitation. They were discovered and first reported as recently as 1877. And although it is the largest grazer of central Asia's deserts, biologists don't even know if the bactrian is descended from the dromedary or vice versa. There isn't even any reliable data on population numbers, with estimates ranging from 1000 to 5000 head. Nor is there reliable data on breeding, though a Russian study in 1980 reported herds made up of 11% juveniles, while more recent studies report 5% juveniles. Our best guess why is that the persistence of drought conditions since the 1970s is to blame.

40 According to the final paragraph, what seems to be happening to wild Asian camel populations?
(A) They are in fierce competition with the dromedaries.
(B) They have been well studied by Russian scientists.
(C) **They are shrinking due to lack of food.**
(D) Their numbers have rapidly rebounded.

Paragraph 6　In Asia, the Gobi's wild bactrian camels look quite distinct from their domestic counterparts. Wild camels are lithe and sleek, their humps small and conical, whereas the dromedaries are stocky and thick-wooled, with floppy, misshapen humps. The fate of these wild camelids in Asia has been less than kind. Living in isolated parts of Mongolia's and

China's Gobi desert, bactrian camels are notoriously difficult to study. They are shy and live in an environment with extremely hot summers, bitterly cold winters, and little precipitation. They were discovered and first reported as recently as 1877. And although it is the largest grazer of central Asia's deserts, biologists don't even know if the bactrian is descended from the dromedary or vice versa. There isn't even any reliable data on population numbers, with estimates ranging from 1000 to 5000 head. Nor is there reliable data on breeding, though a Russian study in 1980 reported herds made up of 11% juveniles, while more recent studies report 5% juveniles. Our best guess why is that the persistence of drought conditions since the 1970s is to blame. (40)

41 The word **drought** in paragraph 6 is closest in meaning to:
(A) **dehydrated.** 乾燥した
(B) depicted. 描写された
(C) denounced. 非難された
(D) decarbonized. 炭素を除かれた

Paragraph 6 In Asia, the Gobi's wild bactrian camels look quite distinct from their domestic counterparts. Wild camels are lithe and sleek, their humps small and conical, whereas the dromedaries are stocky and thick-wooled, with floppy, misshapen humps. The fate of these wild camelids in Asia has been less than kind. Living in isolated parts of Mongolia's and China's Gobi desert, bactrian camels are notoriously difficult to study. They are shy and live in an environment with extremely hot summers, bitterly cold winters, and little precipitation. They were discovered and first reported as recently as 1877. And although it is the largest grazer of central Asia's deserts, biologists don't even know if the bactrian is descended from the dromedary or vice versa. There isn't even any reliable data on population numbers, with estimates ranging from 1000 to 5000 head. Nor is there reliable data on breeding, though a Russian study in 1980 reported herds made up of 11% juveniles, while more recent studies report 5% juveniles. Our best guess why is that the persistence of drought conditions since the 1970s is to blame. (41)

42 Three of the answer choices below provide the correct sequence of events in the history of the vicuna. Put those THREE answers in order. The other three sentences do not belong in this sequence because they express ideas that are not presented in the passage or are minor ideas in the passage. *This question is worth 2 points.*

The vicuna were highly prized by the Incan rulers before the Spanish arrived in South America.

(A) The vicuna evolved from the alpaca.
(B) **Trade of vicuna products was outlawed.**
(C) **Vicuna populations were forced to move to remote locations.**
(D) Vicunas migrated to South America.
(E) **The vicuna were widely slaughtered.**
(F) Vicuna wool and fiber began to lose value.

Paragraph 4   The Spaniards also began killing vicuna, (42-E)which the Incan royalty had vigorously protected. Only Inca rulers could wear the revered vicuna wool, and the penalty for breaking the prohibition was death. New World settlers and their livestock also pushed the wild vicuna higher into the Andes grassland ranges, where hunters continued to stage organized kills for their pelts. (42-C)Vicuna populations diminished and became fragmented.

Paragraph 5   Fortunately for the vicuna, its fiber — with a diameter of 12 micrometers — is the finest in the world. Vicuna garments are some of the most expensive luxury clothing items in the world, so in the 1970s, the species' native countries — Peru, Argentina, Bolivia, Chile, and Ecuador — signed a collective agreement to protect the animal. And in 1975, the Convention on International Trade in Endangered Species of Wild Fauna and Flora, or CITES, prohibited the commercial trade of vicuna products, from hides to wool. (42-B) Today, approximately 220,000 vicuna — over half of which live in Peru — graze the high Andes. Remarkably, they have rebounded to the point where governments are permitting citizens to once again capture and shear the animals for their silky fibers, as South Americans had done for centuries.

和訳

Paragraph 1

　17世紀に、その元祖にあたるオーロックーが死に絶えてしまった牛とは逆に、家畜化されたラクダたちは同類の野生ラクダと幸せに共存している。ラクダ科の動物は3000万年前に北アメリカに源を発し、約1100万年前に二つの部類へと分かれていった。一つ目の部類は最終的にベーリングの土地橋を越えてアジアへと渡り、そこで進化の道筋をたどりフタコブラクダとヒトコブラクダになった。その進化の道筋は大雑把にしか理解されていない。

Paragraph 2

　もう一方は南アメリカに渡り、そこで今日野生のグワナコやビクーナ、家畜のリャマやアルパカとして生き残っている。長年の間、歴史家と科学者たちは、インカ族たちはグワナコを品種改良してリャマとアルパカの両方を生み出したのだと推測した。グワナコはビクーナより大きくてより広い地域に分布している。

　しかし、リャマの先祖が実際にグアナコだということに対し、遺伝子の研究によるとアルパカの先祖は実はビクーナである。(約6000年前、アルパカはビクーナから非常に影響を受けた品種改良によって生み出されたと信じられている。) しかし、種分化は数千年前に起こったことなので、インカ族たちがそれらの品種改良に関わっていなかったのは明らかである。

Paragraph 3

　スペイン人の南米征服がもたらした多くの結果の一つは、ラクダ科の飼育と世話の管理を誤ったことである。

　占領100年足らずの間で、90％にいたる南米の家畜のラクダ科の動物が死滅

し、主に馬に取って代わられた。

　それ以来、ラテンアメリカ人はでたらめに残りのアルパカとリャマをかけあわせてきた。今日アルパカのたったの約20％が遺伝子的に純粋種である。このアルパカとリャマの異種交配の結果、アルパカの毛は著しく太さを増し、アルパカの羊毛の値打ちが下がってしまった。

Paragraph 4

　またスペイン人は、かつてインカ族の王家の人々が活発に保護したビクーナを殺し始めた。インカ人の支配者だけが、崇められていたビクーナの毛皮を着ることができ、その禁止を破ることへの罰は死であった。新世界への移住者と彼らの家畜たちもまた、野生のビクーナをアンデスの奥深くの草地へと追いやった。そこでは猟師たちがビクーナの生皮を捕るために組織化された狩をし続けた。ビクーナの数は減少し、まばらなものになってしまった。

Paragraph 5

　ビクーナにとって幸いなことに、彼らの繊維（直径12マイクロメーター）は世界で最も良質（肌理が細かい）である。ビクーナの繊維でできた衣服は世界で最も高級な服に属するとされ、1970年にビクーナの原産国であるペルー、アルゼンチン、ボリビア、チリ、エクアドルはビクーナを保護するという協定に署名した。

　そして、1975年にCITES（サイテス）は皮から羊毛を含むビクーナの産物の商業貿易を禁止した。今日約22万頭のビクーナ（その半数以上はペルーに生息する）は、アンデスの高所で草を食んでいる。注目すべきは、政府が市民に、かつて南米人が何世紀もの間そうしていたように、そのシルクのような繊維を得るために、もう一度ビクーナを捕まえて毛を刈り込むのを許可するまでに、ビクーナの個体数は回復したことである。

Paragraph 6

　アジアでは、ゴビ砂漠の野生のフタコブラクダは、他の家畜のラクダとはまったく姿が異なる。野生のラクダはしなやかでつやがあり、コブは小さく円錐状をしているのに対して、フタコブラクダはがっちりしていて、毛が濃くだらりと垂れた不格好なコブがある。アジアでの、これらの野生のラクダ科の動物の運命は厳しいものだった。

モンゴルと中国のゴビ砂漠の孤立した地域に生息しているので、フタコブラクダは研究するのが難しいとして知られている。彼らは臆病で、夏は極端に暑く冬はひどく寒く、降水量のほとんどない環境に生息している。

　彼等はごく近年の1877年に発見され、初めて報告された。そして彼らは中央アジアの砂漠で最大の草を食む動物だということにもかかわらず、生物学者はフタコブラクダがヒトコブラクダの子孫なのか、もしくはその逆かどうか知りさえしない。個体数について正確なデータさえなく、おおよその見積もりで1000頭から5000頭に及ぶ。繁殖に関する正確なデータもないが、1980年のロシアの調査で、11％の若いフタコブラクダからなる群れが報告されている一方、最近の調査では5％の若い個体数しか報告されていない。一番考えられる原因は、1970年代からの続く干ばつのせいであろう。

Listening Section

解答 Questions 1 - 5

1 D 2 B 3 A 4 B 5 C

解答のポイント Questions 1 - 5

スクリプト

Narrator : Listen to part of a conversation between two students.

Student 1 : Hey, Emma. Can I talk to you for a moment?
Student 2 : Sure, Scott. What's the matter?
Student 1 : You took Spanish last semester, didn't you?
Student 2 : Last year, actually, but yes, I did. Why? Are you thinking of taking it?
Student 1 : I'm taking it now, in fact, but I'm not sure everything's right with the class.
Student 2 : What do you mean?
Student 1 : Well, I heard you mention before that you studied Spanish for three years in high school, right? I did, too, you see, so what class level did they put you in here?
Student 2 : Uh, I was in the intermediate — no, upper intermediate level. How about you?
Student 1 : I'm listed as being in the lower intermediate level class, but I was really hoping to be higher up so I could really improve my language skills.
Student 2 : Yeah, my class was pretty challenging, but it really helped me to work on my Spanish. I wonder how you ended up in that class.
Student 1 : Well, you had to take, like, a placement test at the beginning of the term, too, right?
Student 2 : Uh, no. No, I didn't. Did you?

Student 1 : Yeah. It took around an hour, an hour and a half. There was, like, a listening section, some reading, some grammar questions, and then we had to write a short passage at the end. No speaking, though.
Student 2 : Oh, yes! Now I remember. They were saying something at the end of last year about introducing some kind of screening test or placement test.
Student 1 : And you didn't have to take one? I wonder why they introduced it.
Student 2 : I don't know, but I guess they found that choosing people's class level based on their high school record meant that too many people ended up in the wrong level class.
Student 1 : So you think I've been put in the lower-intermediate class based on my score on the placement test, and not on my three years of Spanish in high school?
Student 2 : Look, Scott, I don't know. You'd have to ask the department about that. But it makes sense, don't you think? I mean, there are plenty of things I studied in high school that I've forgotten about now, or that I just wasn't so good at. And, no offense to you, but a placement test now says more about your Spanish ability now than how many years you studied in high school.
Student 1 : Yeah. I guess you're right. I mean, I haven't used my Spanish at all since I left high school, and to be honest, I wasn't so hot at it even when I was studying. Oh, well, maybe lower intermediate is the right class for me after all.
Student 2 : And I guess I was lucky I took Spanish last year. I don't know how well I'd have done on that placement test.

Narrator : Now get ready to answer the questions. You may use your notes to help you answer.

スクリプト和訳

Narrator(以下 ***N***）：二人の学生の会話を聴きなさい。

Student 1（以下 ***S1***）：やあ、エマ。少し話せる？
Student 2（以下 ***S2***）：もちろんよ、スコット。どうしたの？
S1：前の学期に、スペイン語の授業をとっていたよね？
S2：（正確には）去年だけど、でも、ええ、とっていたわよ。どうして？ スペイン語の授業をとろうと思っているの？
S1：今もとっているんだけどね、実は。でも、このクラスでほんとにいいのか悩んでいるんだ。
S2：どういうこと？
S1：その、君がスペイン語を高校で3年間勉強したと前に言っていたのを聞いたことがあるけど、そうだよね？ で、僕もなんだよ。それで、去年スペイン語をとった時にここではどのレベルのクラスに入れられたの？
S2：ええと、中級……、あ、違う、中級上のクラスだったわ。あなたは？
S1：僕は中級下のクラスなんだよ。でも、もっと上のレベルのクラスに入りたいと本当に願っている。そうすれば自分の語学力をしっかり上げることができる。
S2：そうね、確かに私のとった授業はけっこう難しかったけど、自分のスペイン語を鍛えるには本当によかったわ。でも、どうしてあなたがそのクラスになってしまったのか、不思議ね。
S1：それはクラス分けの試験のようなものを学期の初めに受けないといけなくて、君も受けたよね？
S2：いいえ、そんなのなかったわ。受けたの？
S1：受けたよ。1時間、いや1時間半くらいかかる試験だった。リスニングといくつかの読解、それから文法問題もあって、その後最後に短い作文もあった。会話はなかったけどね。
S2：ああ、そうそう。今思い出した。そういえば、去年の末に、選抜試験またはクラス分けの試験を導入するとかいう話があったわね。
S1：じゃあ、君はその試験を受ける義務がなかったの？ なんで、導入されたんだろう。
S2：さあね。でもたぶん、高校時代の成績にもとづいてクラスのレベルを決めたら、合わないレベルのクラスに入る人がとてもたくさん出てしまったという結果を見つけたのかもね。
S1：それじゃあ、僕が中級の低いほうのクラスなってしまったのは、クラス分け試験の成績による結果で、高校で3年間スペイン語を勉強したことは関

係ないと君は思うんだね。

S2: ちょっとスコット、わからないわよ。それは、学科に問い合わせなければならないわ。でも、このクラス分けのやり方は正しいと思う。そう思わない？　だって、高校で学んではいたけれど今はもう覚えていないこととか、高校の時からそんなに得意じゃないことってたくさんあるし。それに、気を悪くしないでね、高校で何年勉強したかということよりも、今受けるクラス分け試験のほうが、今現在のあなたのスペイン語力に関してより多くを示すと思うわ。

S1: そうだよね。君が正しいのかも。言われてみれば、高校を卒業してからまったくスペイン語を使ってないし、正直、高校で勉強をしていたときもそんなに熱心ではなかったしね。ま、たぶん中級下のクラスが僕には合っているんだろうな、結局。

S2: 私も去年スペイン語のクラスをとってよかったわ。だって、クラス分け試験があったら、どのくらい上手くやれたかわからないし。

N: それでは問題に解答する用意をしてください。解答の際にメモを用いても構いません。

解答 Questions 6 - 11

6 C　7 A・C　8 B　9 C　10 C　11 B

解答のポイント Questions 6 - 11

スクリプト

Narrator: Listen to part of a lecture in an Economics class.

Professor: Today, we're going to discuss a few basic points about public goods. Now, we come into contact with public goods everyday, but what exactly is, or what constitutes, a public good?

　　Well, public goods can be described as, well, goods that would be unsuccessful, or simply fail in the market, under true market conditions. In other words, not enough would be demanded, or not enough could be supplied at market prices. OK, now, that's putting it in pretty simple terms, but it can serve as a, basic starting point for our discussion.

Now, moving on, it can be said that there are two principal characteristics which define public goods — they are non-excludable, and they are non-diminishable. Now let me give you an idea of what those two terms mean.

Right, first, non-excludability. Well, non-excludability basically means that if some organization were to provide such a good to the public — and of course the users to pay a fee — it would be difficult, or simply impossible, to exclude people who didn't pay from using it as well. Right? That's where the term comes from, because, uh, non-payers cannot be excluded from using the good, or the service, or whatever the good is. And we call such people — the non-payers, that is — we call them "free riders."

Well, let me illustrate the point of non-excludability with an example. OK, a lighthouse is a traditional, and a pretty clear example of a public good. Do you see why? Well, think of it in practical terms. If an organization — you know, whoever — decided to build a lighthouse as a business proposition — if that organization tried asking all the ship owners who, oh, whose ships were steered clear of the rocks by the lighthouse, to pay a fee, well, not enough money would be raised. Why not? Well, it would be very easy for many ships just to see the light and to use its light as a service without paying for it. Hence, a lighthouse, as a business idea, would be a market failure. OK?

Public service broadcasting on the radio — not commercial music or talk shows — but, you know, weather reports, some educational programs, or community announcements, that sort of thing, that would be another example. Anyone could listen to it, but it would be hard to charge a fee, or to get income through advertising.

Now, uh, non-diminishability. Well, this means that whenever an extra person uses the public good, the good is not diminished as a result. You know, it's not used up, or made smaller, or it doesn't decrease in size. Basically, the same amount of the good remains available for other users, no matter how many people use it. Does that make sense?

OK, let's think about it by using a fairly simple example. For instance, let's imagine the case of street lighting. Now, of course, a person who is just, you know, walking along the street, does not use up the light in any way. And no extra light is required if an extra person walks down the street. Therefore, street lighting is non-diminishable — simply because the amount of light, or the availability of the light to other potential users, is not diminished or reduced whenever one person uses it.

Now, you may be thinking that of all this sounds very obvious, but, as we know, private companies or entrepreneurs are only prepared to produce or provide services in areas where profits are likely. So you see the problem, right? Public goods are not profitable, but they are very necessary. Can you imagine if there were no streetlights or lighthouses? Or how about roads? Or armies and navies? You know, these are all well-known examples of public goods. So public goods are almost always provided by the state, and paid for with tax funds.

Narrator : Now get ready to answer the questions. You may use your notes to help you answer.

スクリプト和訳

N：経済学の授業における講義の一部を聴きなさい。

P：今日は、公共財に関するいくつかの基礎的な事項を講義します。私たちは、毎日公共財と出会っています。ですが、公共財とは、正確にいうとどのよう

なものであり、何によって成り立つものなのでしょうか。公共財は、実際の市場条件のもとでは、市場では商品として取り引きされにくいもの、あるいは、失敗しているものであると言えます。換言すれば、十分な需要がないもの、あるいは市場価格では十分に供給され得ないものと言えるでしょう。まあこれはかなり単純な文言になりますが、今日の議論を始めるに基本点としては、これで事足りるでしょう。

　それでは続けます。公共財の定義となる主要な特徴が、二つあると言えます。一つは、排除不可能性。もう一つは否減少性です。では、この二つの用語が何を意味するかを、説明してみましょう。

　まず、排除不可能性です。これは、もしある組織がこの性質を持つ財を提供する—そしてもちろん購入者は代金を支払う—とした場合に、これを使用してもお金を払わない人をこの財を使用することから排除することが困難であるか、あるいはそもそも排除が不可能であることを意味します。よろしいでしょうか？　このことからこの用語が生まれました。なぜなら、支払いをしない人が、この財またはサービス、何にせよこの商品、を使用することから排除されないからです。そして、こうした人々、すなわちお金を支払わない人、を我々はフリー・ライダーと呼びます。

　それでは、この排除不可能性について、例を挙げて説明します。灯台は、昔から知られ、かつとてもわかりやすい公共財の例です。なぜだかわかりますか？　実情に即して考えてみましょう。もし、何らかの組織が—どのような組織でもよいのですが—利益を目的とする事業として、灯台を設置することを決めたとします。その組織が、船の所有者—灯台のおかげで岩と接触することなく航行することができた船の所有者に、利用料金を支払うことを求めても、あまり多くのお金を集めることはできないでしょう。なぜでしょうか。それは、多くの船にとって、お金を支払うことなく灯台を見、そしてその光をサービスとして使うことが、容易だからです。故に、灯台は、商売としては、市場的に失敗であるといえます。よろしいでしょうか。

　ラジオの公共放送、商業的な音楽番組やトークショーではなく、しかしそうですね、天気予報や教育番組、あるいは自治体の広報番組など、そのようなものは、公共財の別の例です。誰でも聴くことが出来て、課金することや、広告により利益を得ることが難しいからです。

　それでは、否減少性についてです。これが意味するのは、公共財は、それをいかに多くの人が使った時でも、減少しないということです。要するに、

使い尽くされることもなく、少なくなってしまうこともない、また大きさが減少することもない、ということです。つまり、どれだけの数の人が利用しても、まったく同じ分量の財が他の人々にも利用可能であり続ける、ということです。分かりますか？

それでは、とても単純な例を用いて考えてみましょう。例えば、街灯の場合を考えてみましょう。当たり前ですが、道を歩いているだけの人が街灯の光を使い切ってしまうということはありえませんね。そしてまた、他の人がその道を歩いても、その人の分の追加の光は必要となりません。したがって、街灯は否減少性を持つと言えます。その理由は単純で、光の量も、他の潜在的な利用者のための供給可能性も、ある一人の人がその光を使う時に減少したり、小さくなったりすることがないからです。

皆さんはおそらく、私がここまでに述べたことはすべて当たり前であると思っていることでしょうが、知ってのとおり、民間企業や起業家は、利益が上がりそうな領域においてのみ、製品あるいはサービスを提供することを考えます。ここに問題があることに気が付きますね？ 公共財はもうけになりませんが、必要不可欠なものです。街灯や灯台がない状況を想像することができますか？ また道路はどうでしょう？ 陸軍や海軍はどうなりますか。そうです、これらはすべて、とてもよく知られている公共財の例です。この理由により、公共財は、ほとんどの場合、国家により供給され、税金をもって賄われます。

N：それでは問題に解答する用意をしてください。解答の際にメモを用いても構いません。

解答 Questions 12 - 17

12 B　13 (A) YES　(B) NO　(C) NO　(D) YES　(E) YES　14 D
15 B・D　16 C　17 B

解答のポイント Questions 12 - 17

スクリプト

Narrator: Listen to part of a lecture in a Business Management class.

Professor: Today, I'm going to introduce you to something known as Transformation Theory, which was, uh, first explained by Dr. George Land in a very influential book titled, uh, quite dramatically, "Grow or Die." It was first published back in the early 1970s, by the way. Anyway, essentially, it's a description of the structure of change in natural systems. In his book, Land used a series of interlocking S-shaped curves to illustrate change, if you can imagine that.

Now, each of these S-curves has two breakpoints. A breakpoint is the moment in time when the rules of survival change. So, two breakpoints per S-curve mean that there are three distinct phases of growth. Let me try and describe these to you.

Phase one is characterized by experimentation, in which the system attempts to make, or uh, find a connection with its environment. Now, it's not unusual for a system — and this applies to any system, whether it's an organism, or a relationship, or just a plain old business — it often happens that a system will die or fail before finding this connection.

Okay? Now, assuming this connection is found, the first breakpoint is reached. It is at this point, then — if you remember — that the rules for success change, from experimentation to replication of success. What this means is that the system must stop searching and, instead, start to make the most of its connection, which might be, uh, a food supply, or market appeal, or just common interests. It does this simply by repeating its formula for success. It's in this phase, phase two, that the system enjoys tremendous growth. In fact, growth is limited only by the environment that provides resources for that growth.

Assuming that the system is allowed these initial conditions for growth without any, uh, any unexpected changes, it will eventually consume all those resources — which is a problem, of course — George Land actually came up with an interesting way of describing this situation. He said, "nothing fails like success," meaning that the very process of succeeding at something actually leads to ultimate failure. Or at least, it will eventually lead to failure unless changes are made. So, at this point in Land's diagram, we have reached a second breakpoint, and once again, the rules for success must change if failure is to be avoided.

At this second breakpoint, the successful system enters a bifurcation, which means it branches out in two ways. Do you remember I told you that Land described change as a series of interlocking S-shaped curves? Well, it's at this second breakpoint that the new S-curve starts to appear. You see, at the same time, the successful system does two things. On the other hand, it begins to open up to innovation and accept information and other resources that were rejected earlier in phase two, and at the same time, it reinvents itself, leading to a new S-shaped growth curve.

So, that's the theory, anyway, but what can it teach us about business? Well, first of all, it's useful for the planning and execution of any system, large or small. What phase is the system currently in? What form of creative thinking is required? How do we know when the rules of survival have changed? You see, Land's theory describes three distinct sets of rules for survival, and the key factor in Land's theory is that the system must be aware of which set of rules currently apply.

Now, if the theory alone doesn't make a lot of sense to you, try thinking of it this way. If we apply the theory to running a business, we end up with some more familiar concepts. Phase one is entrepreneurship, phase two is success and growth, and the final stage can be seen as diversification. That's a very clear and logical process, don't you think? Good. Well, let's look at some actual examples of this.

Narrator : Now get ready to answer the questions. You may use your notes to help you answer.

> スクリプト和訳

N：ビジネス・マネジメントの授業における講義の一部を聴きなさい。

Professor：本日は、皆さんに、変化理論（Transformation Theory）として知られる考えを、紹介したいと思います。この理論は、ジョージ・ランド博士により、「成長か死か」という何ともドラマティックなタイトルが付けられ非常に大きな反響があった彼の著作において、最初に提唱されました。ちなみに、この著作の初版の発行は1970年代の初めに遡ります。それはさておき、本題ですが、この著作は、自然界の様々なシステムにおける構造的な変化を記述したものです。この著作においてランド博士は、連結し連続するＳ字形の曲線を、変化というものを説明するために用いました。頭に思い浮かべられますか。

　さて、このＳ字形の曲線のそれぞれには、二つの転換点があります。この転換点は、生存のためのルールが変わるその瞬間を示しています。したがって、それぞれのＳ字形曲線に二つの転換点があるということは、独立した三つの成長の段階が存在することを意味します。このことについて説明してみましょう。

　第一の段階は、試行的であるという特徴があり、この段階において、あるシステムは、周囲の環境との関係を作り出す、もしくは見出そうとします。さて、このことは、システムにとって特別なことではなく、あらゆるシステム―それが有機体であれ、人間関係であれ、更には昔ながらの単純なビジネスであっても―あてはまることであり、システムが周囲の環境との関係を見出す前に死ぬ、もしくは崩壊することはよくあります。

　お判りでしょうか。さてこの環境との関係が構築されたと仮定した場合に、第一の転換点に達することになります。そしてまさにこの時点において、覚えているでしょうか、成功のためのルールが変わります。ルールは、試行から成功の繰り返しへと変化するのです。このことが意味するのは、当該のシステムが模索するのを止

め、その代わりに、環境との間に築いた関係——それは食料の供給であったり、市場への訴求であったり、あるいは単に共通の利益であったりしますが——この関係を最大限に活用することを始めなければならない、ということです。当該のシステムは、成功の公式をただ繰り返すことにより、この最大化を実行します。この段階、すなわち第二の段階において、システムは飛躍的な成長を実現します。実際、システムの成長は、その成長のための資源を供給する環境によってのみ、制約されることになります。

　成長のためのこれらの主な条件を与えられ、いかなる予期しない変化に見舞われることもなければ、当該のシステムは、最終的にすべての資源を使い尽くしてしまうことになります。もちろん、このことは問題となります。そこで、ジョージ・ランドは、この状況を述べる面白い言い方を思いつきました。彼は言いました、「成功ほどの失敗はない」と。これはつまり、成功するためのまさにその過程は、実は究極の失敗へと至る、という意味です。または、少なくとも変革を実行しない限り、成功は最終的に崩壊へと至ることが示されています。さて、ランドの図式のこの段階において、第二の転換点に到達したことになり、失敗を避けるためには、またしても成功のルールは変わらなければなりません。

　この第二の転換点において、成功を志向するシステムは分岐点にさしかかります。すなわち、道筋が二つに枝分かれします。はじめに私が、ランドは変化を連結し連続するＳ字形の曲線として記述した、と話したことを覚えているでしょうか。そうです、この第二の転換点において、新しいＳ字形の曲線が現れ始めるのです。さて、この時、成功を志向するシステムは、二つのことを実行しています。一方では、革新へと向かい始め、またかつて第二の段階においては採り入れなかった情報や資源を受け入れることを始めます。それと同時に、自己を変革し、新しいＳ字形の成長曲線へと至ります。

　これはあくまで理論ですが、はたしてこれは、ビジネスについて我々に何を教えているのでしょうか？　第一にこの理論は、大小に関わらず、あらゆるシステムを計画し実行するに際し有用です。当該のシステムは、成長のどの段階に今あるのか？　どのような創造的思考が求められているのか？　生存のためのルールが変わった

時、それをどのように察知するのか？　おわかりのように、ランドの理論では、三つの生存のためのルールが説明されていますが、この理論において重要な点は、どのルールが今の状況に適合するかを、当該のシステムにおいて知られなければならないということです。

　理論の説明だけでは釈然としないようなら、このように考えてみましょう。この理論を事業の経営に応用してみると、もっと馴染みのある概念に思い当たることになります。第一の段階は起業の段階であり、第二の段階は成功と拡張の段階、そして最後の段階は多角化の段階ととらえられるでしょう。これは、とても明快で論理的な過程であると思いませんか？　いいでしょう。それでは、このことについて、いくつかの事例を見てみることにします。

N：それでは問題に解答する用意をしてください。解答の際にメモを用いても構いません。

解答 Questions 18 - 22

18 D　19 B　20 A　21 C　22 D

解答のポイント Questions 18 - 22

スクリプト

Narrator: Listen to part of a conversation between a student and a professor.
Professor: Hello there, Michael. Were you looking for me?
Student: Uh, yes, actually, professor. I was hoping you might be able to clear something up for me.
Professor: Well, let me see. I guess I can spare a few minutes before I should be getting to class. What seems to be the problem?
Student: It's the latest assignment, professor. The one you gave on Monday. I know you went over it in class, but like you said, it's different from all our previous assignments, so I guess I'm still not sure I've got everything straight.

Professor: Okay, well, rather than me go through it all again, suppose you tell me first what you think you're supposed to do, and then I'll stop you if you get it wrong.

Student: Uh, okay. I know we're supposed to start by choosing one person or one event from history, right?

Professor: Yes.

Student: Do we really have a completely free choice on that?

Professor: Sure. Why not? I want people to choose something or someone they feel fairly familiar with. Go on.

Student: Here it gets a little unclear. Uh, what I've wrote in my notes is that you want us to research and write about that person or event from a positive, negative, and uh, changing perspectives. Is that right?

Professor: Mmm, yes. Those are probably the exact same words I used, yes.

Student: Okay, but what exactly does it mean?

Professor: Come on, Michael. You're an intelligent person. Tell me what you think it means.

Student: Uh, I suppose one thing you want us to understand is that we should always consult a wide range of sources for our research.

Professor: Absolutely! You see, it's not so confusing when you actually think about it. What else do you think I'm after?

Student: That I'm not sure about, professor.

Professor: Listen. The idea that I really want to get across is that any event can be viewed in different ways. For instance, almost any historical figure who had an impact on his or her society would have been thought of as a hero by some and a villain by others while still living. And then views and judgments about that person will also have changed and evolved over the years since their death.

Student: So — you want us to do more than just look at different sources, right? You also want us to take these different opinions into account, and maybe consider why they exist.

Professor: And also why they may have changed. Yes, Michael. You've answered all your own questions. Okay?

Student: Mmm, yeah, it makes sense to me now, professor. Thanks for clearing that up for me. Now I'd better think about choosing a topic for it.

Narrator : Now get ready to answer the questions. You may use your notes to help you answer.

スクリプト和訳

Narrator（以下 *N*）：学生と教授の会話を聴きなさい

Professor（以下 *P*）：こんにちは、マイケル。私を探していましたか？

Student（以下 *S*）：はい、そうです、先生。先生に解決してほしい悩みがありまして。

P：なるほど。ええっと、授業に行かなくてはならない時間の前に、少しならば時間をとることはできると思います。何が問題に思えるのですか？

S：一番新しい課題についてなのです、先生。月曜日に先生が出したものです。もちろん、先生は授業中にしっかり説明されたことは、わかっているのですが、先生がおっしゃったとおり、これまでの課題とは全く異なっていますよね。なので、僕はすべて正しく理解できているのか、未だによくわからないのです。

P：なるほど。それでは、私がもう一度最初から説明するのではなく、自分は何をすることになっていると思っているのか、まずあなたが言ってみてください。そこでもし、誤解しているところがあればあなたの話を止めますよ。

S：そうですね、わかりました。僕がわかっていることは、歴史の中から、ある一人の人物もしくはある一つの事件を選ぶことになっているということなのですけど、そうですよね？

P：その通りですよ。

S：本当に完全に自由に選んでもいいのですか？

P：もちろんよ。当然でしょう？　私はね、あなたたちに自分がとてもよく知っている事件とか人物を選んでほしいと思っているのよ。続けて。

S：ここからが、少し明確に理解できないところなのです。ええと、僕は授業中、ノートにこう書きました。先生が僕らに求めるのは、肯定的な視点、否定的な視点、そしてええと、変わっていく視点から人物や事件について書くことだと。これも正しいですか？

P：そうね、正しいわ。たぶんそれは私が話したままの言葉ですね。その通り。

S：はい。でも、それって、正確にはどういうことですか？
P：頑張って、マイケル。あなたは知的なのだから、どのような意味だと思うのか、あなたが、私に言ってみなさい。
S：ええっと、僕の考えでは、先生が僕らに理解してほしいことの一つには、まずものを調べるときは、常に幅広い資料に当たることを心がけなくてはならないということだと思います。
P：まさにその通りよ。実際に考えてみると、そこまで複雑なことではないでしょう。じゃあ、私は、ほかには何を求めていると思いますか？
S：そこのところがわかりません、先生。
P：よく聞いてください。私が本当に伝えたかった考えはね、どんな事件も様々な視点から見ることができるということなの。例えば、社会に影響を与えたどんな歴史的人物に対しても、彼らの生存中には、英雄だと考えた人々もいたのだろうし、悪党だと考えた人々もいたことでしょう。それに、その後、その人物についての評価や判断も、死後年月を経るにつれ、変わってしまったり進化していることでしょう。
S：ということは、僕らは異なる資料をただ調べる以上のことが求められているのですね？ また、異なる意見を考慮に入れて、どうしてこうした意見も存在しているのかを、考えることも求められているのですね。
P：それと、どうしてそうした変化が起こったのか、その理由もね。ほら、マイケル、自分の質問に全て自分で答えてしまったじゃない。そうでしょ？
S：はい、やっと理解できました。解決していただいて、ありがとうございました。さあ、これから、この課題のトピックを考えないと。
N：設問に答える準備をしてください。解答の際にメモを用いても構いません

解答 Questions 23 - 28

23 C　24 D　25 B・C・E　26 C　27 A　28 D

> 解答のポイント Questions 23 - 28

> スクリプト

Narrator : Listen to part of a lecture in a History of Science class.

Professor : When looking at the history of science, we often come across instances where different theories and ideas have arisen at almost the same time, and have then competed to gain wide acceptance as the "correct" theory. One particular theory might become more or less popular at any given time, or even rejected outright, for reasons which often have nothing to do with science. I wanna look at one such instance of this today.

Now, although Einstein and others have taken our modern understanding of the nature of light to a much higher level, there was an interesting diversion that occurred in early scientific theories of light. The earliest theories were proposed around the end of the 17th century. In 1690, a Dutch scientist, Christian Huygens, proposed a theory that explained light as a wave phenomenon. So, to begin with, we have the wave theory of light.

However, in 1704, a rival theory comes along, offered by the influential English scientist and uh, natural philosopher, Sir Isaac Newton. Back in 1666, Newton had discovered that white light can be separated into a spectrum of colors, and he theorized that light is composed of tiny particles that are emitted by luminous bodies. Despite Huygens being first to describe a plausible theory of light, it was Newton's ideas which prevailed in the scientific community for close to a century.

Why was this? Well, first of all, Sir Isaac Newton was the greatest figure of the scientific revolution. I mean, he had taken many early discoveries in mechanics and astronomy, added to them many of his own discoveries, and combined them all in a single system to describe and explain the workings of the universe. The system was based on the concept of gravitation, and it used a new branch of mathematics, calculus, that he had invented for the purpose. All of this was set down in Newton's landmark book, Philosophical Principles of Natural Philosophy, which was published in 1687 and which marked the beginning of the modern period of mechanics and astronomy. How could Huygens compete with that?!

I should mention another vitally influential man at this time, the French scientist and philosopher, René Descartes. He had introduced the belief that the universe is a mechanical system that can be described in mathematical terms. Actually, it was then Huygens who perfected the mechanical clock, allowing greater precision in timing events. This was an essential factor in the development of exact sciences such as mechanics.

Anyway, returning to Newton's theory of light, by combining his particle theory with his laws of mechanics, Newton was able to explain many optical phenomena. And the behavior of his particles could be described by the laws of mechanics. So given that Newton's prestige and influence were so great, and the acceptance of the mechanistic philosophy of Descartes and others was so widespread, Newton's particle theory was the dominant one for more than a century. Also, another factor is that, at the time, not enough experimental evidence existed to provide an adequate means for comparing the two theories. This also worked in Newton's favor. Given his fame and achievements, people simply assumed that Newton knew what he was talking about, and trusted him to have all the answers.

The wave theory of light was eventually revived at the beginning of the 19th century when, finally, important experiments were done on the diffraction and interference of light, starting with Thomas Young in 1801. These produced results that could only be interpreted in terms of the wave theory. The polarization of light was another phenomenon that could only be explained by the wave theory. Additional support came in 1864, when uh, James Clerk Maxwell's electromagnetic theory showed that light was just one form of electromagnetic energy. Thus, a century and a half after Newton, the wave theory became the dominant theory of the nature of light.

Narrator : Now get ready to answer the questions. You may use your notes to help you answer.

スクリプト和訳

Narrator(以下 *N*)：科学史の授業における講義の一部を聴きなさい。

Professor：科学史に目を向けると、異なる理論や思想がほぼ同時に現れ、「正しい」理論として広く受け入れられるために、互いに競合するといった事例によく出会います。ある特定の理論がいつでも多かれ少なかれ人気が出るかもしれませんし、逆に即座に拒否すらされてしまうかもしれません。その理由が、全く科学と関わりのない理由によることがよくあるのです。本日はこうした事例の一件に着目したいと思います。

　さて、アインシュタインをはじめとする人々により、光の性質についての今日の我々の理解度は、非常に高い次元にまで引き上げられていますが、光に関する初期の科学的な理論では、興味深い意見の転換が起こりました。最古の理論は、17世紀の終わり頃に提唱されました。1690年、オランダ人の科学者クリスチャン・ホイヘンス（Christian Huygens）は、光を波動の現象であると論じる理論を出しました。したがって、まずは光の波動説です。（ここでの we have は、このクラスで、波動説を話して分かち合っている情報であることを示す。）

しかしながら1704年、一つの競合する理論が現れます。これは影響力のあるイギリスの科学者であり自然哲学者でもある、アイザック・ニュートン卿（Sir Isaac Newton）が提案したものです。時は遡り1666年、ニュートンは白い光を色のスペクトルに分けることができるという発見をし、光を放つ物体が放出する細かい粒子が光を構成しているという理論を出しました。ホイヘンスが最初に妥当な光の理論を説明した人物であるにもかかわらず、一世紀近く科学界を席巻したのは、ニュートンの方でした。

　どうしてこうなったのでしょうか。第一に、アイザック・ニュートン卿は科学革命の最も偉大な人物でありました。つまり、彼は、力学や天文学における初期の数多くの発見を取り上げ、それに彼自身の多くの発見を追加し、宇宙の仕組みを説明するために、これら全てを一つのシステムにまとめ上げたということです。このシステムは引力の概念に基づくもので、彼がそのために考え出していた新しい数学の分野である微積分学を利用しました。これら全ては、1687年に出版されたニュートンの画期的な書物、『自然哲学の数学的諸原理』（*Mathematical Principles of Natural Philosophy*）に書き留められました。この本は近代の力学と天文学の黎明を示すものであります。これほどの功績に対して、どうやってホイヘンスが太刀打ちできるでしょう？

　もう一人、この時代に極めて重要な影響力を持っていた人物についても、言及するべきでしょう。フランスの科学者で哲学者ルネ・デカルト（René Descartes）です。彼は、宇宙は数学用語で説明することのできる、機械的なシステムであるという意見を提案しました。実際は、ホイヘンスがまさに機械式時計の欠点をなくし完成させた人で、時間測定をずっと正確にしました。これは、力学のような精密科学の発展には不可欠な要素であります。

　とにかく、また、ニュートンの光の理論に戻ります。彼の粒子理論と力学の法則を組み合わせることで、彼は数多くの光学上の現象について説明することができた。彼の唱える粒子の行動性質も、力学の法則で説明がつきました。そういうわけで、ニュートンの名声や影響力が絶大であったことや、デカルトやその他の人物による機械論的哲学の受容が広範囲に広まったことが前提にあり、ニュート

ンの粒子理論は一世紀以上もの間優勢理論であったのです。加えてもう一つの要因として、当時は二つの理論を比較するために十分な手段を提供するための、実験的証拠が不足していたことも挙げられます。このことも、ニュートンに有利に働いたのでした。彼の名声と実績を考慮すれば、ニュートンは出鱈目なことは言わない、と人々は単純に思い込んでしまい、彼はなんでもわかっていると信じてしまったのです。

　最終的に、光の波動説が復活するのは、19世紀の初めです。この時代、ついに光の回折や光波の干渉といったことに関する重要な実験が、1801年のトーマス・ヤング（Thomas Young）の研究を皮切りに行われました。これらの実験が示す結果は、光の波動説においてのみ解釈されうるものでありました。偏光といったものも、光の波動説だけが説明しうる現象であります。更なる擁護論が、1864年に現れました。この年、ジェームズ・クラーク・マックスウェル（James Clerk Maxwell）の電磁場理論が、光は電磁波のエネルギーの一つの形にすぎないことを示しました。したがって、ニュートン以後一世紀半の年月を経て、光の波動説が光の性質をめぐる支配的な理論となったのです。

N：設問に答える準備をしてください。解答の際にメモを用いても構いません。

解答 Questions 29 - 34

29 B　30 B　31 A・D　32 (A)YES・(B)NO・(C)YES・(D)YES・(E)NO　33 B・D・E　34 C

解答のポイント Questions 29 - 34

スクリプト

Narrator : Listen to part of a discussion in an Economics class.

Professor : One of the best-known theories about population growth was published over two hundred years ago by Robert Malthus. Now,

Malthus was an English political economist best known for some very pessimistic views. Actually, his ideas were very controversial at the time, because they went against the common intellectual philosophy of the era, which was very optimistic.

What do I mean by optimistic? Well, before Malthus, rapid population growth was seen as a good thing, you see, because more people meant more workers for the economy. However, Malthus saw how much the working poor had to struggle to survive, and so he came to doubt this idea strongly. After developing his ideas, he published "An Essay On The Principle of Population" in 1798, with an expanded version in 1803.

Now, Malthus described how the world's population appeared to be increasing geometrically, y'know, 1, 2, 4, 8, 16 and so on, while resources were only growing arithmetically, like 1, 2, 3, 4, 5. Essentially, resources were limited, but population growth was potentially limitless. Of course, this cannot continue forever since, at some point, the needs of a growing population would become too great for agricultural production to satisfy. This is what Malthus called a "catastrophe" when millions would die, halting population growth naturally.

Well, Malthus's ideas were very controversial, and attacked by many people as just being too negative. In practical terms, though, he had a major influence on many areas of life. Just to list some of them, well, the first British population census was conducted in 1801, partly as a result of the impact of Malthus's ideas on public and political opinion. Um, his ideas strongly influenced many political reforms, especially on issues of poverty and welfare, and Charles Darwin was greatly influenced by Malthus. In fact, in his book "The Origin of Species", Darwin said his own famous theory was an application of Malthus's ideas in a non-human field.

Obviously, we know now that population and agricultural and economic production haven't followed the pattern Malthus expected. The twentieth century especially saw massive geometric population growth, but there hasn't yet been one of his predicted catastrophes. Many modern economists, of course have knowledge that Malthus could never have foreseen. Well, they've tended to criticize Malthus rather heavily, and somewhat unfairly, I think we'd have to say. Well, what do you think? How about population? What might prevent its continued geometric increase? What do you think, uh, Amanda?

Student A : Well, on a large scale, we'd have to factor in war, natural disasters — diseases as well. And the way we live today, y'know, how we think about families and children, that's really slowed down population growth.

Professor : That's right. Malthus didn't account for war, disaster, or disease putting a sudden stop to population growth. And, yes, many factors, including lower infant mortality rates, better education, lifestyle changes, and improved contraception, too — they've all given us more control over population growth. However, let's not underestimate Malthus, you know. He understood the role of contraception could play in checking excessive population growth, but he favored "moral restraint" himself, which included such things as late marriage and sexual abstinence. Anyway, on the other side — the production side — is there anything to do with resources that Malthus didn't foresee? Or are we actually running out of food? Yes, John?

Student B : I don't think we're really running out of resources. I mean, there's no way Malthus could have imagined the improvements in technology. Modern farming is much more efficient and productive than it was 200 years ago. Things like high-yield crop varieties especially.

Student A : Yeah, and distribution is much better now, too. You know, we can get the food to where it needs to go.

Professor : Yes, very true, both of you. Indeed, most food shortages in the world right now are more likely to be caused by some breakdown or obstacle to effective distribution.

Narrator : Now get ready to answer the questions. You may use your notes to help you answer.

スクリプト和訳

Narrator(以下 ***N***)：経済学の授業における議論の一部を聴きなさい。

Professor(以下 ***P***)：人口の増加に関するもっとも有名な理論の一つは、200年以上前にロバート・マルサス（Robert Malthus）によって発表されました。ところで、マルサスはとても悲観的な見解で有名なイギリスの政治経済学者なのです。現実問題として、彼の考えは当時かなり議論を呼ぶものでありました。なぜならば、非常に楽観的なこの時代の一般的な知的哲学思想に、反旗を翻すものであったからです。

　ここでは、楽観的という言葉は、なにを意味するのでしょう？　マルサス以前は、人口の増加は良いことであると見なされていたのです。なぜならば、より多くの人口の存在は、経済活動のためのより多くの労働者の存在を意味するからです。しかし、マルサスは貧しい労働者が何とか生きていくのに苦労しているのを目の当たりにし、この考え方に強い疑問を持つようになったのです。自分の考えを発展させた後、彼は『人口論』（*An Essay on the Principle of Population*）を出版しました。1798年のことです。その増補版は1803年に出版されます。

そこでマルサスは、資源が1,2,3,4,5といったようにただ算数的に増加するだけである一方、いかに、世界の人口が幾何学的に増加していくように見えるのか、つまり1,2,4,8,16……といった具合に増えていくのかを説明しました。本質的に言うと、資源は有限ですが、人口は限りなく増加する可能性があるのです。もちろん、永遠に人口増加は続くことはありません。というのは、ある地点で、人口増加による需要があまりにも多くなりすぎて、農業の生産量が、その需要を満たすことが不可能になる可能性があるからです。これがマルサスのいう「大惨事」です。その時、何百万の人が死に、人口増加に自然と歯止めがかかるのです。

　マルサスの思想はかなりの物議を醸すものであり、あまりにも悲観的過ぎると多くの人の批判の的となってしまいました。しかし実際には、人生の多くの場面に彼の影響が強く及びました。その中のほんのいくつかを挙げてみると、1801年に初めて実施された英国の人口調査は、部分的ですが公共的および政治的な意見に関するマルサスの見解の影響によるものであります。また、彼の思想は多くの政治改革、とりわけ貧困や社会福祉といった問題に、強い影響を与えました。加えて、チャールズ・ダーウィン（Charles Darwin）はマルサスに非常に感化された人です。実際、彼の著書の『種の起源』（*The Origin of Species*）において、ダーウィンは自身の有名な理論は、マルサスの思想を人間以外のものの領域に応用したといっています。

　言うまでもなく、現在我々は人口、農業、経済における生産が、マルサスの予想したパターンに沿うものではないことを知っています。20世紀には、特に爆発的な幾何学的人口増加に直面しましたが、まだ彼の予想する「大惨事」は１つも起こっていません。現在の経済学者の多くは、もちろんマルサスが決して予見することができなかっただろう知識を持ち合わせています。そう、彼らはマルサスを批判する傾向があります。非常に厳しく、そして、幾分不当

にと、言わざるを得ないでしょう。(I-I think we'd have to to say. は、and somewhat unfairly「そして、幾分不当に」についての、教授の意見を示す発言)

さて、どのように思いますか？　人口についてはいかがですか？　人口の幾何学的な増加を食い止めるかもしれないものは一体何でしょうか？　アマンダ、どう思いますか？

Student A（以下 **SA**）：そうですね、大規模に考えると、戦争、自然災害、疾病を含まねばならないでしょう。それと、私たちの今日の生き方です。つまり、家族や子供についての我々の考え方は、現実に人口増加を抑えています。

P：その通りです。マルサスは人口増加を突然止めるものとして戦争、災害、病気を計算に入れなかったのです。そして、多くの要因、例えば幼児の死亡率の低下、教育水準の上昇、生活様式の変化、そして避妊法の進歩などは、我々に人口増加へのより強い管理力を与えてくれます。しかし、マルサスを過小評価するのはよしましょう。彼も避妊が過度の人口増加を阻止する役割を果たすことは知っていました。ただ、彼自身は「道徳的な節制」の方を支持していました。例えば、晩婚や性的禁欲です。では、もう一方の要因、生産サイドで、マルサスが予見することができなかった資源と何か関係はありますか？　または本当に我々の食料は、尽きさせてしまうのでしょうか？　ジョン、どうぞ。

Student B：僕は我々の食料が本当に尽きてしまうとは思いません。と言うか、マルサスには技術の進歩を想像することができたかもしれない、なんてことは、ありえないと思います。

現代の農業は200年前よりもずっと効率的で生産的です。特に、様々な多収穫が可能な作物なんかに関しては。

SA：その通りだわ。また　流通も今はずっと良くなっています。ほら、食料を行くべきところに持っていくことができるでしょう。

P：そうです。二人とも正しい答えですね。確かに、目下のところ起こっている食料不足のほとんどは、効率的な流通の断絶か、妨害により生じている可能性が高いのです。

N：設問に答える準備をしてください。解答の際にメモを用いても構いません。

Speaking Section

解答例・解答のポイント　Question 1

スクリプト

In this question, you will be asked to talk about a familiar topic. After you hear the question, you will have 15 seconds to prepare your response, and 45 seconds to speak.

解答例

410. mp3

Young people are generally much more comfortable and familiar with using modern electronic devices. Many older people, however, feel uncomfortable with them because they didn't exist when they were younger. So, young people can teach older people how to use electronic devices easily.

For example, I have been using computers, e-mail, and the Internet since I was a school student. Also, I've used devices like a mobile phone, DVD player, and car navigation system every day for several years.

However, for my parents, and especially my grandparents, these devices are strange and confusing. So, in my family, it's my responsibility to teach them how to use such devices.

Question 2

スクリプト

In this question, you will be asked to give your opinion about a familiar topic. After you hear the question, you will have 15 seconds to prepare your response, and 45 seconds to speak.

解答例

411. mp3

In my opinion, it's necessary for university students to attend classes.

Universities are places of education, so going to class is the main reason for being there. The subjects studied in university require a great amount of basic knowledge, and if you graduate from university, you can usually get a better job and higher salary. People believe university graduates have more knowledge, but if students don't attend their classes, they are wasting their education, and should not be able to enjoy the benefits of being a graduate.

Attending university is a special privilege for those who are able to attend, and therefore universities must enforce attendance of classes.

Question 3

スクリプト

《 Reading 》

Narrator: Now read the passage about University to Increase Campus Security. You have 45 seconds to read the passage. Begin reading now.

《 Listening 》

Narrator: Now listen to two students discussing this notice.

Man: Can you believe that? I hope this place doesn't turn into a prison. To make matters worse, they're going to make us pay for the increased security. And even worse, they're going to take money out of the student entertainment fees.

Woman: I know. I guess they want to show us that we're all responsible for maintaining security on campus. I think it's a way to get us to try and turn in whoever is behind all those thefts recently. I mean it is a serious problem. My friend had her car broken into last week.

Man: Yes, it is, but why cut into the entertainment fund to cover the costs? This probably means the bands will be lousy this spring festival.

Woman: Hey, look on the bright side. You live in Anderson, right? Well, maybe you won't have to worry so much about someone breaking into your room and stealing your stuff.

Man: Yeah, maybe you're right. I guess it's a small price to pay for being safer. I just think they should find the money to pay for the plan elsewhere. Why not use the alumni fund?

Narrator: The man expresses his opinion about the university's plan to increase security. State his opinion and explain why he holds that opinion.

《 Reading 》和訳

大学構内の治安強化実施のお知らせ

　大学運営本部は、非常勤の構内警備員を新たに2名雇用し、また警備巡回の回数を3月1日から増やすことを決定しました。学生寮および構内の建物裏駐車場A区画からF区画に停められた車上における窃盗の増加のため、これらの対策が必要となりました。アンダーソンおよびウッドウォード・ホールは、校内警備の特別警戒対象となっています。これらの対策のために追加費用は、学生会の催事基金の一部から支給されます。

《 Listening 》和訳

ナレーター：この告知について話している二人の学生の会話を聴きなさい。

男性：これって信じられる？　ここが刑務所みたいにならないことを願うよ。もっといやなのは、大学が学生に治安強化の費用を払わせようとしていることだよ。で、学生催事資金からお金を取って使おうっていうんだから、最悪。

女性：そうよね。でも、大学は、構内の治安を維持することに関しては、私たち皆に責任があることを示したいんじゃないかな。今回の対策は、最近の一連の窃盗の背後にいる犯人を警察に引き渡す為に、学生を協力させるためのものだと思うけど。だって、今の状況は深刻よ。私の友だちも先週車上荒らしに遭ったし。

男性：それはそうだけど、費用を賄うために、なんで催事基金に手を付けるわけ？　これじゃ春の学園祭のバンドの質が悪くなる。

女性：でも、いい面もあるじゃない。あなたはアンダーソンに住んでいるんでしょ。だったら、誰かが部屋に押し入って物が盗まれるのを、これまで

ほど心配しなくてすむんじゃない？

男性：うーん、まあ、そうかもね。安全のための代償としては、安いものだとは思うけど。ただ、今回の対策のためのお金は他から出すべきだと思うんだよね。卒業生基金とかさ。

ナレーター：男子学生は、大学の治安維持強化対策に関して、自分の考えを述べています。この学生の考えと、なぜ彼がそのように考えるのかを、要約しなさい。

解答例

The man thinks the increased campus security presence might be too stifling. The man is especially against funding the plan to increase security by taking money out of the student entertainment fund. He is worried the bands for the spring festival won't be very good this year. He would rather have the funding for more security come from another source like the alumni fund. In the end he seems to agree with the woman to some degree regarding the need for more security.

Question 4

スクリプト

《 Reading 》

Narrator: Now read the passage about Agriculture in Louisiana. You have 45 seconds to read the passage. Begin reading now.

《 Listening 》

Narrator: Now listen to part of a lecture on this topic in an American History class.

Professor:

I want to continue our survey of the development of farming in the southern states by focusing today on Louisiana.

Now, although most of the state consists of similar low-lying terrain, it was only in southern Louisiana — that is, along the coast, and around the Mississippi Delta with its rich, fertile soil — it was only in this area that the plantation agriculture gained a significant foothold. Initially, rice was grown along the lower Mississippi, but sugarcane soon replaced it as the major plantation crop. However, sugar cane farming was generally restricted to areas near the Mississippi, as well as those slow, sluggish streams — the bayous — to the west and south of Baton Rouge. The huge sugar plantations are still there today, and actually still have much of the appearance of the pre-Civil War days, but of course they are now largely mechanized.

A second crop specialization, rice cultivation, was developed immediately west of the sugar area, and bordering on Texas, which is an area of geologically older coastland, with tight, water-holding soil. Now, as I just mentioned, rice had been grown earlier on the Mississippi Delta, but this was using small-scale, labor-intensive methods. However, in the late nineteenth century, Midwesterners experienced in large-scale farming brought their experience to the south, and applied their ideas to rice production. The rice is still grown in huge, water-covered fields, only today, airplanes are used to spread seed and apply fertilizers.

Narrator : The professor describes the development of sugarcane and rice production in southern Louisiana. Summarize and explain the reasons the region's agriculture developed in this way.

《 Reading 》和訳

ルイジアナの農業

　南部は亜熱帯性で北部は温帯性であるルイジアナの気候、低く平坦な地勢、そして肥沃な堆積土壌が、ルイジアナ州を合衆国でも有数の農産地としています。ルイジアナ州の地勢は水によって特徴づけられています。ルイジアナ州には、総延長5,000マイルにおよぶ河川があり、この国の湿地の40%以上がこの州にあります。ミシシッピ川が最も広い流域を占めていますが、レッド川をはじめ他にも多くの河川があり、沿岸部にはバイユーと呼ばれる、きわめてゆるや

かな流れが低地を縫うように分布しています。メキシコ湾岸の平野とミシシッピ川の沖積平野にある地域には湿地と肥沃な三角州があり、米、サツマイモ、サトウキビなどの生産に適しています。内陸部には、松に覆われたなだらかな丘陵と平原が広がっており、綿花の栽培が盛んです。これらの他に主要な作物として大豆や酪農製品もありますが、林業も広く行われています。

《 Listening 》和訳

ナレーター：この話題に関連する、アメリカ史の授業における講義の一部を聴きなさい。

教授：引き続き、南部の諸州における農業の発展を詳しく学んでいくわけですが、今日はルイジアナに目をむけてみたいと思います。

　さて、ルイジアナ州のほとんどは低くなだらかな土地から成りますが、プランテーション農業が発達の足場を築いたのは、州の南部、すなわち沿岸部および豊かで肥沃な土壌を有するミシシッピ三角州が広がる地域、に限られました。はじめは、米がミシシッピ川下流域において栽培されていましたが、すぐにサトウキビがこれに代わって主要なプランテーション作物となりました。しかし、サトウキビの栽培は、おおむねミシシッピ川流域、および、あのゆるく、止まっているかのような細流、そうバイユーです、の一帯、そしてバトン・ルージュの西方と南方の地域に限られていました。サトウキビの大規模なプランテーション栽培は、今でもこれらの地域において行われており、表向きには南北戦争以前の時代のおもむきの多くを残していますが、もちろん大部分は機械化されています。

　二つ目の主要作物である米の栽培は、サトウキビの栽培地域のすぐ西の地域と、テキサスとの州境におよぶ地域において発達しましたが、この沿岸地域の地質は古いため、密に詰まった、水持ちのよい土壌が分布しています。ところで、先ほど、米はかつてミシシッピ三角州において栽培されていた、と言いましたが、これは小規模で労働集約型のやり方でした。しかし19世紀の終わりになると、大規模農業をよく知る、中西部から来た人々が、彼らのやり方を南部へともたらし、米の栽培にそれを応用しました。米は広大な水田で現在も栽培されていますが、今日においてのみ、種を蒔き肥料を撒布するのに飛行機が使われています。

ナレーター：教授は、ルイジアナ州南部におけるサトウキビの栽培と米の生産の発達に関して述べています。この地域における農業の発達の過程とその背景を要約しなさい。

解答例

413. mp3

　Sugarcane and rice became the main agricultural crops in southern Louisiana because the Mississippi River and coastal areas have very rich and fertile soil and lots of water and marshland. Near the Mississippi River, some rice was grown at first but only on a small-scale. Then, sugarcane became the biggest crop, but this was only in places close to the Mississippi Delta and the bayous.

　In west Louisiana, next to Texas, there is older land by the coast which holds lots of water. They started to grow rice there in the nineteenth century when many people who knew about large-scale farming came from the Midwest and started to grow rice in huge fields covered in water.

　Both sugarcane and rice are still the biggest crops in Louisiana today.

Question 5

スクリプト

Narrator: Listen to a conversation between two students.

Man: We're going to have to do something. The student election is only two days away, and I really don't think we've generated enough interest in my proposals as candidate. Any ideas how we can get my message across more effectively in a short time?

Woman: We could really make your posters much better. Every candidate has put up posters in the same places, so if we can redesign your posters so they have a stronger impact, that'll make your name and your message stand out much more compared to the other candidates.

Man: For example?

Woman : Well, one way would be to use bright colors and big letters for your name. We should also think of a short, powerful slogan so everyone remembers your name and what you stand for.

Man : We could do that... but I don't know if it can work in just two days. I really think we should leaflet students. Y'know, stand outside lecture halls and cafeterias and hand out leaflets about me.

Woman : That could work, and quickly too, but it's expensive to do all the photocopying... and many students just don't care. They'll throw away the leaflet as soon as you give it to them, without even looking at it. Everyone looks at the posters, though.

Man : Hmm... we have to do something.

Narrator : The students discuss two possible solutions to the man's problem. Describe the problem. Then state which of the two solutions you prefer and explain why.

| 和訳 |

ナレーター：二人の学生の会話を聴きなさい。

男性：うーん、なんとかしなきゃなあ。生徒自治会（または、生徒会）の選挙まであと二日しかないのに、僕の立候補者としての公約に十分注目が集まっているとは、とても思えないもんなあ。短い時間で効果的に僕の考えを投票者に理解してもらうにはどうしたらいいか、何か案はある？

女性：選挙ポスターをもっとよくすることは、できると思うわ。候補者は皆ポスターを同じ場所に掲示しているわけだから、ポスターを作りなおして、もっと強烈なインパクトのあるものにすれば、あなたの名前とメッセージは他の候補者に比べてもっと目立つようになるはずよ。

男性：たとえばどんなふうに作りなおすの？

女性：そうね、名前にもっと派手な色と大きい文字を使うとか、それに、あなたの名前と主張を覚えてもらう為に、簡潔で説得力のある標語を考え出す必要もあると思うわ。

男性：それもいいと思うけど、でもたった二日で効果があるかな。僕はチラシを配るのがいいと思うんだよね。ほら、講堂とか学生食堂の外に立って、

僕のチラシを手渡すんだよ。
女性：それも効果があるでしょうね、しかも短時間で。でも、印刷（コピー）するのに相当お金がかかるし、チラシは読んでくれない人も多いと思うし。チラシを手渡しても、見もしないですぐに捨てちゃうでしょ。ポスターは皆が見るけどね。
男性：うーん。なんとかしなきゃなあ。

ナレーター：二人の学生は、男子学生の抱える問題に対する二つの解決策を話し合っています。問題がどのようなものであるかを要約しなさい。さらに、二つの解決策のうちのいずれがよいとあなたは考えるか、また、その理由を述べなさい。

解答例

414.mp3

The man is a candidate for the student elections in two days' time, but he's worried that not enough students are interested in him or his proposals. In this situation, I think the man's idea is much better than the woman's. It's much too late to simply change the man's posters by making them brighter or bigger, but by giving leaflets directly to students, the man can communicate his message much more quickly and also in more detail. He can make a more personal appeal to each individual student by showing them how motivated he is and by explaining his ideas to them.

Question 6

スクリプト

Narrator: Now listen to part of a talk in an Economics class.

Professor:

We've spent some time studying profit, which we generally regard as a company's total revenue minus its total costs. However, there are different ways of calculating those costs, which leads to different ideas of profit. Especially, there's a significant difference between economic profit and accounting profit, and if they are confused, some very serious and very costly mistakes can occur. So, I want to clear this up for you now.

With just a few exceptions, such as the cost of equipment or facilities gradually wearing out over time, accountants consider only explicit costs, where money is actually paid out. If we deduct only the costs recognized by accountants — that is, total revenue minus accounting costs — what we're left with is the accounting profit.

Economists, however, have a much broader view of cost, which is the total value of everything given up to produce output. This includes not only the explicit costs recognized by accountants, such as wages or payment for raw materials, but also implicit costs, when something is given up but no money changes hands.

For example, suppose that you used $5,000 of your own money to start a small business at home. Well, as it's your own money, you don't have to pay any interest on a loan, so there are no explicit costs. However, there are implicit ones. First, you've given up the chance to keep that money in the bank and earn a few hundred dollars in interest. Also, using a spare room in your house as office space will save you the cost of renting an office, but it means losing the chance to earn some extra income by renting the room out. By subtracting both the implicit and explicit costs for a company from its total revenue, we get a different measure of profit. This is economic profit.

Narrator: Using points and examples from the talk, summarize and explain the differences between accounting profit and economic profit.

和訳

ナレーター：経済学の授業における講義の一部を聴きなさい。

教授：利益というものに関してこれまで学んできましたが、私たちは一般に、利益は会社の総収益から経費の総額を差し引いたもの、と考えます。ところが、その総経費を計算するにはいくつかの異なる方法があり、したがって利益の概念もこれにより変わることになります。特に、経済的利

益と会計利益との間には大きな違いがあり、これらを混同してしまうと、深刻で大きな損失をもたらす過ちを犯しかねません。そこで、今この違いをはっきりさせたいと思います。

　いくつかの例外、例えば備品や設備など時間の経過に伴い消耗されるものの費用などを除き、会計士が扱うのは明示的な費用、すなわち実際にお金として支払われる形の費用に限られます。この、会計士が扱う費用のみを差し引くと、すなわち、総収益から会計上の費用を引くと、残るのは、会計利益です。

　一方、経済学者は、より包括的な見方で費用というものをとらえ、結果を得るための代償となったすべてのものの総額、が費用であるとします。このとらえ方によれば、費用には、賃金や原材料費など、会計士が扱う明示的な費用に加えて、お金に出入りはなくとも何かが費やされた時に発生する、計算上の（潜在的な）費用が、含まれることになります。

　例を挙げてみましょう。自宅で小規模の事業を始めるために、自分のお金を5,000ドル使ったとします。自費だから、借入金の利子を支払う必要はなく、したがって明示的な費用は発生しません。しかし、計算上の（潜在的な）費用は発生します。まず、この5,000ドルを銀行に預けてその利子として何百ドルかを得る機会を失ったことになります。また、自宅の空いた部屋を事務所として使うことにより、事務所を賃借する費用は節約できますが、その空き部屋を賃貸して副収入を得る機会を失ったことになります。このように、計算上の（潜在的な）経費と明示的な経費の両方を総収益から差し引くことによって、我々は先ほどのものとは異なる利益尺度を得ます。これが経済的利益です。

ナレーター：この講義において述べられた論点と事例を用いて、会計上の利益と経済的利益の違いを要約し説明しなさい。

解答例

According to the professor, accounting profit is calculated by subtracting explicit costs from a company's total revenue. Explicit costs means only costs where the company has to pay out money, such as paying wages to workers or buying raw materials.

On the other hand, to calculate economic profit, we have to subtract both explicit and implicit costs from the company's revenue. An implicit cost is where something is given up by the company apart from just money. For example, if you want to use your own money to start a company, you have to give up the chance to invest that money in the bank.

Writing Section

解答例・解答のポイント　Question 1

《 Reading 》和訳

　「鬼火」とは、多くの人好奇心をそそるがまれにしか見られない、通常、湿地において夜に見かけられる青白い炎の明滅の呼び名のひとつである。この現象にまつわる、死者の霊魂や孤独な旅人を死へとおびき寄せようとする悪霊など、数々の迷信が生まれた。他方、合理的で科学的な説明を見つけるための数々の試みもなされ、「鬼火」の現象を説明する少なくとも2、3の説を科学者たちが提示している。

　提示されたもののうちもっともよく知られる説は、「鬼火」は沼の腐食有機物から発生したメタンガスとリン化水素の酸化により生じる、とするものである。メタンガス、リン化水素ともに可燃性が高く、通常の大気の状態で燃焼する。これらの化合物を実験室で反応させたところ、発光することが確かめられた。2008年には、イタリア人の化学者であるルイジ・ガルラシェリとパオロ・ボシェティは、実験室において「鬼火」を再現することを試みた。彼らはリン化水素を空気と窒素に反応させることにより、淡く冷たい光を発生させることに成功したのである。

　圧電効果の可能性があると思っている科学者もいる。圧電気は、ある種のセラミックや結晶など、曲げられたり圧力をかけられたりすると電気と火花を発生する物質により発生する。これとよく似た現象で、摩擦発光と呼ばれる現象が、Wint-O-Green Lifesavers の発光に見られ、圧電の場合のように物質が曲げられた時ではなく、破砕された時に電気と光が発生する。この考えは、「鬼火」の往々にして不規則な動きをある程度説明する。

　生物発光（生きている生物によって作られる光）も、一説として提唱されている。菌など、ある種の微生物には、ほとんど発熱なしに光を発する化学反応を起こすことができるものがある。この類の発光はメンフクロウに観察されたと報告されている。この説では、フクロウがその巣やねぐらに繁殖している発光性のキノコの類―数種の存在が知られている―に体をすりつけることが一因ではなかろうか、と説明する。それからフクロウが羽毛に発光性の物質をつけ

て飛び回り、その発光物質が時々月の光のような光源から十分な光を反射した結果、「鬼火」のように見えることがある。

《 Listening 》スクリプト

Will-o'-the-wisp is an extensively documented phenomenon and has been the subject of many published articles, radio and television programs. However, the cause has never been satisfactorily explained.

Although those who are less superstitious say that Will-o'-the-wisp is the ignition of the gases rising from the marsh, I doubt it because a common characteristic associated with this phenomenon is its elusive nature. According to accounts of Will-o'-the-wisp, the mysterious lights advance towards you as you advance towards them, recede as you recede, and at other times remain stationary. How could a light produced from burning gas have the form described and move as described without having any visible connection with the earth?

One of the arguments offered against explanations for a piezoelectric effect is that most of the mechanisms simply can't produce the energy needed for visible luminescent phenomena. In the cases of both the piezoelectric and triboluminescent models, most of the rocks involved would insulate against electricity, and so they would absorb any currents produced by ground activity before any sort of discharge.

Barn owls have been said to have come in contact with luminous fungus inside the tree hollows in which they roost. The fungus usually mentioned is the well-known Honey Fungus (Armillaria mellea), which causes wood to glow. However, the articles covering the bioluminescent honey fungus go on to suggest that this is not the correct explanation for Will-o'-the-wisp. The glowing part of this honey fungus could very likely be the mycelium growing in the wood, not external fruiting parts or spores or exudation. For feather contamination to take place by these means, the wood would have to be broken up into particles. Wood fragments and fungal fibers are unlikely to adhere to feathers for long, given the frequent feather maintenance of birds by preening in order to ensure their aerodynamic properties and insulation.

Therefore, contamination of owls' feathers by luminescent fungi from decaying wood within tree hollows is an unlikely explanation for Will-o'-the-wisp.

《 Listening 》和訳

　「鬼火」は大々的に報告され、また多くの文献やラジオまたはテレビの番組などにおいて扱われてきました。しかし、その原因の納得のいく説明は未だありません。

　迷信にとらわれない人たちは、「鬼火」は沼地から立ち上る気体が発火するものだろうと言いますが、私はこの説を疑問視しています。というのは、「鬼火」には、とらえどころのないという特徴があるからです。「鬼火」の目撃報告によると、この不思議な光は、それに近づくと近寄り、それから退くと退く、とのことです。また、別の場合には、静止しています。気体の発火による光が、空中に浮遊した状態で、このような形態をとり、このような動きをすることがあるでしょうか。

　「鬼火」圧電効果説に対する反論の一つは、圧電効果の説明される仕組みのほとんどでは、可視発光現象に必要なエネルギーを生み出すことができない、というものです。圧電気の説も摩擦発光説においても、これらの説に関わる岩のほとんどは、電気を絶縁するため、地活動が出した電流を、放電が起こる前に、吸収してしまうでしょう。

　メンフクロウが、そのねぐらとする樹木の幹の穴の中で発光性の菌類と接触することがあることは、これまでにも言われてきました。この説に言われる菌類とは、よく知られたナラタケ（Armillaria mellea）ですが、これが樹木を光らせます。ところが、発光性のナラタケに関する研究文献の多くは、これは「鬼火」の現象の正しい説明とはならない、と言い始めています。ナラタケの発光部分は、樹木の組織内部に入り込んだ菌糸部分である可能性が極めて高く、外部に露出した子実体や胞子や滲出物ではありません。フクロウの羽毛がナラタケ由来の発光物質にまみれるためには、樹木が破砕された状態にならなければなりません。鳥類には、飛行力学特性と断熱性の確保のために、羽毛をくちばしで頻繁に手入れする習性を考慮すると、樹木のかけらにせよキノコの繊維にせよ、羽毛に付着した状態を長時間維持することはなさそうです。したがって、フクロウの羽毛が穴の中で、朽ちた木から出たキノコ由来の発光物質にまみれ

る、との説は、「鬼火」の現象の説明として成り立つことはなさそうです。

解答例

The professor challenges several theories on the possible causes of "Will-o-the-wisp," a phenomenon in which small flickering flames (usually bluish in color) appear at night in areas such as marshes. In the reading passage, there are many suggested scientific possibilities for this phenomenon, including oxidation of gases, piezoelectric effects and bioluminescence. However, the professor refutes each of these theories with detailed explanations.

First, regarding oxidation of gases, the reading passage describes how Will-o-the-wisp is likely generated by the oxidation of methane gases and hydrogen phosphide produced by the decay of organic material in bogs. Both chemicals are highly flammable and will ignite under normal conditions. In an Italian study, two researchers successfully created a similar type of light by mixing phosphine, air and nitrogen. However, the professor says the erratic movements of the light, such as how they move towards you as you advance towards them, could not be produced from burning gas without a visible connection with the earth.

Second, the article discusses how Will-o-the-Wisp is probably created by piezoelectricity, which is generated by materials such as ceramics and crystals that create electricity or sparks when bent or squeezed. Similarly, in triboluminescence, in which electricity and light are generated when something is broken. As an example, it mentions the sparks created by Wint-o-green Lifesavers candy. On the other hand, the professor argues this point, stating that not enough energy is created in these types of situations to produce visible luminescent phenomena. He adds that in both cases of piezoelectricity and triboluminescence, most of the materials involved would insulate against electricity and absorb any currents.

Finally, regarding bioluminescence, the reading passage mentions that this process of light production by living organisms is another possible explanation. Some microorganisms like fungi can produce chemical reactions that do not require heat to make light. For instance, barn owls are used as an example and how they rub against luminescent fungi. Then, the owls carry the fungi on their feathers, which can reflect light from sources such as the moon. However, the professor disagrees with this notion, explaining that the owl example actually is flawed. He says that the fungus usually associated with owls is the honey fungus. This fungus could be glowing because of the mycelium inside the wood. But, he describes how it is unlikely that the wood would be broken up into small enough particles and probably wouldn't stick to their feathers for long.

For these reasons, the professor refutes the claims made in the reading passage.

Question 2

解答例

Standard Model

In choosing a place to live, I would consider several factors, including rent, size, and location. Both living in a dormitory on campus and living in an apartment in the community have advantages and disadvantages. To explain my preference with regard to this issue, I will compare major advantages and disadvantages of the two options.

First, I will discuss an advantage of living in a dormitory. If I live in a dormitory, I can learn how I should associate with others. There are many other students living in the same dormitory. To live comfortably in a dormitory, I must cooperate with them. This is beneficial to me because interpersonal skills are important for career success. There are also disadvantages of living in a dormitory. In order to associate with other students living in the same dormitory, I must make effort to develop a good relationship with them. Consequently, I will lose some of my time for study and other personal activities. This is frustrating.

I will discuss an advantage of living in an apartment. If I live alone in an apartment, I feel independent. I also have more freedom if I live alone. However, rent for an apartment is usually high, and it is inconvenient and costly to commute to campus if my apartment is located far away from it.

As I compare these advantages and disadvantages, I conclude that I would choose to live in an apartment if I have enough money. Living in an apartment allows me to keep a more flexible life-style. For instance, if I live in an apartment, I can really relax and refresh myself by taking a bath for long time. In contrast, if I live in a dormitory, I can only take a shower, which I can't occupy for long time when the place is crowded with other students. Likewise, if I live in a dormitory, it is difficult for me to do what I want to do when I want to do it. For this reasons, I would prefer living in an apartment to living in a dormitory.

解答例 2

Simple Model

Both living in dormitories on campus and living in apartments in the community have advantages and disadvantages. That is why we find students at both places. Before I conclude on my preference, I intend to clarify the advantages and disadvantages of the two options.

First, I will explain an advantage of living in dormitories. There are many students living in dormitories. We must be cooperative with one another when we live in a dormitory. Then we can learn how we should associate with others in such a group setting. This is beneficial for us because we will have such situations in business and other jobs. Living in dormitories is a good preparation for our future. Secondly, I will introduce an advantage of living in an apartment. I can feel very independent when I live alone. Also it gives me more freedom.

I considered all these things and concluded that I would choose to live in an apartment if I have enough money. Though I can make many friends by living in a dormitory, it is impossible to be alone and do what I want to do when I want to do it. On the other hand, living in an apartment allows me a more flexible life-style. For instance, I like to take a bath for a long time. This is my family's life-style. I usually spend thirty minutes to wash my body and take another thirty minutes to stay in the bathtub. It helps to activate my blood circulation and good for controlling my weight. Also, by sweating in the bath, I can eliminate all odor of my body regardless of what I have eaten on that day. However, if I live in a dormitory, I can only take a shower and I can't occupy the shower room for such a long time when the place is packed with other students. In an apartment it's free and I can really relax and refresh myself. Thus, I prefer living in an apartment to living in a dormitory.

第2部

リスニング・スペシャルトレーニング

解答の手引き

リスニング・スペシャルトレーニング

解答 Questions 1 - 5

1 A 2 A 3 C 4 D 5 C

スクリプト／解答のポイント

　Good morning listeners. Welcome once again to the WCHB series,(1) "Listen and Learn." With the approach of summer you may have noticed trees in our area blossoming and their fruit ripening. But have you ever wondered how fruit ripens, especially after it has fallen from a tree or vine? The answer is relatively simple. A single chemical called ethylene is produced by the fruit itself,(2) and it is this chemical that causes the fruit to ripen.(3) When the fruit produces increased amounts of ethylene, the ethylene affects the fruit physiologically. The fruit begins to "breathe" oxygen, and the oxygen supply in turn raises the internal temperature of the fruit.(4) This increased internal temperature allows the ripening process to begin with fruits becoming sweeter, less green in color and softer: in short, delicious. Until our next broadcast, this is Jane Anderson wishing you a fruitful day.(5)

1 What is the audience listening to?
- (A) **A radio broadcast.**
- (B) A political discussion.
- (C) A sales promotion.
- (D) A health documentary.

2 What is the source of the ethylene described in the talk?
- (A) **The fruit itself.**
- (B) The air surrounding the fruit.
- (C) The spray applied by farmers.
- (D) The tree or vines to which the fruit is attached.

3. **According to the speaker, what does ethylene do?**
   (A) Makes fruit greener in color.
   (B) Increases fruit production.
   (C) Causes fruit to ripen.
   (D) Discourages attacks by fruit flies.

4. **According to the speaker, when fruit "breathes" oxygen, what begins to happen?**
   (A) The fruit loses its sweetness.
   (B) The fruit falls off the tree.
   (C) Bees begin to pollinate the fruit.
   (D) The temperature inside the fruit increases.

5. **Listen again to**
   "This increased internal temperature allows the ripening process to begin with fruits becoming sweeter, less green in color and softer: in short, delicious."

   Why does the speaker say this?
   "in short, delicious."

   (A) To mention that she likes fruit.
   (B) To indicate that some fruits taste better than others.
   (C) To summarize the result of ripening.
   (D) To note that fruit ripens quickly.

   スクリプト和訳

   リスナーの皆さん、おはようございます。WCHBシリーズ「リッスンアンドラーン」へまたようこそ。夏の到来とともに、あなたは我が地域の木に花が咲いたり、果実が熟していることにお気づきになったかもしれません。しかし、今までに果実が特に木や蔓から落ちた後どのように熟すのか不思議に思ったことはありませんか？ 答えは比較的簡単です。果実自身によって作られるエチレンと呼ばれる一つの化学物質が原因で果実は熟すのです。果実が多量のエチ

レンを作ると、エチレンは果実に生理学的に影響を与えます。果実は酸素による「呼吸」をし始め、そして酸素の供給が果実内部の温度を上げます。上昇した内部温度のために成熟の過程が始まり、それとともに果実が甘くなり、色が緑でなくなり、柔らかくなります。要するにおいしくなるのです。では、次回の放送をお楽しみに、ジェーン・アンダーソンでした。皆さんが実り多き一日を過ごされますように。

重要単語
- **blossom**：花が咲く
- **ripen**：熟する
- **vine**：蔓（植物）
- **ethylene**：エチレン（炭水化物）
- **oxygen**：酸素

解答 Questions 6 - 10

6 A　7 A　8 D　9 B　10 D

スクリプト／解答のポイント

Someone just asked where the world's most accurate clock is.(6) And the answer will probably surprise you. It's outside our solar system. In fact, it's an electromagnetic signal from trillions of miles away.(7) And was sent out some 16,000 years ago. Let me explain. This unusual clock is actually a pulsar or a star collapsed to planet size. And it spins over 600 times every second. Can you imagine that? Faster than all early known pulsars. Like all pulsars this clock's spin rate is slowing.(8) But unlike other pulsars, this one's rate of decrease is regular.(9) As long as the law stays even, it can be even taken into consideration. One astronomer, I forget his name right now, thinks the pulsar's spin is more regular,(10) in fact, than the vibrations of atomic clocks. If this is true, scientists may one day regulate their clocks by this star. And speaking of regulating clocks, this class' timepiece is about 5 minutes fast. So don't leave just yet.

6 **Why does the speaker talk about pulsars?**

(A) To answer a question.
(B) To settle a debate.
(C) To suggest future research projects.
(D) To describe a newly discovered planet.

7 What does the speaker say about the electromagnetic signal?
(A) **It comes from a great distance.**
(B) It's produced by a group of stars.
(C) It comes from a nearby planet.
(D) It's about to disappear.

8 According to the speaker, in what way is the pulsar's rate of spin changing?
(A) It's becoming more like that of the Earth.
(B) It's growing erratic.
(C) It's becoming more regular.
(D) **It's slowing down.**

9 Listen again to
"But unlike other pulsars, this one's rate of decrease is regular. As long as the law stays even, it can be even taken into consideration. One astronomer, I forget his name right now, thinks the pulsar's spin is more regular, in fact, than the vibrations of atomic clocks."

Why does the professor say this?
"One astronomer, I forget his name right now, thinks the pulsar's spin is more regular, in fact, than the vibrations of atomic clocks."

(A) To ask students to recall the name of an astronomer.
(B) **To emphasize the regularity of the pulsar's spin.**
(C) To explain how atomic clocks work.
(D) To name the astronomer who found the pulsar.

10 According to the speaker, what may scientists use some day to keep precise time?

(A) A solar clock.
(B) A magnet.
(C) An atomic calendar.
(D) **A pulsar.**

スクリプト和訳

　世界で一番正確な時計はどこにあるのでしょうか、との質問が今、ある方からありました。ですがその答えに、皆さま方はおそらく驚くことでしょう。世界で一番正確な時計は我々の太陽系の外側にあるのです。実のところ、それは何兆マイル離れたところから送られてくる電磁信号で、およそ１万6000年も前に発せられたものであります。説明いたします。実際のところを申し上げますと、この聞き慣れない時計は、惑星の大きさにつぶれたパルサーという電波天体や恒星のことなのです。これは毎秒600回もの回転をしております。想像することはできますでしょうか。これは、今まで知られていたすべてのパルサーよりも、高速で回転をしております。すべてのパルサー同様、この時計の回転率は低くなりつつありますが、しかしこの時計の回転率の減少の割合は、他のパルサーと異なり、規則的であるのです。この法則が一定であり続ける限り、我々は減少率さえ考慮することが可能です。今すぐに名前を思い出すことができないのですが、ある天文学者の考えでは、このパルサーの回転は、実際に、原子時計の振動よりも一定であるとのことのです。もしもこの考えが正しい場合、いつの日か、科学者がこの星を通じて時計を調節することが、可能になるかもしれません。ところで時計の調節について言うと、この教室の時計はだいたい５分間進んでおります。だから、まだ帰ってはいけませんよ。

重要単語

- **solar system**：太陽系
- **electromagnetic**：電磁気の
- **trillions**：兆
- **pulsar**：パルサー、脈動星
- **collapse**：つぶれる、崩壊する
- **spin**：回転
- **astronomer**：天文学者
- **vibration**：振動
- **regulate**：規則づける
- **timepiece**：計時

解答 Questions 11 - 15

11 B　12 C　13 B　14 B　15 A

スクリプト／解答のポイント

　Everybody back on the bus? If it gets too stuffy, feel free to open a window. Okay next on our tour, we'll see a grist mill. For those of you unfamiliar with these mills, they were the places where grain was ground into flour. <u>Often these mills were the first buildings to be built in early settlements.</u>(11) Farmers from outlying farms would sometimes transport their grain a distance of twenty miles to the mills. <u>They would then trade their surplus grain for other necessary items.</u>(12) Stores soon opened near the mills and families began to settle nearby because of these conveniences. <u>Many towns, including this one, were begun this way.</u>(13) If you look to your left, the grist mill is coming up next to the farmhouse. <u>Have your cameras ready,</u> (14) <u>we'll be stopping for just 10 minutes.</u>(15)

11 In the type of settlements described by the speaker, which building was probably the oldest?

　(A) The grocery store.
　(B) The gristmill.
　(C) The church.
　(D) The school.

12 What did farmers trade for the supplies they needed?

　(A) Cash.
　(B) Credit.
　(C) Grain.
　(D) Gold.

13 What usually happened after a grist mill was built in an area?

　(A) Local stores lost business.

(B) **A new town was established.**
(C) Less farmland was used to produce grain.
(D) Farmers built gristmills on their own property.

14 At the end of the talk, what will the listeners most likely do?
(A) Unpack for the night.
(B) **Take photographs.**
(C) Sit down to dinner.
(D) Grind flour.

15 Listen again to
"If you look to our left, the grist mill is coming up next to the farmhouse. Have your cameras ready, we'll be stopping for just 10 minutes."

Why does the speaker say this?
"Have your cameras ready,"

(A) **To prevent students from failing to take pictures.**
(B) To highlight the historical importance of a building.
(C) To emphasize the beauty of a town.
(D) To warn students not to leave their cameras behind.

> スクリプト和訳

みんなバスに戻っていますか？ 息苦しいなら、自由に窓を開けてください。よろしいですね、では次の見学場所では穀物の製粉所を見ます。これらの製粉所になじみのない方のために申しますと、それらは小麦の穀粒を挽いて小麦粉にしていた場所のことです。これらの多くの製粉所は入植時代の初期に建設されたものです。離れた農場にいる農夫はときおり、穀物を製粉所まで20マイルの距離を運びました。そして余った穀物を他の必需品と交換したものでした。すぐに製粉所の近くに店が開き、これらの便利さのため近くに家族が定住し始めました。この町を含む多くの町が、このように始まりました。左手を見て下さい。農家の隣に穀物の製粉所が見えてきます。カメラを用意してください、10分だけ止まりますよ。

重要単語

- **stuffy**：風通しの悪い
- **grist mill**：穀物の製粉所
- **grain**：穀物
- **ground into**：粉にされた
- **flour**：小麦粉
- **outlying farm**：離れたところにある農場
- **surplus**：余剰の
- **settle**：落ち着く、定住する

解答 Questions 16 - 20

16 B　17 D　18 C　19 A　20 B

スクリプト／解答のポイント

　The meteorological society is pleased to welcome you to its monthly meeting. Our topic this evening will be changes in atmosphere and climate. (16) In particular, we will be talking about the marked increase of carbon dioxide levels in our atmosphere.(17) And the fact that one surprising consequence of this is an increase in tree fertilization at certain altitudes.(18) We've been warned by scientists in recent years that our burning of coal and oil or fossil fuel is increasing the carbon dioxide level in the air. This increase in carbon dioxide might cause long term climatic changes that may prove harmful to us in various ways. On the other hand, some researchers are suggesting that the increased level of carbon dioxide may have an unexpected benefit.(20) Namely a fertilization effect. Specialists who wish to determine the rate of tree growth by examining tree rings in certain areas of the United States, have found that at high elevations, the growth rate of trees has accelerated sharply since 1960.(19) Based on climatic records for these sights warmer summers and increased rainfall have been ruled out as causes of this rapid growth. The only other explanation appears to be the rising carbon dioxide level in the atmosphere. We will now divide into smaller groups for further discussion of this subject.

16　**What is the main topic of the talk?**

(A) The burning of different types of fossil fuels.
(B) **An unexpected effect of changes in the atmosphere.**
(C) Warnings by scientists not to use fertilizers.
(D) Recently discovered tree species.

17. What does the speaker say about the carbon dioxide level of the atmosphere?
(A) It has decreased steadily.
(B) It has been stable.
(C) It has fluctuated.
(D) **It has increased noticeably.**

18. According to the speaker, what has been most affected by the carbon dioxide level?
(A) Record-keeping.
(B) Rainfall.
(C) **Tree growth.**
(D) Fertilizers.

19. According to the speaker, what have researchers found to be one unusual result of certain climatic changes?
(A) **The increased fertilization of trees.**
(B) The increased oxidation of coal.
(C) The reduced burning of fuels.
(D) The reduced layering of fossils.

20. Listen again to
"*On the other hand, some researchers are suggesting that the increased level of carbon dioxide may have an unexpected benefit. Namely a fertilization effect.*"

Why does the speaker say this?
"*Namely a fertilization effect.*"

(A) To show how much carbon dioxide level has increased.
(B) **To specify the point of his discussion.**
(C) To introduce a new topic.
(D) To support the ideas proposed by the researchers.

> スクリプト和訳

　気象協会は皆さんを月例会に喜んでお迎えします。今夜の話題は大気と気候の変化です。特に、大気中の二酸化炭素レベルの著しい上昇についてお話しします。このことの一つの驚くべき結果が高地での木の多産化の進行であると言うこともね。近年科学者達は、石炭や石油つまり化石燃料を燃やすことが、大気中の二酸化炭素のレベルを上げることになると警告してきました。この二酸化炭素の増加は、様々な点で我々に有害である長期の気候変化を引き起こす可能性があります。その一方で、研究者の中には二酸化炭素レベルの上昇が思わぬ利益をもたらすかもしれないと示唆しています。すなわち、多産化の効果です。合衆国のある地域で木の年輪を調べることで木の成長率を測定したいと望んでいる専門家達は、高地での木の成長率が1960年以来急速に加速してきていることに気付きました。これらの場所の気候記録に基づいて、以前より温暖な夏と降雨量の増加は、この急速な成長の原因としては除外されました。唯一の説明は、大気中の二酸化炭素レベルの上昇であるように思われる訳です。さて、この議題を詳しく議論するために、これから小さなグループに分かれましょう。

> 重要単語

- **meteorological**：気象学の
- **elevation**：高さ、高地
- **marked increase**：きわだった上昇
- **accelerate**：加速させる
- **carbon dioxide**：二酸化炭素
- **rule out**：除く
- **fertilization**：肥沃化、多産化
- **appears to be**：〜のように見える
- **altitudes**：高さ、高度
- **divide into**：〜に分かれる
- **fossil fuel**：化石燃料
- **tree rings**：年輪

解答 Questions 21 - 25

21 B　22 A　23 D　24 B　25 D

> スクリプト／解答のポイント

　I'm glad that all the members of our zoology class could come down to the zoo today to continue our study of animal adaptation. As you know, some animals are able to move between domestic and wild environments with relatively little difficulty. The first example of this that we will see here at the zoo is the wild burro. As you are probably aware, burros are relatives of the horse. Wild burros in the United States are the descendants of pack animals brought here three centuries ago by Spanish explorers, (21) and these pack burros were in turn, the descendants of wild African asses. (25)　About 100 years ago, gold prospectors came to the mountains and deserts of the western United States. (22)　Most of the prospectors were accompanied by steadfast companions, burros. These animals were used along with the mule trains that served many mining operations. But when the gold and silver mining died out, many of the prospectors turned their burros loose. (23)　They joined the wild burros that were already roaming the hills and canyons, the descendants of those brought by the Spanish. The prospectors knew that their burros were hearty animals, completely able to take care of themselves in the wild. The fact that there are over 11,000 wild burros living in the western states today, testifies to their great adaptability. (24)

21 Who first brought the ancestors of wild burros to North America?
　(A) Early miners.
　(B) Spanish explorers.
　(C) African naturalists.
　(D) Early industrialists.

22 What were the prospectors looking for?
　(A) Gold.
　(B) Settlements.
　(C) New routes for the railroads.
　(D) New sources of water.

23 **What was done with many of the burros when the prospectors no longer needed them?**

(A) They were sent to zoos.
(B) They were given to miners.
(C) They were raised commercially in herds.
(D) **They were set free.**

24 **What is the main reason that the speaker wants the students to study the burro?**

(A) Burros are relatives of the horse.
(B) **Burros can adapt easily.**
(C) Burros are common farm animals.
(D) There are many burros in the United States.

25 **Listen again to**
"Wild burros in the United States are the descendants of pack animals brought here three centuries ago by Spanish explorers, and these pack burros were, in turn, the descendants of wild African asses."

What does the professor imply when she says this?
"and these pack burros were, in turn, the descendants of wild African asses."

(A) That Spanish explorers took pack burros back to Africa.
(B) That burros can't live long.
(C) That African asses are already extinct.
(D) **That burros are highly adaptive.**

| スクリプト和訳 |

　動物の適応の研究を続けるために今日動物園に来ましたが、クラスの全員が参加できたことを嬉しく思います。ご存知のように、動物の中には飼い慣らされた環境と野生の環境の間をほとんど苦労なしに行き来できるものがいます。我々がここの動物園で見る最初のこの例が野生のロバです。おそらく気付いて

いると思いますが、ロバは馬と同族です。合衆国にいる野生のロバは、スペインの探検家によってここに300年前に連れてこられた荷運び用の動物の子孫です。そしてこの荷運び用のロバは、野生のアフリカロバの子孫でした。約100年前、金採掘者が合衆国西部の山や砂漠へとやってきました。金採掘者のほとんどは、忠実な仲間であるロバを連れていました。これらの動物は多くの採掘作業を提供したロバ用荷車とともに使われました。しかし、金と銀の採掘が無くなったとき、採掘者の多くはロバを解き放ちました。それらは丘や渓谷をすでにうろついていた野生のロバ、すなわちスペイン人によって連れて来られたロバの子孫に加わりました。金採掘者達は自分たちのロバが野生でも完全にひとりで生きていける頑健な動物であると知っていました。今日、西部の州に住んでいる野生のロバが1万1000頭以上いるという事実が、その高い適応性を証明しています。

重要単語

- **zoology**：動物学
- **gold prospectors**：金鉱山採掘者
- **animal adaptation**：動物の適応
- **be accompanied by 〜**：〜をともなって
- **with little difficulty**：ほとんど苦労なしに
- **steadfast companion**：忠実な仲間
- **burro**：小型ロバ
- **mule trains**：馬車、ラバ用荷車
- **relative**：同族、同種
- **turn 〜 loose**：〜を解放する、解き放つ
- **pack animal**：荷運び用の動物
- **roam**：うろつく
- **descendant**：子孫
- **canyon**：渓谷
- **explore**：開拓する
- **hearty**：頑健な、丈夫な
- **in turn**：交代で、順に
- **testify**：証言する、証明する、立証する

解答 Questions 26 - 30

26 A　27 C　28 A　29 B　30 A

> スクリプト／解答のポイント

　Thank you for coming to this meeting for students who will be remaining on campus during the 10 day winter break. (26) (27) As the dean of students it is my responsibility to explain the vacation arrangements and have you fill out forms (29C) giving the dates you will be on campus. To reduce heating costs, Butler Hall will be the only dormitory open. (29A) All the other dorms will close at 5:00pm on Friday, February 7th. And will not reopen until 6:00pm on February 16th. Once we have your completed forms we will assign you a room in Butler Hall. Please move all the belongings you will need to your temporary accommodations by the 7th, as it will not be possible to reopen the other dorms during these 10 days, once they have been closed. (30) Most college facilities will be closed during the vacation. (28) These facilities include the gymnasium, the college store, and the dining halls. The library and computer center will be open (29D) though on a reduced schedule. Only the post office and the college administration offices will maintain their regular hours. Since I imagine most of you are staying here to finish up academic projects of one sort or another, let me wish you luck with your work. If you have any special problems, please do not hesitate to contact me at the Dean's office.

26 Which group of students is the speaker addressing?
　(A) **Those who will be on campus during a vacation period.**
　(B) Those who work part-time in the administration offices.
　(C) Those who normally live in Butler Hall.
　(D) Those who will be moving on campus in a few months.

27 For how long will the dormitories remain closed?
　(A) One weekend.
　(B) Five days.
　(C) **Ten days.**
　(D) Two weeks.

28 Which statement is true about college facilities during the vacation period?
   (A) **Most facilities will be closed.**
   (B) Only a few facilities will be closed.
   (C) Most facilities will operate on a reduced schedule.
   (D) All facilities will be open.

29 Which topic is not discussed by the speaker?
   (A) Which dormitory will be open.
   (B) **Where students will eat.**
   (C) Whether any forms need to be filled out.
   (D) Whether the computer center will be open.

30 Listen again to
"Please move all the belongings you will need to your temporary accommodations by the 7th, as it will not be possible to reopen the other dorms during these 10 days, once they have been closed."

What does the speaker imply when he says this?
"Please move all the belongings you will need to your temporary accommodations by the 7th,"

   (A) **That students can return to their current rooms after the winter break.**
   (B) That students should vacate their current rooms completely.
   (C) That the earlier a student moves his or her belongings, the better room he or she will be assigned.
   (D) That students will not be assigned rooms if they fail to move their belongings by the 7th.

スクリプト和訳

　10日間の冬休みにキャンパス内に留まる学生向けの会議に参加いただき、ありがとうございます。学生部長として、休みの間の取り決めについての説明を

行い、皆様方にキャンパスに滞在する日数を用紙に記入していただくことが私の責務です。光熱費の節約のために、バトラー・ホールだけを使用可能な寮といたします。すべての他の寮は、2月7日金曜日午後5時には、閉館します。そして、2月16日午後6時まで開館することはありません。皆様の記入済み申し込み用紙を受け取ったら、バトラー・ホールの部屋を皆様方に割り振ります。7日までに、一時的な宿泊に必要なすべての所有品を移動させてください。この10日の間、閉鎖の後はその他の寮に入ることは出来ませんよ。休みの間、ほとんどの大学の施設は閉鎖されています。ジム、学生生協、食堂といった施設もその中に含まれています。利用時間は縮小されておりますが、図書館とコンピューター設備の使用は可能です。普段通りのスケジュールで運営されているのは、郵便局と大学の本部のみです。ここに留まるほとんどの方は、様々な研究課題を終わらせるためだと思うので、皆様方の研究が上手く進むことを祈っております。どんな種類の問題であっても何かございましたら、学生部長の部屋に遠慮なさらずいらしてください。

重要単語

- **dean of students**：学生部長
- **fill out**：記入する
- **dormitory**：寮
- **assign**：(宿題などを)課す
- **temporary**：一時的な
- **accommodation**：住まい
- **facility**：施設
- **gymnasium**：体育館
- **college administration office**：大学事務局

解答 Questions 31 - 35

31 A   32 D   33 A   34 D   35 B

スクリプト／解答のポイント

Good afternoon. As you know, this is a course in beginning political theory. We'll be meeting each Monday, Wednesday and Thursday at 8:00 for the next 12 weeks. <u>Each Monday I'll give you a lecture on a different concept in political thought. I might talk about justice, for example.</u>(35) On Wednesday, you'll hand in a 1-page paper on the topic, and as a group, we will discuss the issues involved. On Thursday, I'll return your paper with suggestions for revision. Also on Thursday, we'll explore through lecture and discussion, (32) what prominent political thinkers have had to say about the topic. Over the weekend, you'll revise your paper, and hand it in on the following Monday. I'll grade only the revised paper. (33) Keep these papers brief, because I'll accept no papers that exceed a single page. (31) I'll be available on Tuesday and Friday (34) afternoons to discuss your papers with you. Are there any questions?

31 How long should each paper be?
(A) **No more than one page.**
(B) At least one page but no more than eight pages.
(C) At least eight pages but no more than twelve pages.
(D) At least twelve pages.

32 What is the format of this course?
(A) Lecture only.
(B) Discussion and laboratory.
(C) Lecture and laboratory.
(D) **Lecture and discussion.**

33 What must a student do with a paper that is returned on Thursday?
(A) **Rewrite it.**
(B) Present it to the class.
(C) Use it to study for the final exam.
(D) Incorporate it into a longer paper.

34 When will the speaker be available to discuss papers?
(A) Before class on Tuesdays.
(B) After class on Thursdays.
(C) Over the weekend.
(D) **On Tuesday and Friday afternoons.**

35 Listen again to

"Each Monday I'll give you a lecture on a different concept in political thought. I might talk about justice, for example."

Why does the professor say this?
"I might talk about justice, for example."

(A) To specify her topic for the next Monday.
(B) To help students get a better idea of their assignment.
(C) To suggest that she is not sure what to talk about.
(D) To name an especially important political concept.

スクリプト和訳

こんにちは。ご存じの通り、この授業は政治理論の入門クラスです。これからの12週間、月曜日、水曜日、そして木曜日の8時にお会いすることになります。毎週月曜日は、私が政治思想の様々な概念についてお話しします。例として、司法などについてお話をするでしょう。水曜日には、当該の話題についての1ページのレポートを提出していただき、グループになり関連する事柄について議論をします。木曜日は、書き直しのためのアドバイスを書いたレポートの返却をいたします。また木曜日には、講義や議論を通じて、当該の話題について重要な政治思想家達が何を語ったのかを追及したいと思っています。週末にレポートを修正して、週明けの月曜日に提出してください。書き直したレポートについてのみ成績を出す予定です。レポートは簡潔に書いてください。1ページを超えるものは受理しませんよ。火曜日と金曜日の午後に、このレポートについてお話をすることができます。何か質問はありますか？

重要単語

- **justice**：司法
- **revision**：修正
- **revise**：修正する
- **explore**：探る
- **prominent**：有名な
- **hand it in**：提出する
- **exceed**：超える

解答 Questions 36 - 40

36 A 37 D 38 D 39 D 40 C

スクリプト／解答のポイント

If there are no more questions about the evolution of male and female roles in society, I'd like to move on to the evolution of the human diet. As you may or may not be aware, we anthropologists (36) have been debating for years about just what foods prehistoric humans ordinarily consumed. (37) We know that nonhuman primates eat little meat. (40) They are essentially herbivores, depending on plants for food. Yet existing hunting and gathering societies eat a great deal of meat. What was the diet of prehistoric humans? One school of thought was held that prehistoric humans were carnivores, with males playing the key role in food gathering. The other has held that they were largely herbivores, with females playing the dominant food gathering role. Recent evidence based on food debris and tools, wear patterns on teeth and strancheum retention, suggest that prehistoric humans had a balanced diet and were omnivores, eating both plants and meat. (38) A team that examined tools and animal bones at a site in east Africa where prehistoric humans lived, has found evidence of butchering animals for food. But the team believes that plants were also widely eaten. Other researchers have examined teeth under an electron microscope to look for the different wear patterns that are characteristic of herbivores and carnivores. (39) Their results support the idea that early humans were omnivores. A technique from geo-chemistry, the measurement of strancheum levels, also supports this idea. Strancheum, a major element in the earth's crust, is retained at different rates by plants and animals. Herbivores retain more strancheum than carnivores. When 10,000-year old human bones were tested, the levels were lower than for herbivores, but higher than for carnivores.

36 What is the speaker's profession?
  (A) Anthropologist.

(B) Nutritionist.
(C) Historian.
(D) Geochemist.

37 The speaker is primarily concerned with what group?
   (A) Nonhuman primates.
   (B) Existing hunting and gathering societies.
   (C) Contemporary city dwellers.
   (D) Prehistoric humans.

38 According to the speaker, the amount of strancheum in a fossil bone depends on what factor?
   (A) Where the bone was found.
   (B) How deeply the home was buried.
   (C) How long ago the animal lived.
   (D) What the animal ate.

39 What does the speaker think about the diet of prehistoric humans?
   (A) It was identical to that of nonhuman primates.
   (B) It contained only insignificant traces of strontium.
   (C) It is not possible to generalize about the diet of prehistoric humans.
   (D) Prehistoric humans were not exclusively herbivorous or carnivorous.

40 Listen again to
   "As you may or may not be aware, we anthropologists have been debating for years about just what foods prehistoric humans ordinarily consumed. We know that non-human primates eat little meat."

   What does the professor mean when he says this?
   "As you may or may not be aware,"

   (A) That the topic is very exciting.

（B）That students should already be familiar with the topic.
（C）That he assumes that the topic could be new to some students.
（D）That the topic is not the focus of his lecture.

> スクリプト和訳

　社会における男性と女性の役割の変化について、もし質問がなかったならば、人間の食生活の変化について話を進めたいと思います。皆様方は気が付いているかどうかわかりませんが、我々人類学者は何年にもわたって、先史時代の人類が日々何を食べていたのか、ずっと議論をしております。人間を除く霊長類がほとんど肉を食べないことを、我々は知っております。彼らは本質的に草食動物で、食糧を植物に頼っています。ですが、存在している狩猟採集社会では非常に多くの肉が消費されています。先史時代の人類の食生活は、どのようなものだったのでしょうか？　ある学説では、先史時代の人類は肉食性であり、食糧の採集において男性が中心的な役割を果たしていたとの主張がなされています。それに対し、彼らは主に草食性であり、食糧採集の中心的な役割は女性が担っていたと主張する学説もあります。しかし、食物の残骸や道具、歯の傷み具合、そしてストロンチウムの保有量から示される証拠が示すのは、先史時代の人類はバランスのとれた食生活を送り、植物も肉も食した雑食性であったということであります。先史時代の人類が住んでいた東アフリカのある場所で発見された道具や動物の骨を調査したとある研究チームは、食べるために動物を屠殺していた証拠を見つけました。しかし、このチームは、植物も幅広く食されていたのではないかとも考えています。他には、草食性であることの特徴と、肉食性であることの特徴を示す異なる歯の傷み具合を探すために、電子顕微鏡を用いて歯を調べている研究者たちもいます。彼らの発見は、初期の人類が雑食性であったことを支持するものです。また、ストロンチウムのレベルを測定することのできる地球科学の研究方法も、この考えを肯定するものであります。ストロンチウムは地殻を形成する主要な要素に数えられます。これを植物や動物が異なる割合で持っているのです。草食動物は肉食動物と比べると、より多くのストロンチウムを持っています。1万年前の古代の人類の骨を調べると、ストロンチウムの割合は草食動物としては少なく、また肉食動物としては高かったのです。

重要単語

- **evolution**：進化
- **debris**：残り物
- **anthropologists**：人類学者
- **retention**：保持
- **primates**：霊長類
- **omnivores**：雑食動物
- **herbivores**：草食動物
- **butcher**：屠殺する、解体する
- **school of thought**：ある考えをもった学派
- **electron microscope**：電子顕微鏡
- **carnivores**：肉食動物
- **geo-chemistry**：地球化学
- **dominant**：支配的な、優勢な、重要な
- **crust**：地殻

解答 Questions 41 - 45

41 B　42 C　43 C　44 D　45 D

スクリプト／解答のポイント

　A disaster was prevented yesterday when the Coast Guard rescued a woman who was sailing in a race from Virginia to Rhode Island. Since the race was a competition in single-handed sailing,(41) the woman had no companions on board with her at the time of the accident. She had been leading the race all day, when she encountered a brief storm off the coast of Long Island.(42)　The unexpected gale threw her off course,(43) and damaged her boat, but she was still able to radio for help. A patrol boat and helicopter from Long Island were sent out to sea to search for her. Their job lasted only 50 minutes. The woman was located within an hour after her first call for help.(45)　The patrol boat brought the woman safely into port.(44) Although she can't complete the race, the woman is uninjured. She plans to sail home in a few days as soon as repairs are completed on her boat.

41　What was the woman doing when the accident occurred?

　　(A) Watching sailboats.
　　(B) Competing in a race.

(C) Working for the Coast Guard.
(D) Repairing a boat.

42 What were the weather conditions at the time of the accident?
(A) There was no wind.
(B) It was clear and sunny.
(C) It was stormy.
(D) There was heavy fog.

43 What happened to the woman?
(A) She was thrown overboard.
(B) She hurt her hand.
(C) She was blown off course.
(D) She ran aground.

44 How was the woman rescued?
(A) By a companion.
(B) By a fisherman.
(C) By another sailboat.
(D) By a patrol boat.

45 Listen again to
"A patrol boat and helicopter from Long Island were sent out to sea to search for her. Their job lasted only 50 minutes. The woman was located within an hour after her first call for help."

Why does the speaker say this? *"Their job lasted only 50 minutes."*

(A) To indicate that the rescue team failed in the mission.
(B) To emphasize the difficulty of the search.
(C) To criticize the rescue team for giving up too early.
(D) To note that the search was successful.

スクリプト和訳

昨日、沿岸警備隊がヴァージニアからロードアイランドまでヨットレースをしていた女性を救出し災難は防がれました。そのレースは独力帆走の競技だったため、その女性が事故に遭った時、船上に仲間はいませんでした。彼女は一日中レースの先頭に立っていましたが、そのときロングアイランド沖で短い嵐に遭遇しました。予期せぬ強風が彼女をコースからそらせ、船に損傷を与えましたが、彼女はまだ無線で助けを呼ぶことが可能でした。彼女を捜すため、ロングアイランドからパトロール艇とヘリコプターが海へ送り出されました。わずか50分で彼らの仕事は終わりました。その女性は最初に助けを求めてから1時間以内に位置をつきとめられました。パトロール艇はその女性を無事港まで連れ戻したのです。彼女はレースを完走することは出来ませんでしたが、怪我はしていません。彼女は数日後、船の修理が終わったらすぐに家に船で帰るつもりとのことです。

重要単語

- **single-handed sailing**：独力帆走
- **companion**：仲間
- **encounter**：出会う
- **a brief storm**：短い嵐
- **gale**：強風
- **radio for help**：無線で救助を求める

解答 Questions 46 - 50

46 D　47 A　48 A　49 B　50 A

スクリプト／解答のポイント

OK everybody, can we start the meeting now? I'm Mike Johnson, the chairperson of the graduation committee for this year. You've all been selected as representatives to plan the graduation ceremonies.(46)　I'm sending around a sheet of paper for you to fill in your name and telephone number. Also, please write down what part of the ceremonies you would like to work on.(47)　Remember, as a representative, you will have a lot of responsibilities, so only sign up if you feel you have the time to participate.

(48) (50) When everyone has finished writing down the information, please return the paper to me. At our next meeting, one week from today, (49) we'll start to discuss the details of the ceremonies.

46 What is the purpose of the meeting?
 (A) To determine who will graduate this year.
 (B) To discuss the seating arrangement.
 (C) To choose the chairperson of the ceremonies.
 (D) To begin planning the graduation ceremonies.

47 What should the students write on the paper?
 (A) Their names, phone numbers, and job preference.
 (B) The names and addresses of their guests.
 (C) The names of the committees they worked on last year.
 (D) Their dormitory name, address, and phone number.

48 Who should sign up?
 (A) Only students who have time for the work.
 (B) All the students who are at the meeting.
 (C) Only students who have a telephone.
 (D) All the students who worked on the project last year.

49 When is the next meeting?
 (A) In an hour.
 (B) Next week.
 (C) In one month.
 (D) Next year.

50 Listen again to

"I'm sending around a sheet of paper for you to fill in your name and telephone number. Also, please write down what part of the ceremonies you would like to work on. Remember, as a representative, you will have a lot of responsibilities, so only sign up if you feel you have the time to participate."

What does the speaker imply when he says this? *"Remember, as a representative, you will have a lot of responsibilities, so only sign up if you feel you have the time to participate."*

(A) That participation requires commitment.
(B) That the ceremonies will take long time.
(C) That he wants everyone to participate.
(D) That he wants to discourage people from signing up.

スクリプト和訳

さて皆さん、ただ今からミーティングを始めてもよろしいですか？ 私は、マイク・ジョンソン、今年度卒業委員会の委員長です。皆さんは卒業式のセレモニーを計画するために代表として選ばれました。皆さんに名前と電話番号を記入してもらう用紙を回します。また、セレモニーのどの部分に関わりたいかも書いてください。代表として多くの責任があることを忘れないでください。ですので、参加する時間があるように思える場合のみ、署名してくださいね。皆さんが情報を記入し終えたら、私のところまで戻してください。今日から1週間後の次のミーティングでは、セレモニーの詳細について議論を始めます。

重要単語

- **chairperson**：議長
- **committee**：委員会
- **representative**：代表

解答 Questions 51 - 55

51 D 52 B 53 A 54 C 55 C

> スクリプト／解答のポイント

　Let's look back in history to an earlier way of life. At one time, children didn't have to learn any more than how to cope with their physical environment. (52) They had to learn to be careful around moving objects, to draw back when they got too close to something dangerous. (55) They didn't need a special school to learn these things, other than the school of experience. Nor was a school necessary for them to learn how to survive, because their parents taught them all they needed to know about how to hunt, and to till the soil. (51) But as societies became more complex, people depended more on others who were living far away. (53) So, it became important for children to learn to read and write. When money was created, they needed to learn to count, and calculate. Children had to know these things in order to survive in this new, expanded environment. Because such skills could not be learned simply through first-hand experience, (54) schools became necessary so that children could be taught, what we now call, the "Three R's": Reading, 'Riting, and 'Rithmatic.

51 What did children need to learn how to do in the earliest times mentioned by the speaker?
   (A) Count money.
   (B) Read and write.
   (C) Draw moving objects.
   (D) Hunt and farm.

52 Why was formal education in schools not necessary for a long time?
   (A) Teachers came to children's homes.
   (B) Children acquired the information they needed by direct experience.
   (C) Children taught one another in small supervised groups.
   (D) Parents instructed their children in the "three R's."

53 What changes in society first made it important to teach children the "Three R's"?

   (A) **A new dependence on people far away and the use of money.**
   (B) The introduction of a new alphabet and numerical system.
   (C) Outmoded methods of farming and ineffective means of transportation.
   (D) Larger family units and greater financial hardships.

54 What is the topic the speaker will most likely discuss next?

   (A) The various means of survival taught by parents in contemporary society.
   (B) The importance of history instruction in the first schools.
   (C) **The increasingly complex skills subsequently taught in schools.**
   (D) The problems involved in the construction of new schools.

55 Listen again to

"At one time, children didn't have to learn any more than how to cope with their physical environment. They had to learn to be careful around moving objects, to draw back when they got too close to something dangerous."

Why does the professor say this?
"They had to learn to be careful around moving objects, to draw back when they got too close to something dangerous."

   (A) To tell students about her own experience in childhood.
   (B) To describe what children are most interested in.
   (C) **To give examples of what children had to learn in their early days.**
   (D) To emphasize the carelessness of children.

スクリプト和訳

  歴史を振り返って昔の生活様式を見てみましょう。昔は、子供達は自然環境に対処する方法以上のことを学ぶ必要はありませんでした。彼らは動いている物体に注意したり、危険なものに近づき過ぎたとき、身を引くことを学ぶ必要

がありました。これらのことを学ぶために、経験という学習以外、特別な学校を必要としませんでした。生き残る方法を学ぶための学校も必要ではありませんでした。なぜなら彼らの親が狩りの仕方や、土地の耕し方について知る必要のあるすべてを教えてくれたからです。しかし、社会が複雑になるにつれて、人は遠く離れたところに住んでいる他人に依存するようになりました。そこで子供達が読み書きを覚えることが重要になったのです。お金が創り出されると、子供達は数えたり計算できたりするようになる必要が出てきました。子供達は、この新しく広がった環境において生き残るために、これらのことを知る必要がありました。そのような技術は単純に直接の経験から学ぶことが出来なかったので、子供たちがいわゆる「3R（読み書き算）」を教わるために学校が必要になりました。

重要単語

- **cope with**：処理する
- **calculate**：計算する
- **physical environment**：物理的な環境
- **expand**：広がる
- **till the soil**：土地を耕す
- **first-hand experience**：直接の体験
- **draw back**：身を引く
- **'Riting, 'Rithmatic = writing, arithmetic**

解答 Questions 56 - 60

56 B　57 A　58 D　59 A　60 D

スクリプト／解答のポイント

　Today, I'm going to discuss crime and punishment in the early 19th Century in the United States. (58) In those days, punishments for crimes committed tended to be much more severe than those which are typically handed down today. In the majority of states, capital punishment was far more common, especially when the perpetrator was seen as having a great physical advantage over the victim, or the motives for the crime could not be made clear or understandable to the jury attending the case. This "eye for an eye" philosophy, which had its roots in the ancient Egyptian "Code of Hammurabi," had a broad appeal to an America more conservative than today's America, with its broader ethnic and religious makeup. "Justice swift and sure" seemed to many to have suffered a setback, when a number of states forfeited the right of their judiciary to sentence convicted murderers to death, (56) but a number of landmark cases gave the lawmakers in those states little alternative. The most widely publicized of these involved a woman known as "The Tiger Lady of Chicago." This woman, convicted of the brutal murder of her own child and ex-husband, was sentenced to the electric chair by the Supreme Court of the State of Illinois. Just days after the sentence was carried out, new evidence led to the trial and conviction, for the same crime, of one of the very men who had testified against the woman during her trial. The popular movement away from capital punishment that case generated, (59) along with the fact that it had never been an effective deterrent to crime, resulted in what we have today, a few states hanging on to capital punishment but the majority opting for life imprisonment.(57) (60)

56 Capital punishment was usually utilized in what sort of cases?
 (A) Theft.
 (B) Murder.
 (C) Fraud.
 (D) Rape.

57 What sort of punishment often replaced capital punishment?
 (A) Life imprisonment.
 (B) Public beatings.
 (C) Forced labor.
 (D) Jury duty.

58 When was capital punishment most common in America?
 (A) In the early 1980s.
 (B) In the early 1990s.
 (C) In the mid 1800s.

(D) In the early 1800s.

59 What is the main idea of this lecture?
(A) The decline of the popularity of capital punishment.
(B) The ability of one landmark case to change American law.
(C) The growth of the American legal system.
(D) The increasing popularity of capital punishment.

60 Listen again to
"The popular movement away from capital punishment that case generated, along with the fact that it had never been an effective deterrent to crime, resulted in what we have today – a few states hanging on to capital punishment but the majority opting for life imprisonment."

What does the professor imply when he says this?
"along with the fact that it had never been an effective deterrent to crime,"

(A) That a particular case made capital punishment less effective.
(B) That the movement failed although it was popular.
(C) That capital punishment had never been implemented.
(D) **That multiple reasons justified the abolishment of capital punishment by many states.**

| スクリプト和訳 |

今日は合衆国19世紀初頭の犯罪と刑罰についてお話します。当時、犯罪に対する刑罰は、今日典型的に言い渡される刑罰よりもはるかに厳しい傾向にありました。大多数の州で、死刑は今よりもはるかによくあることでした。特に加害者が被害者に対して大きな肉体的利点を持っている場合や、犯罪の動機が明らかにされなかったり、陪審員に理解できるようにされなかった場合はそうでした。古代エジプトのハンムラビ法典をルーツとするこの「目には目を」の考え方は、今日の倫理・宗教上の構成が幅広いアメリカ人よりも保守的であった当時のアメリカ人に広く訴えかけました。多くの州で、裁判官の有罪判決を受けた殺人者に死刑を宣告する権利を剥奪したとき、多くの人にとって「素早く

決定する、確かな正義」が、挫折したように思われました。しかし多くの転換点となる事件が起きたとき、それらの州の立法者には他に取るべき手段がほとんどなかったのです。

　これらの事件のうち最も広く知られているものは、シカゴのタイガーレディとして知られている女性に関するものです。この女性は、自分の子供と元夫を残虐に殺した罪に問われて、イリノイ州の最高裁判所に電気イスの刑を宣告されました。刑が執行されたわずか数日後、新しい証拠が見つかり、その女性の審理中に反対証言をしていた他ならぬその男性が、同じ犯罪に対して、審議され有罪判決を受けました。その事件が生み出した死刑廃止の民衆運動が、死刑が決して有効な犯罪抑止力でなかった事実と合わせて、少数の州が死刑に固執しているが、今日我々が持っている大多数の州は終身刑を選択する状況を生み出しました。

重要単語

- **punishment**：刑罰、罰
- **severe**：厳しい
- **be sentenced to**：〜に刑として課される
- **capital punishment**：死刑、死刑を課すべきこと
- **sentence**：罪の刑
- **perpetrator**：加害者、犯人
- **trial**：裁判
- **motive**：動機、動機付け
- **widely publicized**：広く報じられる
- **conviction**：有罪判決、罪

- **jury**：陪審員
- **testify against**：〜に対して反対に証言する、証明する
- **ethnic and religious makeup**：倫理、宗教上の構成
- **justice swift and sure**：素早く決定する、確かな正義
- **suffer a setback**：挫折する
- **forfeit**：〜を剥奪する、没収する
- **judiciary**：司法制度
- **convict**：有罪に課す
- **landmark**：目印、特色のあること

解答 Questions 61 - 65

61 C　62 C　63 D　64 D　65 D

> スクリプト／解答のポイント

　Thank you for coming here today. As most of you already know, I'm Mrs. Jackson, Dean of Student Affairs. <u>I'll try to make this as quick as possible, since I know how much you have to do in these last two weeks before graduation.</u>(61) I'm going to give you three forms that must be completed before you'll be able to graduate.(64) <u>To cut down on the confusion, each one is a different color.</u>(65) The green one is for ordering the caps and gowns that you must wear during commencement. Please return this form to the business office, or to me, no later than next week, with a check for ten dollars, which is the rental fee for the cap and gown. Next, the yellow form goes to the library to be signed. <u>The librarian will sign it only if you've returned all the books you've borrowed and have paid any outstanding fines.</u>(63) Finally, you should have the pink form signed by someone in the maintenance office, after they have had your room inspected and found everything in order. <u>This way, we know your room has been left in good condition.</u>(62) The three different colors should make it easy for you to remember that you have three important tasks to complete. All forms must be returned to me at least a week before graduation. Good luck to you all, and I'll be seeing you next week.

61　When does the talk take place?
　(A) On course-registration day.
　(B) During the first week of classes.
　(C) A short time before the end of the semester.
　(D) During the graduation ceremony.

62　What will having the pink form signed in the maintenance office indicate?
　(A) All furniture repairs have been listed.
　(B) Room charges have been refunded.
　(C) The room is in good condition.
　(D) Students are permitted to pay by check.

|63| **What must students do before the librarian will sign the yellow form?**

(A) Register for graduate courses and pay tuition.
(B) Sign their library cards.
(C) Show copies of their final grades.
(D) Return all library books and pay any fines.

|64| **Why is it important for the students to turn in all of the signed forms before graduation?**

(A) So that the administration can issue guest invitations.
(B) So they can have their rooms cleaned free of charge.
(C) So they can prove they are outstanding students.
(D) So they'll be allowed to graduate on time.

|65| **Listen again to**

"I'll try to make this as quick as possible since I know how much you have to do in these last two weeks before graduation. I'm going to give you three forms that must be completed before you'll be able to graduate. To cut down on the confusion, each one is a different color."

What does the speaker imply when she says this?
"I'll try to make this as quick as possible since I know how much you have to do in these last two weeks before graduation."

(A) That students tend to confuse the forms.
(B) That she wants students to work harder so that they can graduate.
(C) That it will take two weeks for students to complete the forms.
(D) That she does not want to make students feel more stress.

> スクリプト和訳

今日はここに集まってくれてありがとう。ほとんどの皆さんは既にご存知かとは思いますが、私は学生部事務局長のジャクソンです。卒業前の2週間、皆さんがどれ程忙しいか分かっていますから、出来るだけ早く済まそうと思います。卒業のために必ず記入してもらう3枚の用紙を渡します。混乱を防ぐため、

それぞれを違う色にしてあります。緑色の用紙は、卒業式に着用が義務づけられている帽子とガウンを注文するためです。この用紙は来週までにビジネスオフィスか私に戻して下さい。帽子とガウンのレンタル代金10ドルを添えて下さい。次に、黄色の用紙は、図書館に行ってサインしてもらわなければなりません。図書館員がサインするのは、皆さんが借りていた本をすべて返し、未払いの罰金を払ってからです。最後に、ピンク色の用紙を管理部の誰かにサインしてもらわないといけませんが、それは、部屋が検査されて、すべて元通りになっているのを確認した後です。このやり方で、部屋が良い状態のまま残されているのが分かるのです。3枚とも色が異なっているので、しなければならない課題が3つあることを覚えておきやすいはずです。少なくとも卒業の1週間前には、すべての用紙を私のところまで提出しなければなりません。皆さん、頑張ってください。では来週お会いしましょう。

重要単語

- **Commencement**：開始、学位授与式、卒業式
- **outstanding fine**：未払いの罰金
- **inspect**：検査する

解答 Questions 66 - 70

66 D　67 A　68 B　69 A　70 B

スクリプト／解答のポイント

　Today, I'd like to talk about another interesting plant that grows in the desert. (66) It is called the saguaro. The saguaro is an unusual leafless plant that has several branches that extend upward. It may stand more than fifty feet tall and weigh as much as ten tons. (70) It bears white flowers and a small edible fruit. This giant plant has been able to survive in regions with very little rainfall for several reasons. First of all, it has a large column-like trunk that holds great quantities of water. (67) After a rainstorm, the trunk swells and conserves water. (68) During dry periods, it becomes smaller as it uses the water. Secondly, the huge plant absorbs water quickly and easily since its numerous roots are close to the ground surface. (69) Lastly, because the plant lacks leaves, little water is lost through evaporation. These special features have made the saguaro especially adaptable to the extreme weather conditions of the desert.

66 In what type of climate is the saguaro plant found?
  (A) Cold and dry.
  (B) Warm and humid.
  (C) Cool and rainy.
  (D) Hot and dry.

67 Why is the saguaro plant unusual?
  (A) It can store water.
  (B) It has many roots.
  (C) It is more than 10 feet tall.
  (C) It bears small white flowers.

68 What happens to the plant when it rains?
  (A) It loses its flowers.
  (B) It expands to hold water.
  (C) It bends down to the ground.
  (D) It grows more leaves.

69 Why does water enter the saguaro plant quickly?
  (A) Its roots are not deep.
  (B) It is very tall.
  (C) Its leaves absorb water.
  (D) It has many branches.

70 Listen again to
  "The saguaro is an unusual leafless plant that has several branches that extend upward. It may stand more than fifty feet tall and weigh as much as ten tons. It bears white flowers and a small edible fruit."

What does the professor imply when he says this?
"It may stand more than fifty feet tall and weigh as much as ten tons."

(A) That the saguaro has never been accurately measured nor weighed.
(B) That some saguaros grow very large.
(C) That most saguaros are small.
(D) That the saguaro grows quickly.

> スクリプト和訳

　今日は、砂漠に育つ面白い植物についてお話ししたいと思います。それは、サグアロと呼ばれています。サグアロは上に広がる枝をいくつか持つ葉のない植物です。50フィート以上の高さになり、10トンもの重さになる場合があります。白い花を咲かせ、小さな食べられる実をつけます。いくつかの理由でこの巨大な植物は、数シーズンをごく少量の降雨しかない地域で生き残ることが出来ます。まず第一に、それは大量の水を保持する大きな円柱のような幹を持っています。嵐の後、その幹は水を保存し膨れ上がります。乾期の間、それは水を使うにつれて小さくなります。第二に、その巨大な植物は、たくさんの根が地表近くにあり、水をすばやく容易に吸収します。最後に、その植物には葉がないので、蒸発によって水がほとんど失われません。これらの特徴のおかげで、サグアロは砂漠の極端な気候条件に特別に適応できるようなったのです。

> 重要単語

- **saguaro**：サグアロ（背の高いサボテンの一種）
- **swell**：膨れる
- **leafless**：葉のない
- **absorb**：吸収する
- **extend upward**：上に広がる
- **numerous**：多くの
- **bear**：実がなる
- **surface**：表面
- **edible fruit**：食べることができるフルーツ
- **evaporation**：蒸発
- **trunk**：幹

> 解答 Questions 71 - 75

71 C　72 A　73 A　74 D　75 D

> スクリプト／解答のポイント

　The state of Maine's most celebrated summer tourist is a 200-pound harbor seal named Andre. Recently, <u>Andre returned to Rockport,</u> (71) Maine to begin another vacation. This furry aquatic mammal arrived in his hometown 65 hours after being set loose in the Atlantic Ocean near Marblehead, Massachusetts. Andre, who spends winters at an aquarium in Boston, was only a few days old when his parents abandoned him in Rockport nearly twenty years ago. It was then that a kind man, Mr. Harry Goodridge, began to take care of the baby seal. He thought a seal would be fun to have as a companion. Mr. Goodridge cared for the seal until a few years ago when he arranged for him to spend winters in the Boston Aquarium and to be set free each summer. No one knows <u>why Andre returns the long distance to his birthplace every summer.</u> (72) <u>Since Andre became famous, he has been given the title of honorary harbor master in Rockport, and the town erected a granite statue of the seal.</u> (73) <u>Andre himself unveiled it,</u> (74) <u>using his teeth to pull off the cloth.</u> (75)

[71] Where was Andre born?
　(A) In Atlantic City.
　(B) In Marblehead, Massachusetts.
　(C) In Rockport, Maine.
　(D) In Boston, Massachusetts.

[72] What does Andre do each year that is so unusual?
　(A) Returns to his birthplace.
　(B) Communicates with humans.
　(C) Abandons his parents.
　(D) Calls long distance.

[73] How was Andre recently honored?
　(A) A granite statue was dedicated to him.
　(B) He was allowed to spend winters in an aquarium.

(C) He was set free in the ocean.
(D) He was fed well.

74 Who unveiled the town's monument?
(A) Mr. Goodridge.
(B) A dentist.
(C) The aquarium director.
(D) **Andre.**

75 Listen again to
"Since Andre became famous, he has been given the title of honorary harbor master in Rockport, and the town erected a granite statue of the seal. Andre himself unveiled it, using his teeth to pull off the cloth."

Why does the speaker say this?
"Andre himself unveiled it, using his teeth to pull off the cloth."

(A) To explain why Andre became famous.
(B) To note that the statue was an accurate copy of the seal.
(C) To indicate that Andre broke the gift by accident.
(D) **To show how impressive the ceremony was.**

スクリプト和訳

メイン州の最も有名な夏の観光客は200ポンドの体重を持つアンドレという名のゴマフアザラシです。最近、アンドレは休暇を始めるために、メイン州ロックポートに戻ってきました。この毛のふさふさした海洋哺乳動物は、マサチューセッツ州マーブルヘッド近くの大西洋を離れてから65時間後に、彼の故郷に到着しました。ボストンの水族館で冬を過ごすアンドレは、ほぼ20年前、ロックポートで両親に捨てられたとき、生後数日しか経っていませんでした。親切な男、ハリー・グッドリッジ氏がその赤ん坊のアザラシの世話をし始めたのはそのときのことでした。彼は、アザラシを仲間に持つと楽しいだろうと考えたのです。グッドリッジ氏は、数年前までそのアザラシを世話していましたが、アザラシが、冬はボストンの水族館で過ごし、夏が来るたびに自由に放されるよ

うに手答をつけました。なぜアンドレが毎年夏になるとはるばる生まれ故郷まで戻っていくのかは、誰にもわかりません。アンドレは有名になったので、ロックポートの名誉港長の地位を与えられました。そして、その町はそのアザラシの花崗岩の像を建てました。アンドレ自身が、布をはぎ取るのに歯を使いながら、除幕式を行いました。

重要単語

- **celebrated**：有名な
- **seal**：アザラシ
- **furry aquatic mammal**：毛のふさふさした海洋哺乳動物
- **aquarium**：水族館
- **abandon**：放棄する、あきらめる
- **harbor master**：港長、港務所長
- **erect**：建てる
- **granite**：花崗岩

解答 Questions 76 - 80

76 D　77 B　78 A　79 D　80 A

スクリプト／解答のポイント

One of my main goals in this survey course of American painting, sculpture, and architecture is to train you to see.(76) I want you to increase your stock of visual experiences by using the slide library(77) at least five hours a week. The library, which is maintained by the Art History Department, is located in the basement of the Arts Center and is open seven days a week. By the end of this course, I expect you to be able to identify 2,000 slides of various American works of art. Slide identification questions will appear on the weekly exams and the final. During each of the ten weeks of this course, I will show a set of 200 slides during my lectures.(78) You should plan on looking at each set twice in the slide library, once before the week's lectures and once after. This pattern of three exposures will improve your visual memory. Please do not remove the slides from the slide library. Doing so is cause for dismissal from the course.(80)Although becoming familiar with 2,000 slides may sound difficult, experience has shown me that this is the best way to increase the visual abilities of (79) students such as yourselves who have never taken an art history course before. (79) (80)

76. Who is the speaker?
   (A) An artist.
   (B) A professor of library science.
   (C) A doctor specializing in vision.
   (D) A professor of art history.

77. What is the main topic of the talk?
   (A) The history of the slide library.
   (B) The use of slides in the course.
   (C) The material to be tested that day.
   (D) The outline of the course.

78. At what point during the semester would this talk be given?
   (A) The beginning.
   (B) Just before the first weekly exam.
   (C) Halfway through the course.
   (D) Just before the final exam.

79. The course is designed with what kind of people in mind?
   (A) Those who have visual disabilities.
   (B) Those who intend to become artists.
   (C) Those who have no interest in painting.
   (D) Those who have never taken art history before.

80. Listen again to
   "Although becoming familiar with 2,000 slides may sound difficult, experience has shown me that this is the best way to increase the visual abilities of students such as yourselves, who have never taken an art history course before."

Why does the professor say this?
"experience has shown me that this is the best way"

(A) **To encourage students to follow the professor's instruction.**
(B) To note that there is no other means to attain the goals of the course.
(C) To remind students of the fun of studying art history.
(D) To convince students that identifying 2,000 slides is actually easy.

スクリプト和訳

　アメリカの絵画・彫刻・建築についての、この概説講義の主な目的の一つは、皆さんが見るための訓練をすることです。私は皆さんに少なくとも週に5時間はスライド図書館を使って、芸術作品を見る経験の蓄積を増やして欲しいと思います。その図書館は、芸術史学科が維持しているのですが、アートセンターの地下にあり、週7日開いています。このコースが終わるまでに、皆さんが2000枚のアメリカの様々な芸術作品のスライドを識別できるよう期待していますよ。スライドを識別する問題は、毎週のテストと期末テストで出題されます。この10週間のコース期間中毎週、講義時間内に200枚1セットのスライドを見てもらいます。各セットをスライド図書館で2回、1回は授業の前に、もう1回は授業の後に、見るように計画してください。このように3回経験する形式は皆さんの視覚的記憶を向上させるでしょう。スライドはスライド図書館から持ち出さないでください。そうすることは、コースから追放される原因となります。2000枚のスライドに精通することは、難しく聞こえるかもしれませんが、これまでの経験から、この方法が、今までに美術史のコースを取ったことがない皆さんのような生徒の視覚能力を高める最良のやり方なのです。

重要単語

- **survey course**：概説講義
- **sculpture**：彫刻
- **exposure**：さらす(さらされる)こと、露出、暴露
- **dismissal**：放棄、退去、解雇、解任、罷免

解答 Questions 81 - 85

81 C   82 C   83 B   84 D   85 C

スクリプト／解答のポイント

I would like to follow-up the discussion we had at our last meeting about natural sources of medicines, by talking now about the drug, quinine. <u>For three centuries quinine, obtained from the bark of the Cinchona tree, was one of the most valuable of all drugs. It was the only medicine effective in treating a disease called malaria.</u>(82)(85) The Cinchona tree is native to South America. <u>Around 1640, the Spanish conquerors of Peru discovered the power of the bark in curing malaria and they took supplies of the bark back to Europe.</u>(81) Powdered Cinchona bark became very popular in Europe for the treatment of malaria. <u>The demand for quinine became so great that Cinchona trees were cut down and stripped of their bark until the supply in South America was almost completely exhausted.</u>(83)(84)

81 When did the Spanish first begin to use quinine?

(A) In A.D. 600.
(B) During the third century.
(C) More than three hundred years ago.
(D) In the 1940's.

82 What is quinine used for?

(A) Curing leather.
(B) Treating deep cuts.
(C) Curing a disease.
(D) Preserving food supplies.

83 What happened while quinine was being exported to Europe?

(A) Quinine dropped in value.
(B) Cinchona trees almost disappeared.

(C) Quinine was often mixed with other substances.
(D) Cinchona supplies were cut off by the Peruvians.

84 Why were Cinchona trees cut down?
(A) To make room for settlements.
(B) To provide a fuel supply.
(C) To make a road through Peru.
(D) To get all the bark off.

85 Listen again to
"For three centuries, quinine, obtained from the bark of the Cinchona tree, was one of the most valuable of all drugs. It was the only medicine effective in treating a disease called malaria."

Why does the professor say this?
"It was the only medicine effective in treating a disease called malaria."

(A) To show how threatening malaria is.
(B) To provide a fuel supply.
(C) To show how valuable quinine is.
(D) To identify the cause of malaria.

| スクリプト和訳 |

　天然資源の薬について前回の講義から議論を続けたいと思いますが、今日はキニーネという薬についてお話します。300年の間、キナの木の皮から得られるキニーネは、すべての薬の中で最も貴重なものの一つでした。それは、マラリアという病気を治療する上で、唯一効果のある薬でした。キナの木は南米の原生植物です。1640年頃、ペルーを征服したスペイン人が、マラリアを治療するその木の皮の力を発見し、その木の皮をヨーロッパに持ち帰りました。粉状にされたキナの木の皮は、マラリアの治療薬としてヨーロッパ中で評判になりました。キニーネに対する需要が非常に大きくなったため、ついには南アメリカでの供給はほぼ完全に使い尽くされるまで、キナの木は切り倒され、その皮が剥ぎ取られました。

重要単語

- **quinine**：キニーネ（マラリアの特効薬）
- **the bark of Cinchona tree**：キナの木の皮
- **be native to ～**：～原産である、～に自生する
- **conqueror**：征服者
- **strip off**：～を剥ぎ取る
- **be exhausted**：使い尽くされた、枯渇した、疲れ切った

解答 Questions 86 - 90

86 A　87 B　88 D　89 B　90 B

スクリプト／解答のポイント

　In my last lecture, I touched on the sanitary conditions of rural households in the early nineteenth century. Today, I would like to begin with a discussion of American cities of the same period.(86)　Because of their dense population, American cities of the early nineteenth century were often far more foul-smelling than the farmyards.(87)　City streets were thickly covered with horse manure. Few neighborhoods were free of the stench of tanneries and slaughterhouses. New York City's accumulation of garbage was so great that it was generally believed that the actual surface of many streets had not been seen for decades.(90)　In most cities, hundreds or even thousands of free-roaming pigs scavenged the garbage.(88)　One exception was Charleston, whose streets were patrolled by buzzards. By converting garbage into pork, pigs kept city streets clearer than they otherwise would have been, but the pigs themselves befouled the streets and those who ate their meat-primarily poor families ran greater than usual risks of infection.(89)

86　What is the speaker's main topic?

　(A) **Sanitation in American cities of the nineteenth century.**
　(B) Sanitary conditions in early American farm houses.
　(C) The care and feeding of pigs in the early United States.

(D) A comparison of urban and rural living conditions.

87 According to the speaker, what was true of American farmyards of the early nineteenth century?

(A) They were full of garbage.
(B) They were cleaner than cities of the time.
(C) They were extremely crowded.
(D) They had no pigs.

88 According to the speaker, what was the primary function of pigs in American cities?

(A) They provided food.
(B) They clean city streets.
(C) They chased uninvited guests from homes.
(D) They consumed much of the street garbage.

89 What does the speaker imply about the meat of the city pigs?

(A) It was sold cheaply.
(B) It was not fit for consumption.
(C) It was considered a rare delicacy.
(D) It was difficult to obtain.

90 Listen again to

"City streets were thickly covered with horse manure. Few neighborhoods were free of the stench of tanneries and slaughterhouses. New York City's accumulation of garbage was so great that it was generally believed that the actual surface of many streets had not been seen for decades."

Why does the professor say this?
"New York City's accumulation of garbage was so great that it was generally believed that the actual surface of many streets had not been seen for decades."

（A）To illustrate how fast the city's economy was growing.
（B）To explain how bad the sanitation of the city was.
（C）To criticize the exaggerated story about the overpopulated city.
（D）To praise the effort of the city's residents to preserve traditional landscapes.

> スクリプト和訳

　前回の授業では、19世紀初期の田舎の家庭の衛生状態について触れました。
　今日は、同時期のアメリカの都市についての議論から始めたいと思います。密集した人口のため、19世紀初期のアメリカの都市は、農家の庭よりもはるかに強い悪臭を放っていました。都市の通りは馬糞で厚く覆われていました。皮なめし工場や屠殺場の匂いがしない界隈はほとんどありませんでした。ニューヨーク市のゴミの蓄積は非常に大量だったので、多くの通りの表面は何十年もの間見られたことがないと一般的に信じられていました。ほとんどの都市で、何百、何千匹もの、自由にうろつきまわる豚がゴミを漁っていました。一つの例外は、チャールストン市で、その通りは、アメリカハゲタカが巡回していたのです。ゴミを豚肉に転換することで、豚は都市の通りを、彼らがゴミを漁らなかった場合よりはきれいにしていました、しかし豚自身が通りを汚し、またその肉を食べる者は—主に貧しい家族は—普通よりも病気に感染する大きな危険を冒していたのです。

> 重要単語

- **touch on ~**：~について触れる、言及する
- **tannery**：皮なめし工場
- **sanitary condition**：衛生状態
- **slaughterhouse**：屠殺場、食肉処理場
- **dense population**：密集した人口
- **free-roaming**：自由にうろつく
- **foul-smelling**：悪臭に満ちた
- **scavenge**：（ごみ・残飯などを）漁る
- **horse manure**：馬糞
- **buzzard**：アメリカハゲタカ
- **stench**：悪臭
- **befoul**：~を汚す、不潔にする

解答 Questions 91 - 95

91 B **92** A **93** A **94** B **95** A

スクリプト／解答のポイント

Welcome to our introductory course on nutrition. This first lecture will center on a very valuable member of the bean family, the soybean. The soybean is a highly nutritious bean, which also can serve as a meat substitute. Some people call soybeans incredible. Let me give you some examples of why the soybean is so special. First of all, when it is made into meal, it enhances animal feeds. Secondly, as soy flour, it similarly enriches the baked goods we humans eat.(92) Thirdly, as soy chips or flakes, it is often included in cereals. And lastly, in some countries, for example, China, the soybean is processed into virtually all fresh milk consumed there.(91) It is also the basic ingredient of textured vegetable protein, which brings a meat-like taste and feel to vegetarian dishes.(93) For many years, soybeans were thought of in the United States only as a commercial agricultural crop.(94) Now, however, the soybean is being raised in backyard gardens. It is easy to grow and, as I pointed out before, beneficial in many ways.(95)

91 What is the main idea of this lecture?
 (A) Soybeans are known in China.
 (B) Soybeans have many uses.
 (C) Soybeans are easy to grow.
 (D) Some people like soybeans.

92 What soybean product can be used to enrich baked goods?
 (A) Soy flour.
 (B) Soybean leaves.
 (C) Soybean oil.
 (D) Soy sauce.

93 What is one important attribute of the soybean?
(A) **It is a meat substitute.**
(B) It is often used for backyard decoration.
(C) It is a complete milk substitute.
(D) It is easily processed into flour at home.

94 In the past, what was the main reason soybeans were grown in the United States?
(A) As an expensive food item.
(B) **As a commercial agricultural crop.**
(C) As an ingredient in Chinese cooking.
(D) As a vegetable in most backyard gardens.

95 Listen again to

"For many years, soybeans were thought of in the United States only as a commercial agricultural crop. Now, however, the soybean is being raised in backyard gardens. It is easy to grow and, as I pointed out before, beneficial in many ways."

What does the speaker imply when she says this?
"Now, however, the soybean is being raised in backyard gardens."

(A) **That raising soybeans has become common.**
(B) That soybeans grow better in the shade.
(C) That the professor raises soybeans.
(D) That the United States does not export soybeans anymore.

> スクリプト和訳

　栄養学の入門コースへようこそ。この最初の講義は、豆科内でも非常に価値ある種類、大豆に重点を置きます。大豆は非常に栄養価の高い豆で、肉の代用品にもなります。大豆は信じられないほど素晴らしいと言う人もいます。大豆がなぜそれほど特別か、例を挙げましょう。まず第一に、あらびきの粉にすると、動物の飼料の質を高めます。次に、大豆粉として、我々人間が食べる焼い

た食品の質を同様に高めます。第三に、大豆チップスや大豆フレークとして、シリアルのなかに含まれます。そして最後に、ある国では、例えば、中国では、大豆は加工されて、そこで消費されるほとんどすべての新鮮なミルクになります。大豆は、野菜料理に肉のような味と食感をもたらす植物性タンパク質の原料でもあります。長年の間、大豆は、合衆国では、単に商業的農産物として考えられていました。しかし、今では大豆は裏庭の家庭菜園で育てられています。大豆は育てるのが簡単で、前に指摘したように、多くの点で有益です。

重要単語

- **nutrition**：栄養学、栄養分、食べ物
- **animal feed**：動物の飼料
- **center on**：〜に重点を置く、〜に集中する
- **soy flour**：きなこ、大豆粉
- **soybean**：大豆
- **basic ingredient**：原料
- **meat substitute**：肉の代用品
- **textured vegetable protein**：植物性タンパク質
- **meal**：あらびき粉、食事
- **a meat like taste and feel**：肉のような味と食感
- **enhance**：(強さ・量・機能・質などを)増す、高める、強化する

解答 Questions 96 - 99

96 C　97 D　98 C　99 D

スクリプト／解答のポイント

　Today I will continue my discussion of the behaviorist school of psychology and tell you about what I feel are some problems related to behaviorism. (96)　The psychologist wishes to understand human behavior and the human mind. He or she must, therefore, design methods of investigating human beings as they actually live. (97)　The behaviorist school of psychology, however, has done almost all of its studies under laboratory conditions. Behaviorism seems to want the respectability of the natural sciences but it uses the methods of 50 years ago. (99)　Furthermore, behaviorist studies often do not make any great contributions, but the author will cover this up with mathematical tables and statistics, which are not important for the study. <u>To investigate human behavior in a more natural setting is difficult, I admit.</u> (98) Nevertheless, there are at least two ways to carry out such a task.

96 What is the main topic of the lecture?

(A) Laboratory methods in psychology.
(B) How to make psychology respectable.
(C) A critique of behaviorist psychology.
(D) Recent advances in theoretical psychology.

97 What does the speaker think is the best way to study human psychology?

(A) Use experimental data only.
(B) Ask people's opinions on various matters.
(C) Use statistical data based on scientific models.
(D) Observe people in real-life situations.

98 What does the next part of the lecture most probably deal with?

(A) Further criticisms of behaviorist psychology.
(B) Criticism of other theories of psychology.
(C) Methods of studying human behavior in natural settings.
(D) New designs in equipment for psychology laboratories.

99 Listen again to

"The behaviorist school of psychology, however, has done almost all of its studies under laboratory conditions. Behaviorism seems to want the respectability of the natural sciences, but it uses the methods of 50 years ago."

What does the speaker imply when he says this?

"Behaviorism seems to want the respectability of the natural sciences but it uses the methods of 50 years ago."

(A) That the history of behaviorism is old.
(B) That psychology owes much to natural sciences.
(C) That psychologists are generally more respected than natural scientists.
(D) That behaviorism has not attained its goal.

スクリプト和訳

　今日は心理学の行動主義学派についての議論を続けましょう、また行動主義に関する問題について私が感じていることをお話しします。心理学者は、人間の行動と人間の精神を理解したいと願っています。彼または彼女は、それ故、実際に生きている人間を調べる方法を考え出さなければなりません。しかしながら、心理学の行動主義学派は、その研究のほとんどすべてを実験室条件下で行ってきました。行動主義は、自然科学の体面を欲しているようですが、50年前の方法を使っています。さらに、行動主義の研究は、大きな貢献をしていないことがほとんどですが、この著者は、このことを研究にとって重要ではない数学的表や統計を使って包み隠そうとしています。人間の行動を、より自然な環境で調べることが困難なことは、認めます。しかしながら、そのような課題を果たす方法が少なくとも2つあります。

重要単語

- **behaviorist school**：行動主義学派
- **behaviorism**：行動主義
- **respectability**：体面、社会的地位、世間体
- **mathematical tables and statistics**：数学的表や統計
- **cover up**：包み隠す、覆い隠す

解答 Questions 100 - 105

100 A　101 C　102 B　103 D　104 D　105 B

スクリプト／解答のポイント

　Millions of acres of land where all kinds of wildlife make their homes have been ruined in recent years. This land has been ruined by federally-approved water projects(101) such as dams, built in violation of a rarely enforced law passed in 1934.(100) According to this law, all projects to modify a body of water can be carried out only after a thorough study to discover what damage may be caused to the wildlife in that area. Many states have not complied with the law. In three southern states, Alabama, Louisiana and Mississippi, (102) about 1.2 million acres of wildlife habitat have been covered with water because of dams which have been constructed there. Another plan to build a dam in Tennessee was fought because it would flood large areas of wildlife habitat, particularly endangering a species of small fish called the snail darter. (103) The proposed dam would also destroy several important archaeological sites including the ancestral capital of the ancient Cherokee Indian nation. (105) To prevent any further destruction, the public must become accurately informed(104) about the advantages and disadvantages of our national water projects. Only then can we be assured that existing laws will be enforced.

100 According to the speaker, why have many animals and birds lost their homes?
(A) Because of the enforcement of laws regarding wildlife.
(B) Because of ancient Cherokee Indian.
(C) Because of lack of water.
(D) Because of the excavation of archaeological sites.

101 What kinds of projects does the 1934 law deal with?
(A) Wildlife.
(B) Archaeological.
(**C**) **Water.**
(D) Soil.

102 According to the speaker, how many southern states have lost land because of dams?
(A) Two.
(**B**) **Three.**

(C) Four.
(D) Five.

103 Why have people fought a plan to build a dam in Tennessee?
(A) Because it would flood farm land and destroy homes.
(B) Because many people would lose their jobs.
(C) Because valuable topsoil would be washed away.
(D) Because it would endanger fish and destroy archaeological sites.

104 According to the speaker, who can prevent further destruction?
(A) The Cherokee Indians.
(B) The federal government.
(C) Lawyers.
(D) An informed public.

105 Listen again to
"*Another plan to build a dam in Tennessee was fought because it would flood large areas of wildlife habitat, particularly endangering a species of small fish called the snail darter. The proposed dam would also destroy several important archaeological sites, including the ancestral capital of the ancient Cherokee Indian nation.*"

What does the speaker imply when she says this?
"*The proposed dam would also destroy several important archaeological sites, including the ancestral capital of the ancient Cherokee Indian nation.*"

(A) That Cherokee Indians have proposed the construction of a dam in Tennessee.
(B) That the damage caused by the proposed dam would be extensive.
(C) That the proposed dam would not cause damage to wildlife.
(D) That constructing a dam is more beneficial than preserving cultural heritage.

スクリプト和訳

　近年あらゆる種類の野生動物が住んでいる何百万エーカーの土地が破壊されてきました。1934年に制定されたがめったに施行されない法律に反して、連邦政府が認可したダムなどの水利事業によってこの土地は、破壊されてきました。この法律によると、水域の形態を変えるプロジェクトはすべて、地域の野生動物にどのような被害が与えられるか十分な検討がされてから初めて遂行できることになります。多くの州がこの法律を守っていません。南部の3州、アラバマ、ルイジアナ、ミシシッピ州において、約120万エーカーの野生動物の生息地が、そこに造られたダムのために水に覆われてしまいました。テネシー州にダムを造るもう一つのプロジェクトは、反対されました。なぜならダムが出来れば、広い領域にわたる野生動物の生息地を水浸しにし、特に、スネール・ダーターと呼ばれる小さな魚の種を絶滅の危機にさらすことになるからです。

　提案されたダムが出来れば、古代のチェロキーインディアン国家の先祖代々の首都を含む幾つかの重要な遺跡発掘現場も、破壊されることになります。さらなる破壊を防ぐために、一般市民は、国の水利事業の良い点と悪い点について正確に知らされなければなりません。そのとき初めて、私達は現存する法律が施行されると確信できるのです。

重要単語

- **in violation of ～**：～に違反して
- **modify a body of water**：水域の形態を変える
- **thorough study**：徹底的な調査
- **cause damage to ～**：～に被害を与える
- **comply with ～**：～に従う
- **temporary**：一時的な
- **wildlife habitat**：野生動物の生息地
- **snail darter**：スネール・ダーター（スズキ目パーチ科の小さな矢魚）
- **archaeological site**：遺跡発掘現場
- **ancestral**：先祖代々の

解答 Questions 106 - 110

106 C　107 C　108 B　109 A　110 B

> スクリプト／解答のポイント

　Treat yourself. Go first class to London.(108)　Fly Lux Airways. We'll do a luxurious job of serving (106) you in a very businesslike way. We leave Chicago at an excellent time, 6:45 every night, (107) and arrive in time for you to have a full day of business in London the day you land.(109)(110) And Lux Airways gives you such excellent food and such warm service that you get to London relaxed, rested, and ready for a day's work. And that's the way you want to arrive. Right? Treat yourself. Lux Airways to London. First class, and we mean, first class. See your travel agent in Chicago. Fly with Lux!

|106| **What special kind of services is the airline advertising?**
　(A) Quick service.
　(B) Economical service.
　(C) Luxury service.
　(D) Individual service.

|107| **What is said about departure?**
　(A) It's always prompt.
　(B) It's during business hours.
　(C) It's in the evening.
　(D) It's first thing in the morning.

|108| **What is the plane's destination?**
　(A) Luxembourg.
　(B) London.
　(C) Ireland.
　(D) Chicago.

|109| **What kind of traveler does the airline want to attract?**
　(A) Wealthy businessmen.
　(B) Vacationing families.

(C) Airline employees.
(D) Tourist groups.

110 What can be assumed about the arrival time?
(A) There are various arrival times.
(B) Early in the morning.
(C) Late at night.
(D) Approximately 6:45am.

スクリプト和訳

　贅沢をしましょう。ファーストクラスでロンドンへ行きましょう。ラックス航空で空の旅を。
　我々はてきぱきと皆さんに仕え、素晴らしいサービスを提供致します。シカゴを毎晩6時45分という丁度良い時間に出発し、ロンドンでは着いたその日に一日中ビジネスが出来る時間に到着します。ラックス航空は皆さんに最高の食事と暖かいサービスを提供しますので、ロンドンに着く頃には、リラックスして十分な休息が取れ、一日の仕事に向かう準備が出来ています。そんな到着の仕方を皆さんは望まれている筈です。そうですよね？　贅沢をしましょう。ラックス航空でロンドンへ。ファーストクラス、それも最上級のファーストクラスを提供致します。シカゴのお馴染みの旅行代理店にお問い合わせ下さい。ラックス航空で空の旅を！

重要単語
- **luxurious job**：快適なサービス
- **businesslike**：てきぱきした、きちんと仕事をする、能率的な

解答 Questions 111 - 115

111 D　112 A　113 A　114 C　115 C

スクリプト／解答のポイント

Today we have a slide presentation on the jellyfish. (111) The jellyfish is not really a fish at all, (115) but rather a type of free-swimming coelenterate. It gets its name from the transparent, (112) jelly-like substance of which its body is composed. As you can see in this slide, their bodies are more or less bell-shaped with a proboscis that hangs down like the clapper of a bell. The mouth is located at the end of this clapper and leads into the stomach.

Most of the species start life as buds on the bodies of adult animals. These buds later separate and lead a free existence, swimming by opening and closing their bell-shaped bodies. (113) They have needle-like organs that are used for defense and to kill their prey. In some species, these organs are strong enough to cause serious injury to people. (114) In some Asian countries, jellyfish are consumed as food. But so much of their bodies consists of water that there is little left of them when they are dried.

111. Where is the talk probably taking place?
- (A) In a harbor.
- (B) At an aquarium.
- (C) On a bus.
- **(D) In a classroom.**

112. Why was the animal given the name jellyfish?
- **(A) Because of its transparent body.**
- (B) Due to its odd shape.
- (C) Because of their sweet taste.
- (D) Due to the way it attacks enemies.

113. How does the jellyfish swim?
- **(A) By altering the shape of its body.**
- (B) By lowering and raising its "clapper."
- (C) By spitting out its needles.
- (D) By shedding its buds.

114. What part of the jellyfish sometimes injures people?
- (A) Its "clapper."

(B) Its stomach.
(C) **Its needle-shaped organs.**
(D) Its teeth.

115 What kind of sea creature is the jellyfish?
(A) Bell fish.
(B) Water fish.
(C) **Not a fish.**
(D) Sweet fish.

```
スクリプト和訳
```

　さて今日は、クラゲについてのスライドショーを見ていただきます。クラゲは魚類ではなく、ある種の自由遊泳性の直腸動物です。ジェリーフィッシュという名前は、体を作っている透明でジェリーのような物質から来ています。このスライドで見られるように、その体は、大体ベルのような形で、ベルの舌のようにぶらさがっている口先きが付いています。口腔はこの舌の先に付いていて胃へと通じています。

　ほとんどの種が大人のクラゲの体に付いている子芽とし生まれます。これらの子芽は後に分離し、自由な存在になり、ベルのような体を開いたり閉じたりして泳ぎます。針のような器官を持っていて、これは防御や獲物を殺すために使います。種によっては、これらの器官は人に大けがをさせるぐらい強力なものです。いくつかのアジアの国々では、クラゲを食料としています。しかし、体の大部分が水で出来ていますので、乾燥させるとほとんど残っていません。

```
重要単語
```

- **jellyfish**：クラゲ
- **coelenterate**：腔腸動物
- **proboscis**：口先き
- **clapper**：(鈴・鐘)の舌
- **bud**：子芽、芽体、芽状突起
- **prey**：餌食

解答 Questions 116 - 120

116 A　117 A　118 A　119 A　120 A

> スクリプト／解答のポイント

　Today, I'm going to discuss transportation and communication <u>in the early 19th century in the United States.</u>(119)　At that time, inland waterways provided North America's most popular form of long distance transportation. Travel by river was often more convenient than taking a wagon over primitive country roads, especially when shipping heavy loads of farm products or household goods.　Where the natural waterways were inadequate, shallow canals were built.　<u>The Erie Canal, opened in 1825,</u>(118) <u>connected the Great Lakes with the upper Hudson River.　It allowed settlers in the Great Lakes region to send their crops eastward to New York City</u> at the mouth of the Hudson,(120) at a much lower cost.　<u>From there, crops could be shipped to other Atlantic ports.</u>(116)　The construction of the Erie Canal also encouraged westward migration along inland waterways and helped populate the frontier.　The city of Detroit grew up between two of the Great Lakes. Later a canal joined the Great Lakes with the Mississippi River system and Chicago became a thriving city.　Politically, the waterway system united the nation in a way few had imagined possible.　<u>By the mid 1800's, faster and cheaper railroads became more popular</u>(117) and the canal system declined.

　Railroads could be used year round whereas canals were often frozen in the winter.　During the first third of the century however, transportation on rivers, lakes and canals aided greatly in the growth of the United States.

　Next week, we'll discuss the railroads in greater detail.

|116| **What was usually transported from west to east?**
　(A) **Agricultural products.**
　(B) Manufactured goods.
　(C) Settlers.
　(D) Farm animals.

|117| **What new system soon replaced inland waterways?**
　(A) **Railroads.**
　(B) Highways.

(C) Wagon trails.
(D) Sea routes.

118 When was inland waterway travel most popular?
(A) **In the early 1800's.**
(B) In the mid-1800's.
(C) In the late 1800's.
(D) In the early 1900's.

119 What is the main idea of this lecture?
(A) **The role of inland waterways in the nation's growth.**
(B) The development of New York City as a seaport.
(C) The growth of the railroads.
(D) The disappearance of the canal system.

120 What was the initial main result of the completion of the Erie Canal?
(A) **It connected the Great Lakes region with New York City.**
(B) It connected Detroit with New York.
(C) It connected Chicago with New York.
(D) It connected the Great Lakes with the Mississippi River.

スクリプト和訳

　本日は、19世紀初頭のアメリカ合衆国における、輸送機関と交通機関について議論をしたいと思います。この時代、内陸部を通る水路が、北アメリカに最も普及した長距離輸送の形を提供しました。水路での移動が、未開の田舎道を荷馬車で走るより、よっぽど便利だったということはよくありました。とりわけ、とても重い農産品や家財の積み荷を運ぶときはそうでした。自然の水路では不十分な場合は、浅い運河が建設されました。例えば、エリー運河は1825年に開通され、五大湖とハドソン川上流を結びました。これにより、五大湖地域の住民は、収穫物をハドソン川の入り口であるニューヨーク市へと東へ向かって運ぶことが、とても安い料金でできたのです。更に、そこから収穫物を他の大西洋の港へと送ることも可能になりました。加えて、エリー運河の建設は、水路を伝って内陸部へと進む西部への移住をも促進し、フロンティアの人口増

加の助けともなりました。デトロイトも五大湖の2つに挟まれる形で成長していきます。後に、運河により五大湖とミシシッピ川は結び付けられ、シカゴは繁栄しました。政治的には、こうした運河はほとんど誰も予想しなかったような様子で、国を結び付けていったのです。しかし、1800年代の半ばまでには、迅速かつ安価な鉄道がますます人気となり、運河は衰退してしまったのでした。

　鉄道は一年中利用することができますが、一方の運河は冬になると頻繁に凍結してしまいました。とはいうものの、19世紀の初頭の3分の1の間は、河川、湖、そして運河における輸送がアメリカ合衆国の発展にかなり貢献しました。

　それでは来週、鉄道についてさらに詳しく議論をしたいと思います。

重要単語
- **inland waterways**：内陸水路
- **wagon**：荷馬車
- **canal**：運河
- **primitive**：粗野な、未発達の
- **populate**：入植する、住む

解答 Questions 121 - 125

121 A　122 C　123 C　124 C　125 C

スクリプト／解答のポイント

　Today, I would like to continue our discussion of insect life cycles by considering the Periodical Cicada, (121) which has the longest life cycle (125) of any known insect. (124)

　In the United States, there are two species of these insects. The northern species has a life cycle of 17 years. The southern species has a shorter life cycle, of 13 years. As is the case with about 20 percent of all insects, the Periodical Cicada undergoes incomplete metamorphosis. It is first an egg, then a nymph, then an adult. There is no pupa stage.

　In June, during their week or so of adult life, the females lay eggs on twigs. (122) By August, the nymphs hatch and drop from the twigs to the ground. They dig into the ground, where the northern species stays for 17 years, and the southern species stays for 13 years. There they grow, eating the sap from small roots (123) and shedding their external skeletons four times as they become larger.

The mature nymphs eventually crawl out of the ground at dusk in late May or early June, and climb the nearest shrub, tree or fence. Their mud-covered external skeletons split, and the white adults emerge. By the following morning, the adult's color has darkened. Then the mating calls, for which the cicadas are well known, fill the forests, and the cycle begins anew.

When the adults emerge from the ground, they do so in vast numbers. Because there are so many, people often mistake them for locusts. Unlike locusts, however, cicadas are not significant agricultural pests.

121. What information about cicadas does the speaker emphasize?
 (A) **The length of their life cycle.**
 (B) The damage they do to crops.
 (C) Their time of emergence.
 (D) Their ability to make noises.

122. Where do cicadas lay their eggs?
 (A) Under the ground.
 (B) On the surface of the ground.
 (C) On twigs.
 (D) In muddy puddles.

123. What do cicada nymphs eat?
 (A) Bacteria.
 (B) Small insects.
 (C) Root sap.
 (D) Young plants.

124. What kind of class is the speaker most probably addressing?
 (A) Geography.
 (B) Forestry.
 (C) Biology.

(D) Engineering.

125 **What can be said about the cicada's metamorphosis?**
(A) They change their body by 20%.
(B) Changes usually occur in winter.
(C) The longest.
(D) Like that of locusts.

> スクリプト和訳

　さて今日も、昆虫の生命サイクルについての議論を続けたいと思います。周期ゼミという、知りうるどの昆虫のなかでも最も長期間の生命サイクルを持つセミについて、考察をしていきます。
　アメリカ合衆国には、この種の昆虫が2種類います。北部にいる17年の生命サイクルを持つ種類と、南部の13年というもう少し短い生命サイクルを持つ種類です。すべての昆虫の20パーセントがそうであるように、この周期ゼミも不完全変態を通ります。すなわち、最初は卵で、次に幼虫になり、そして成虫になるのです。サナギとしての段階がありません。
　6月、成虫として生きる約1週間に、メスは木の枝に卵を産み付けます。そして8月になると、幼虫が孵化し、枝から地面へと落ちていきます。その後地面の中へと進み、北部における種は17年の間、一方南部における種は13年間、そこに留まります。ここで彼らは、細い根から汁を吸って成長し、大きくなるにつれ4度脱皮を重ねるのです。
　成長した幼虫は、5月の末ごろか6月の初頭の日暮れに、ついに地面へと這い出てきて、一番近くにある低木、もしくは高木やフェンスをよじ登ります。そこで、土にまみれた外皮が破れ、白い色をした成虫が姿を現します。次の朝になるまでには、この成虫の色は黒ずんでしまいます。その後、セミの鳴き声として聞き慣れた、交尾期の鳴き声が森に満ち溢れ、また新しいサイクルが始まるのです。
　成虫が地面から出てくる時期、膨大な数が現れます。あまりにも数が多いので、よくイナゴと勘違いされてしまいます。ですがイナゴと違い、セミは農業にとってそこまで深刻な害虫ではありません。

> 重要単語

- **Periodical Cicada**：17年ゼミ（周期ゼミ）
- **sap**：樹液
- **As is the case with 〜**：〜の場合と同様
- **sheds their external skeletons**：脱皮する
- **metamorphosis**：変態
- **at dust**：黄昏時に、日暮れに
- **nymph**：幼虫
- **mating call**：交尾期の鳴き声
- **pupa**：さなぎ
- **mistake A for B**：AをBと間違える
- **twig**：小枝
- **locust**：バッタ、イナゴ
- **hatch**：孵化する

解答 Questions 126 - 130

126 D   127 C   128 D   129 B   130 D

スクリプト／解答のポイント

Today, before you start practicing your orchestra pieces, I want to show you how different kinds of materials can affect the sound of musical instruments. (126) I've recently read about an experiment that several people did with brass instruments.

First, I'll show you a lacquered brass French Horn. Do you see how the lacquer keeps the instrument shiny? Second, here is a horn from which I have removed the lacquer. And here is a third horn, a silver-plated one.(127) Silver tarnishes easily and has to be polished frequently. Lacquer, on the other hand, protects a horn against corrosion,(130) and so the horn doesn't require polishing.

What's significant about these differences is that for years, French Horn players have complained because they felt that the sound of their horns was deadened or diminished by lacquer.(128)

It seems that the orchestra players have a legitimate complaint after all. The experiment with the three horns showed that when the lacquer was removed, the instruments sounded much clearer. But if the silver plate was removed, it made little difference in the sound.

Now, I'll first play the lacquered horn, then I'll play the horn from which I've taken off the lacquer. Finally, I'll play the silver-plated one. (129)

See if you can hear the differences, especially between the lacquered and unlacquered ones. Then we'll go on to our regular practice session.

126 What is the main point of the talk?
　(A) How to benefit more from various practice techniques.
　(B) How silver-plating and lacquer can make an instrument heavier.
　(C) How to test whether instruments have been well-cared for.
　(D) How the tone quality of an instrument is affected by its surface.

127 What is the speaker comparing?
　(A) The differences among kinds of lacquer.
　(B) The differences in plating techniques.
　(C) Three horns with different finishes.
　(D) Three different types of musical instruments.

128 What have French Horn players complained about over the years?
　(A) The necessity of polishing unlacquered instruments.
　(B) The way the prices of instruments keep going up.
　(C) The difficulty of removing corrosion from their horns.
　(D) The way lacquered horns produce a weaker sound.

129 What is the speaker going to do at the end of his talk?
　(A) Remove lacquer from all the instruments.
　(B) Play each of the instruments he has described.
　(C) Show the listeners how to polish the horns.
　(D) Repeat the sounds until they are clearer.

130 What is the main reason for using lacquer on the instruments?
　(A) To polish them and make them look shiny.
　(B) To increase their sound quality.

（C）So one doesn't need to use silver plating.
（D）**To protect them from damage.**

> スクリプト和訳

　今日は、オーケストラ作品の練習を始める前に、異なる素材が楽器の音にどのように影響を与えるかを皆さんに見せたいと思います。私は最近、数人の人が金管楽器に行った実験について読みました。

　まず、真鍮にラッカーがしてあるフレンチホルンをお見せします。ラッカーが楽器をピカピカに保っているのが分かりますか？　次に、ここに私がラッカーを取り除いたホルンがあります。そして、これが3つ目のホルンですが、銀メッキのホルンです。銀はすぐに輝きを失うので頻繁に磨く必要があります。一方で、ラッカーはホルンを錆びることから守るので、ホルンを磨く必要がありません。

　これらの違いで何が重要かというと、長年、フレンチホルンの演奏者は、ラッカーによってホルンの音が鈍くなったり、小さくなったりすると感じ不平を言っていたことです。

　奏者は結局、正当な不平を言っているように思われます。3つのホルンの実験によって、ラッカーを取り除いた場合、楽器はずっとクリアな音になると分かりました。しかし、銀メッキを取り除いた場合、音にほとんど違いは生じませんでした。

　今から、最初にラッカーのホルン、次にラッカーを取り除いたホルンを演奏します。最後に、銀メッキのホルンを演奏します。

　さて皆さんは、特にラッカーをした楽器とラッカーを取り除いた楽器の違いが聞き分けられるでしょうか。

　それから、いつもの練習に移ります。

> 重要単語

- **orchestra piece**：オーケストラ用の作品
- **tarnish**：輝きを失う、変色する
- **brass instrument**：金管楽器
- **corrosion**：腐食、浸食
- **brass**：真鍮
- **deaden**：弱らせる、鈍らせる
- **lacquer**：ラッカー
- **legitimate**：合法な、正当な、筋の通った
- **silver-plated**：銀メッキの

解答 Questions 131 - 135

131 A 132 D 133 B 134 C 135 A

スクリプト／解答のポイント

Good afternoon class. Today I would like to continue our discussion of fish that are used for commercial purposes by talking about the carp. Originally found in Asia,(131) the carp was popular because it was easy to raise, cheap to feed, and a good source of food. By the 12th century the fish had been taken to Europe by missionaries, and was growing well in ponds in Germany and Poland. The European immigrants who came to North America in the 1870's were unhappy that there were no carp to eat or to sell and immediately began importing them.(132) The project was very effective, and in a short time carp were being distributed throughout the country. In fact, the project was too successful. The carp multiplied so quickly that the fish farmers could make no money selling them,(133)(135) and the fish spreading into the lakes and rivers began to eat the water plants(134) that native fish and other wildlife needed to survive. The government did everything possible to get rid of them, but the carp population did not disappear. Today the importation of carp is banned in 33 states. Of the carp under private control, thousands are kept in ponds as living decorations because of their beautiful colors. There are plans to use others to keep waterways free of unwanted plants, and also to sell them as food. But the problem of the carp remains.

131 **Where was the carp originally found?**
(A) Asia.
(B) Germany.
(C) Poland.
(D) The United States.

132 Why did the immigrants want to import carp?
(A) They would eat nothing else.
(B) They had no food.
(C) They wanted a reminder of home.
(D) They wanted to eat and to sell them.

133 What problem was encountered in raising carp in the United States?
(A) Most people didn't like to eat them.
(B) The number of carp increased too rapidly.
(C) There were too many import regulations.
(D) It was too expensive to feed them.

134 What do carp eat?
(A) Small wild animals.
(B) Other fish.
(C) Water plants.
(D) Pond decorations.

135 Why was the importing of carp to North America "too successful"?
(A) Farmers couldn't make any money for selling carp.
(B) They disappeared.
(C) There wasn't enough food for them.
(D) People wanted to eat water plants, native fish and wildlife.

> スクリプト和訳

皆様、こんにちは。本日も商業のために利用される魚について、引き続き議論をしたいと思っております。そこで、コイについてお話いたします。もともとアジアで発見されたもので、非常に人気が高いものでした。その理由は、育てるのが簡単で、エサにもお金がかからず、食糧源としてとても便利だったからです。12世紀までには、この魚は宣教師によってヨーロッパへと移植され、ドイツとポーランドの池ですくすくと成長していきました。1870年代北アメリカに移住したヨーロッパ人は、食糧にするための、また商売をするためのコイがアメリカにいないことを嘆き、さっそくコイを移入し始めます。この事業は

とても効力を発し、まもなくコイはこの国中に広められました。ですが実のところ、これはあまりにも成功し過ぎてしまったのです。コイの数がかなりの勢いで増加したため、養殖業を営む人々はコイを売ってお金を稼ぐことができなくなってしまい、また湖や川に広がったこの魚は、もともとそこに生息していた固有の魚やその他の野生生物に不可欠な水草を食べ始めてしまったのです。そこで、政府はできる限りのことをすべて行い駆除しようとしましたが、コイの数が減少することはありませんでした。今現在では、33の州で、コイを移入することは禁じられています。ですが、個人的な範囲で、数千ものコイがその美しい色により、生きる装飾品として池で飼育されています。また、その他のコイに関して、水路に生える余分な草を取り除くために利用する計画や、食糧として売る計画もあります。とはいうものの、コイに関する問題は未解決のままです。

重要単語

- **carp**：鯉
- **missionary**：宣教師、使節、伝道師
- **multiply**：数が増える、増殖する

解答 Questions 136 - 140

136 D　137 D　138 C　139 A　140 B

スクリプト／解答のポイント

Cotton fabric has been taken for granted for as long as anyone can remember. Cool and lightweight, cotton is one of the most easily-maintained natural fabrics, and therefore the most common. (136) It is almost certain that each of you today is wearing at least one article of clothing made completely or partially of cotton. Part of the reason for this is Eli Whitney, and his concern for the waste of time and energy he witnessed as a young man in 19th century America. The governments of several southern states offered prizes for anyone who could come up with a way to separate the cotton fibers from the seeds of the plant, and Whitney accepted the challenge.

The machine he invented, the cotton gin, allowed a single laborer to separate up to fifty pounds of cotton fibers from the troublesome seeds,(139) a vast improvement over the single pound a worker using only his hands had been able to do before.(137)(140) He did collect the prizes, but his dreams of wealth were never realized, since people simply copied his design themselves, paying nothing to Whitney for being the originator of the machine.(138)

136. What development greatly contributed to the popularity and affordability of cotton fabric?
(A) The discovery of cotton in North America.
(B) The development of a seedless variety.
(C) Improved agricultural methods.
(D) Improvement of the method of processing cotton.

137. How much more efficient was the new machine than hand labor?
(A) Twice.
(B) Ten times.
(C) Five times.
(D) Fifty times.

138. According to the speaker, how much credit did the inventor actually receive?
(A) Enough to make him extremely wealthy.
(B) Enough to help him establish an empire.
(C) Almost none at all.
(D) None at all.

139. What did Eli Whitney invent?
(A) A machine that separated cotton seeds and fibers.
(B) An apparatus that planted cotton efficiently.
(C) A device that harvested cotton efficiently.
(D) A chemical that dissolved cotton fibers.

140 **Why were the cotton seeds troublesome?**

(A) They required a great deal of water.
(B) **They were difficult to separate from the cotton plants.**
(C) They were easy to copy.
(D) They were cool and lightweight.

スクリプト和訳

　非常に長い間、綿織物はあって当たり前のものとして享受され続けています。涼しくて軽いので、綿は最も維持管理しやすい自然素材の布の一つに数えられ、その結果最もありふれています。今日出席なさっているあなた方が来ている服も、100パーセントかもしくは数パーセント、綿を素材としていることは、ほとんど確実です。その理由の一つに、イーライ・ホイットニー（Eli Whitney）の存在があります。19世紀のアメリカで若者であった彼が目にした時間と労力の無駄に対する関心がその理由なのです。幾つかの南部州の政府は、綿の繊維を苗木の種子から取り分ける方法を思いついた者には褒賞を与えるといい、ホイットニーはその挑戦を引き受けたのです。彼の発明した綿繰機という機械は、一人の労働者が、この厄介な種子から綿繊維を50ポンドも取り分けることを可能にしました。これは、これまで一人の労働者が手で取り分けることのできた1ポンドに比べ、非常に大きな進歩です。そして彼は褒賞を受けました。しかしながら、彼のお金持ちになりたいという夢が実現することは無かったのです。なぜならば、この機械の発明者としてのホイットニーに一切お金を支払うことなく、彼の発明した設計を他の人々が簡単に模倣してしまったからです。

重要単語

- **cotton fabric**：綿織物
- **natural fabric**：天然繊維
- **come up with ～**：～を思いつく
- **cotton fiber**：綿花、綿繊維
- **cotton gin**：綿繰り機、コットンジン

解答 Questions 141 - 145

141 A　142 C　143 D　144 C　145 D

> スクリプト／解答のポイント

　Scientists believe that when the oceans were young they contained only a trace of salt, and that the level of salinity(141) has been growing gradually. (142) Over the years rains have worn away the rocky mantle of the continents. Minerals released by this erosion have been carried to the sea by the flow of river water.(145) This water adds several billion tons of salt to the ocean annually.

　There are other sources of oceanic salinity, too. One source is underwater volcanic action.(143) These eruptions occur along the mid-ocean ridge and release great amounts of salt into the sea each year.

　However, these sources of salt don't increase the actual mineral composition of the water by much because of the enormous chemical requirements of marine life. Oysters, clams, snails and other mollusks use salt to build shells and skeletons.(144) Coral reefs also consume large amounts of salt.

　Also, some salt leaves the ocean through the process of evaporation. As salts escape into the atmosphere, they go into the creation of raindrops. This is why the coast receives more rain than landlocked areas. You see, more salt exists in the atmosphere near the ocean, thereby attracting increased moisture and producing rain.

|141| What is the topic of this talk?
　(A) **The salinity of the ocean.**
　(B) Pollutants found at sea.
　(C) The composition of coral reefs.
　(D) The weather patterns of coastal areas.

|142| What does the speaker say about the ocean's level of saltiness?
　(A) It is measured annually.
　(B) It is highest at the ocean's surface.
　(C) **It has increased over time.**
　(D) It has decreased over time.

143 What is one of the sources of oceanic salinity mentioned in the talk?
 (A) Seaweed found in kelp beds.
 (B) Industrial waste.
 (C) Meteorites.
 (D) Underwater volcanoes.

144 Why does the speaker mention oysters and clams?
 (A) They are more nutritious than freshwater shellfish.
 (B) They contribute to the salinity of the ocean.
 (C) They use salt to build their shells.
 (D) They inhabit coral reefs.

145 What does the speaker mention about the rocky mantle?
 (A) It contains traces of salt.
 (B) It produces evaporation and thus rain.
 (C) It erupts at the mid-ocean ridge.
 (D) Its erosion produces minerals such as salt.

> スクリプト和訳

　科学者達は、海が出来たばかりの頃は極微量の塩しか含んでおらず、塩分濃度は徐々に増していったと考えています。長年にわたって、雨が大陸の岩石のマントルをすり減らしました。この浸食によって出てきた鉱物が川の流れによって海に運ばれてきました。この水が年間数十億トンもの塩を海水に加えているのです。

　海水の塩分には別の源もあり、一つの源は、水面下の火山活動です。これらの噴火は、中央海嶺に沿って起こり、毎年大量の塩を海へ放出します。

　しかしながら、これらの塩の源は海水の実際のミネラル構成を余り増やしません。なぜなら、海洋生物が大量の化学物質を必要とするからです。二枚貝や巻き貝や他の軟体動物は、貝殻や骨格を作るために塩を使います。珊瑚礁もまた大量の塩を消費します。

　そして、塩の一部は蒸発の過程を通じて海から去って行きます。塩が大気中に逃れるにつれて、塩が雨滴を作り始めます。こういうわけで、海岸は、内陸地域よりもたくさん雨が降ります。お分かりでしょうが、海に近い大気中には

より多くの塩が含まれます。それによって、ますます多くの湿気を引き寄せ雨を作り出すのです。

重要単語

- **a trace of 〜**：微量の〜
- **oyster**：牡蠣、二枚貝
- **salinity**：塩度、塩分
- **clam**：ハマグリ、アサリ、二枚貝
- **wear away**：すり減らす、摩滅させる
- **snail**：巻き貝
- **rocky mantle**：岩石のマントル
- **mollusk**：軟体動物
- **erosion**：浸食
- **evaporation**：蒸発
- **erruption**：噴火
- **landlocked area**：内陸地域
- **mid-ocean ridge**：中央海嶺

解答 Questions 146 - 150

146 B　147 A　148 C　149 D　150 D

スクリプト／解答のポイント

Good morning class. Last time we started to talk about some crops and traditions of early agricultural based societies.(146) We had said that corn was the one food that dominated the food growing activities of those early American Indian tribes that relied on farming for food. The early farmers of the American Indians planted lots of varieties of corn, including the kind of corn that we eat today as popcorn.(147)

The corn was prepared in different ways. It could be eaten fresh from the field. Sometimes it was boiled. Sometimes the corn was roasted or parched. But most of the corn was dried on the cob, and later it was ground into flour. (148) The advantage of this method was that dried corn could be stored for long periods of time without spoiling.

The American Indians harvested the corn twice. The first harvest was the green corn, or sweet corn,(150) harvest. This harvest was accompanied by a ceremony of thanksgiving. The farmers thought that this celebration would protect the farmers from disaster.

The final harvesting of the ripe corn and the harvest ceremony took place about six weeks later. During this harvesting the farmers pulled back the husks of corn and braided them together. Big bundles were prepared this way and were dried for use later on throughout the winter.

After the corn was eaten, the farmers used the dried husks to make all sorts of different things, like mats, moccasins, dolls and ceremonial masks. (149)

146 What class might the speaker be teaching?
(A) Statistics.
(B) Cultural Anthoropology.
(C) Micro Economics.
(D) Meteorology.

147 What is the main subject of this talk?
(A) The history and traditions of early corn farmers.
(B) The growing cycle of Indian corn.
(C) Differences between the two corn harvests.
(D) Various ways to prepare corn.

148 According to the speaker, how was most of the corn prepared?
(A) It was first boiled and then dried.
(B) It was braided in bundles and steamed.
(C) It was dried and then ground into flour.
(D) It was roasted and wrapped in husks.

149 After the farmers ate the corn from the second corn harvest, what did they do with the husks?
(A) They braided them with animal hair for clothing.
(B) They bundled them together for fuel.
(C) They used them to insulate their homes.
(D) They made various items from them.

150 Which of the following correctly describes the Indians' corn harvests?
(A) First harvest: Yellow corn;　　Second harvest: Five months later.
(B) First harvest: Green corn;　　Second harvest: Yellow corn.
(C) First harvest: Ripe corn;　　Second harvest: Thanksgiving corn.
(D) First harvest: Sweet corn;　　Second harvest: Six months later.

> スクリプト和訳

　みなさん、おはようございます。私たちは前の授業から、農業に基盤を置く初期の社会にあった収穫物とそれに関する伝統についての議論を始めました。そこで話したことは、トウモロコシが農業に依存する初期アメリカのインディアンの部族が行っていた食糧生産の中心にあった食物の一つであったということでしたね。アメリカ・インディアンの最初の農民は、今でも我々が食べているポップコーンとしてのトウモロコシを含む、多くの種類のトウモロコシを植えました。

　しかしトウモロコシの下準備には、異なる様々な方法がありました。畑から収穫して、そのまま生で食べることのできたものもありました。ときには、茹でることもありました。また火で炙ったり、日光で乾燥させたりする場合もあったのです。ですが、ほとんどのトウモロコシの場合は穂軸のまま乾燥させ、その後ひいて粉末状にしました。この方法の長所は、乾燥したトウモロコシは長い間腐ることなく保管することができる点です。

　アメリカ・インディアンはトウモロコシを2度収穫しました。1回目の収穫はグリーンコーンまたはスイートコーンでした。この収穫は感謝祭の儀式を伴うものでした。農民たちはこのお祝いが自分たちを災害から守ってくれると考えました。

　6週間後、最後の熟したトウモロコシの収穫と収穫の儀式が行われました。この収穫の時に農民たちはトウモロコシの皮を引きはがし、それらを束ねました。大きな束はこのように準備され、そして後の冬を通して利用する為に乾かされました。

　トウモロコシが食べられた後、農民たちは乾いた皮をあらゆる異なる種類の物を作る為に使いました。例えばマット、靴、人形、そして儀式用のお面などです。

重要単語

- **roast**：焼く、炙る
- **husk**：トウモロコシの皮
- **parch**：炒る、炙る
- **braid**：編む、束ねる
- **cob**：トウモロコシの穂軸
- **moccsin**：靴、室内履き
- **green corn**：未熟な柔らかいトウモロコシ

解答 Questions 151 - 156

151 D　152 A　153 C　154 D　155 D　156 A

スクリプト／解答のポイント

Good morning. This is Art 102A for undergraduate students only.(151) Please check your class cards to make sure you are in the right section. Although this class is called Color and Design,(152) we will be working only with black and white the first semester.(153)　In other words, we will begin by learning basic design principles and become acquainted with materials and techniques before getting involved in the complexities of color. During the first part of each class period, I will be showing slides relevant to your current assignments.(156)　We will also spend part of each period on a critique of your work. In other words, you will hang up your designs and we will discuss their good and bad points.(154)　Any remaining time will be used for questions and answers and for work on current projects. You will have one project due each week. The first project, due Wednesday, will be a design 8 1/2 by 11 inches using only black rectangles on a white background.(155) The rectangles may be any size, and you may use as many as you wish. See you next week.

151 Who is the speaker addressing?

(A) Engineers.
(B) Photographers.
(C) Fashion designers.
(D) College students.

152 What is the class called?
  (A) **Color and Design.**
  (B) Black and White.
  (C) Materials and Techniques.
  (D) First Design Principles.

153 What will the class work on during the first semester?
  (A) The blending of colors.
  (B) The checking of color cards.
  (C) **Black and white design.**
  (D) Basic slidemaking.

154 What is a critique?
  (A) A shape.
  (B) A design technique.
  (C) A way to hang pictures.
  (D) **A discussion of a person's work.**

155 What should the first design be composed of?
  (A) Colored circles.
  (B) White squares.
  (C) Eleven triangles.
  (D) **Black rectangles.**

156 What will happen at the beginning of each class?
  (A) **The teacher will show slides related to current projects.**
  (B) The students will only work with black and white.
  (C) They will spend time critiquing their work.
  (D) Discussion of good/bad points, Q & A, and current work.

スクリプト和訳

おはようございます。このクラスは美術102A、学部生のみを対象とした授業です。正しいクラスにいるか、時間割表で確認してください。この授業は色彩

と設計という名前が付いていますが、第一学期では白と黒だけを取り扱いたいと思います。要するに、まず始めは設計原理の基礎を学び、色の複雑な側面に取り掛かる前に、素材と技術に慣れるのです。それぞれの授業の最初の部分では、君たちが取り掛かっている課題に関係するスライドをお見せしようと考えております。また、君たちの作品について批評をする時間も、それぞれの時間に持ちたいと思います。つまり、自分の設計を披露し、その良い点、悪い点を話し合うのです。そして、残りの時間は質疑応答やそのときに行っている課題に取り組む時間です。それぞれの週に締め切りの課題を一つ出します。最初は、水曜が締め切りのもので、白を背景に黒の長方形だけを使う8.5×11インチの設計です。長方形はどんな大きさでも構いません。また、好きなだけ使ってください。それでは、また来週お会いしましょう。

重要単語

- **undergraduate student**：学部生、大学生
- **semester**：学期（半年ごとの前期・後期のこと。年4回ごとの学期は quarter）
- **become acquainted with ～**：（人と）親しくなる、（物に）精通する
- **get involved in ～**：～に関与する、巻き込まれる
- **relevant to ～**：～と関連がある
- **assignment**：宿題、課題
- **due Wednesday**：水曜日が締め切りの
- **rectangle**：長方形

解答 Questions 157 - 161

157 C 158 A 159 D 160 A 161 C

スクリプト／解答のポイント

People who grow vegetables in urban areas must be aware of an invisible enemy in the soil. Lead. The lead comes from exhaust fumes of automobiles and chips of lead based paint.(157) This lead can be absorbed by plants, and then by people when they eat the plants. The lead is hazardous to the neurological system, particularly in children under six years of age. The risk is reduced if the garden site is located away from roads.(158) It's important to have the soil tested regularly to determine the lead concentration. (161) One way to keep the lead in the soil and out of the vegetables is to add lime and organic material rich in bacteria to the soil. (159) Lead buildup is greater in leafy green vegetables such as lettuce and spinach. (160) So vegetables that bear fruit, such as tomatoes, squash and cucumbers should be planted instead. Of course all produce should be washed carefully before consumption.

157. What is the speaker's main point about urban vegetable gardens?
(A) They rarely produce enough crops to be worth the trouble.
(B) They are so contaminated with lead that they shouldn't be used.
(C) **The lead concentration in them can be reduced by taking precautions.**
(D) The produce grown in them must be washed before being eaten.

158. According to the speaker why should urban gardens be located away from roads?
(A) **To decrease exposure to exhaust fumes.**
(B) To lower contamination from roadside salt.
(C) To improve plants' ability to form fruit.
(D) To limit the amount of bacteria in the soil.

159. What is the effect of adding lime and organic material to the soil?
(A) The amount of lead in the soil can then be measured.
(B) Bacteria in the soil are destroyed.
(C) The fruit of the plants is protected.
(D) **Less lead is absorbed by plants.**

160. According to the speaker, which vegetable probably contains the most lead?
(A) **Lettuce.**
(B) Tomatoes.
(C) Cucumbers.
(D) Squash.

161 What may be the best way to determine lead concentration?

(A) Expand proximity to exhaust fumes and paint chips.
(B) Test children under six years-old regularly.
(C) The soil should be tested regularly.
(D) Test the plants regularly.

> スクリプト和訳

　都市部で野菜を栽培している人は、土に存在するある目に見えない敵の存在に、注意しなくてはなりません。それは鉛です。鉛は車の排気ガスや、鉛をベースにした塗料の剥がれた欠片から発生します。そして、この鉛を植物が吸収し、その後この植物を食べることで、人が摂取してしまう可能性があるのです。鉛は神経系に悪影響を与え、とりわけ6歳以下の子供には危険です。このリスクは、もし道路から庭が離れていれば軽減されます。定期的に鉛の濃度を測定することが重要です。土に鉛を封じ込め、植物に吸収されないようにする一つの方法が、石灰とバクテリアがたくさん生息する有機物を土に撒くことです。鉛の蓄積がより大きくなるのは、レタスやホウレン草のような緑色の葉物野菜です。なので、実をつける野菜、例えばトマト、カボチャ、そしてキュウリのような野菜を代わりに植えるとよいでしょう。もちろんどんな収穫物も、摂取する前には丁寧に洗うべきです。

> 重要単語

- **lead**：鉛
- **lead buildup**：鉛の蓄積
- **exhaust fume**：排ガス
- **spinach**：ホウレンソウ
- **chips of lead based paint**：鉛が入っているペンキの破片
- **hazardous**：有害な、危険な
- **squash**：カボチャ
- **neurological system**：神経系統
- **cucumber**：キュウリ
- **lead concentration**：鉛濃度
- **produce**：農産物、野菜や果物
- **lime**：石灰
- **organic material rich in bacteria**：バクテリアが豊富な有機物質

解答 Questions 162 - 165

162 A   163 B   164 D   165 B

スクリプト／解答のポイント

Today we will begin a unit on my favorite period of American history, the Civil War. (162) Let me warn you now, I wrote my doctoral dissertation on this topic, so we might end up spending more time than usual on it. (165) In the past, when you've studied the Civil War, you've probably learned about the various battles and generals. While they may be important, as far as I'm concerned, such material is not as historically relevant as the political, economic, and social factors that led to the outbreak of this war. (163) In order to explore these factors in some depth, we will supplement the textbook with readings in historical journals. These journals contain essays by several noted historians who wrote about the causes of the Civil War. I've put these journals on two-hour reserve in the library. We'll begin our study by reading the first essay listed in the syllabus. Be prepared to discuss this essay in class next Monday. (164)

162 When did the class start studying the Civil War?
(A) Today.
(B) Last Monday.
(C) Three weeks ago.
(D) At the start of the semester.

163 What feature of the Civil War will probably be emphasized in this unit?
(A) Its battles.
(B) Its causes.
(C) Its conclusion.
(D) Its journalists.

164 **What will the class do on Monday?**
   (A) Answer questions in the textbook.
   (B) Review an important battle.
   (C) Write an essay about the Civil War.
   (D) Discuss an article from a historical journal.

165 **Why might the class spend a lot of time discussing the Civil War?**
   (A) It's one of the most important events in US history.
   (B) The professor wrote her thesis paper on the Civil War.
   (C) There are so many important generals and battles.
   (D) There are so many essays and journals on two-hour reserve in the library.

スクリプト和訳

　本日から取り掛かる単元は、アメリカ史の中でも、私の得意な時代である南北戦争です。今君たちに警告をしておきますね。私はこのトピックに関する博士論文を書きました。だから、いつもよりも多くの時間をこの単元に割くことになるでしょう。以前に南北戦争について勉強をしたとき、みなさんはたぶん様々な戦いや多くの将軍について学んだことでしょう。確かにこのことは重要ですが、私の知る限り、これらのものには政治的、経済的、そして社会的な要因としてこの戦争の引き金になったものほどの歴史的重要性はないのです。幾分掘り下げてこれらの要因について考察するために、教科書の補足として歴史学の定期刊行物を読みます。これらの定期刊行物には、南北戦争の原因について書いた数人の著名な歴史家の論文が載っています。これらの定期刊行物を、2時間貸出できるリザーブ図書として、図書館に入れておきました。授業は、シラバスに書いてある最初の論文を読むことで始めたいと思います。次の月曜日の授業にこの論文について議論するために、予習をしておいてください。

重要単語

- **unit**：単元
- **general**：将軍、軍司令官
- **doctoral dissertation**：博士論文
- **relevant**：関連のある、重要な
- **end up 〜**：〜することになる
- **outbreak**：勃発
- **in the past**：これまでに、過去において

- **tow-hour reserve**：２時間の制限
- **syllabus**：講義要項、教授細目（開講されるコースで行われる授業の概要が記されたもの。最初の授業で配布され、授業内容・日程、試験方法・日程、教科書、宿題、実験、実習、成績の付け方などが書かれている）

解答 Questions 166 - 170

166 C　167 D　168 A　169 B　170 A

スクリプト／解答のポイント

　Do you really want to go back to college and get a degree but think you are too old? Well, you're never too old. In fact, older students are often welcomed.(166) They have a recognized record of success (167) and they are often more motivated and better disciplined than many young students. Why not try a single non-credit course (168) to whet your appetite and help you define your goals? (170) Call your local college (169) or university for further information. Remember you're never too old.

166 To whom is this announcement directed?
- (A) Young students.
- (B) College professors.
- **(C) Adults who want to finish college.**
- (D) Technicians who are training for jobs.

167 Why are older students welcomed?
- (A) They discuss their problems openly.
- (B) They talk more in class.
- (C) They discipline others.
- **(D) They are very reliable.**

168 What are returning students advised to do first?

(A) **Try one course.**
(B) Consult a counselor.
(C) Define a full program.
(D) Decide on a professional goal.

169 How does the announcer suggest that one get further information?

(A) By returning to college and asking.
(B) **By calling a nearby college.**
(C) By talking to another student.
(D) By checking a college catalog.

170 Why does the announcement suggest trying a single, non-credit course first?

(A) **To get motivated to take classes again and a better idea of career plan.**
(B) The cost can be a bit expensive for some students.
(C) The homework workload may be a bit too difficult for some students.
(D) It may be difficult to fit with older students' work schedule.

スクリプト和訳

本当は大学に戻って学位を取りたいけれど、年を取りすぎていると思っていませんか？ 年を取りすぎているなんてことは決してありません。実際、年齢の高い学生は歓迎されることがよくあります。彼らは優れた実績を認められていますし、しばしば若い学生よりやる気があり、規律が行き届いています。自分の意欲を刺激し目標を見極めるのに役立てるため、単位の付かないコースをひとつ試してみてはいかがでしょう？ 詳しい情報が欲しい方は、地元の短大や大学にお電話下さい。忘れないでください、年を取りすぎているということはありませんよ。

重要単語

● **degree**：学位
● **motivated**：やる気のある

- disciplined：規律のある、しつけの良い
- whet your appetite：興味を深める、意欲をそそる

解答 Questions 171 - 175

171 C　172 A　173 D　174 B　175 C

スクリプト／解答のポイント

　Good afternoon students. My name is Jane Murphy and I am a representative of the Travel-Ease Company.(171)　Your school has selected our company to make the arrangements for the upcoming student summer trip.(172)　Each of you will be signing up individually,(175) but there are several points you all need to be familiar with. I've already passed out yellow papers with a list of important information. Please follow along with me as I go over each point.(173)　As you can see, the list is rather long, so I'd appreciate it if you'd wait until we've completely covered the information sheet before asking any questions. Some of your questions might be answered as we go along. After we've finished reading over the paper, please don't hesitate to raise your hand if you have any concerns.(174)

171　Who is the speaker?
　(A) A school administrator.
　(B) A member of the student government.
　(C) A company representative.
　(D) A graduate student.

172　Why are the students at the meeting?
　(A) They plan to take a trip.
　(B) They are interested in summer jobs.
　(C) They want to become travel agents.
　(D) They have to write papers about the class trip.

173 What does the speaker ask the students to do?
(A) Return the yellow sheet to her.
(B) Write questions on their papers as she speaks.
(C) Make a list of the items she covers.
(D) Read along as she reviews the sheet.

174 How should the students indicate that they want to ask a question?
(A) By writing on a piece of paper.
(B) By raising their hands.
(C) By interrupting the speaker.
(D) By following the speaker when she leaves.

175 How are the students expected to sign up?
(A) By asking questions.
(B) By contacting Jane Murphy at Travel-Ease.
(C) Individually.
(D) By checking the information sheet.

スクリプト和訳

こんにちは。私はジェーン・マーフィーと申しまして、トラベルイーズカンパニーの販売代理人です。来るべき夏の学生旅行の手配をするため、あなた方の学校に我が社を選んでいただきました。皆さんには個別に申し込んでもらいますが、全員に知っておいていただく必要のあることがいくつかあります。既にお配りした黄色の書類に重要な情報のリストがついています。一つ一つチェックしていきますので、話についてきていただければと思います。ご覧のとおりリストはかなり長いですので、我々の情報の説明が一通り終わるまで待ってから質問していただけますと幸いです。進んでいくうちに、幾つかの疑問には答えているかもしれません。書類を読み終えた後で、気になる点がある場合は遠慮なく手を挙げてくださいね。

重要単語

- **sign up**：登録する、参加する、署名する
- **pass out**：配る、配布する

- **follow along**：後について行く、話についていく、理解する
- **go over**：チェックする、点検する
- **concern**：心配、懸念、関心

解答 Questions 176 - 180

176 D 177 B 178 C 179 A 180 B

スクリプト／解答のポイント

　I'm sure you realize that your research papers for this freshman English course(176) are due in six weeks. I have looked at the index cards you handed in with your proposed topics and have made appropriate comments. The most frequent error was proposing a topic too broad to be handled well (180) in the space of a 15-page paper. Here is what we will do during the next two weeks. Today is Monday, by Friday I want your preliminary outline. Please incorporate the suggestions I made on topics in your outline. Next week I will have a conference with each of you.(177)　I have posted a schedule on my office door. Please sign your name to indicate the time you are available for an appointment. In the conference, we will discuss your preliminary outline.(178)　You will then make the necessary revisions and hand in your final outline. The final outline is due two weeks from today on Monday the 15th. Use the model of outline style in your textbook. Your preliminary outline should be no more than two pages long. Begin your outline with a thesis statement.(179)　Do you remember what a thesis statement is? It's a precise statement of the point you intend to prove. Be sure to include both an introduction and a conclusion in your outline. To sum up, your 2-page outlines are due at the end of this week. Follow the textbook style and include a thesis statement, an introduction, and a conclusion.

176 **What is the main topic of the speaker's talk?**

- (A) Conferences.
- (B) Index cards.
- (C) Examinations.
- (D) **Research papers.**

177 When will conferences be held?
- (A) Immediately.
- (B) **The following week.**
- (C) In two weeks.
- (D) At the end of the semester.

178 What is the purpose of the conference?
- (A) To narrow down the research topic.
- (B) To give a model of outline style.
- (C) **To discuss the preliminary outline.**
- (D) To prepare a thesis statement.

179 What term does the speaker define?
- (A) **Thesis statement.**
- (B) Research paper.
- (C) Final outline.
- (D) Conclusion.

180 What was the most frequent error by students in proposing their topics?
- (A) They chose irrelevant topics.
- (B) **They chose too broad a topic.**
- (C) They only submitted a preliminary outline.
- (D) They didn't include a clear thesis statement.

スクリプト和訳

きっと皆さんお気づきだと思いますが、この１年生の英語コースの研究論文は６週間後に提出期限が来ます。皆さんが、提出したインデックスカードと提

案した主題に目を通して、適切なコメントをしておきました。最もよくある間違いは、範囲が広すぎて15ページの論文で上手く扱えない主題を提案していることです。以下が次の2週間で行う作業です。今日は月曜日ですから、金曜日までに予備の概略を提出すること。主題に関して私が示唆したことを概略に組み入れてください。来週、皆さん一人一人と相談をします。私のオフィスのドアにスケジュールを貼っておきました。都合の良い時間に名前を書き込んでください。相談では、予備の概略について議論します。それから必要な修正を行って、最終の概略を提出してください。概略の最終版は、今日から2週間後の15日月曜日が締め切りです。教科書にある概略のスタイルの見本を使うように。予備の概略は2ページ以内におさえてください。概略は主題文から始めましょう。主題文とは何か覚えていますか？ 証明しようとする点を簡潔に述べたものです。概略には必ず、序文と結論の両方を入れて下さい。要約すると、2ページの概略は今週末が締め切りです。教科書のスタイルに沿って、主題文、序文、結論を入れて下さい。

重要単語

- **research paper**：研究報告、研究論文
- **introduction**：序文
- **preliminary outline**：予備の概略
- **incorporate**：組み込む、盛り込む
- **have a conference with ~**：~と協議する、相談する
- **revision**：構成、修正
- **thesis statement**：主題文

解答 Questions 181 - 185

181 A　182 D　183 B　184 C　185 B

スクリプト／解答のポイント

I would like to give you a very brief outline of how educational philosophy in the United States has changed over the past two centuries. (181) First, in the colonial era, the main goal of education was to train people for religious and moral purposes and to promote good behavior. (182) Later on, reformers such as Horace Mann called for public education for all and professional training for teachers. (183) As opposed to educators of the colonial period, later educators wanted this public education to be free from religion.

Later in the 19th century John Dewey began teaching his theory of "Learning by Doing." Even more importantly he stressed that school was not just a period of preparing for life but was a period of life itself. (185) Lastly, in this century the shift of population from the countryside to the cities has made schools more concerned with social problems. (184) As you can see trends in educational philosophy have changed a great deal in 200 years.

181 What is the main subject of the lecture?
(A) The history of educational philosophy in the United States.
(B) How education in the United States has improved.
(C) Education in the United States before 1900.
(D) Different types of schools in the United States.

182 What was the role of education in the colonial period?
(A) To train philosophers.
(B) To help fight against England.
(C) To educate all students.
(D) To improve moral behavior.

183 What is Horace Mann known for?
(A) He was the first trained teacher.
(B) He wanted education for all.
(C) He wanted to use non-professional teachers.
(D) He was in favor of private schools.

184 What has characterized education in the United States in this century?
(A) It has been anti-religious.

(B) It has changed many times.
(C) **It has been socially oriented.**
(D) It has been concerned with rural problems.

185 **What is John Dewey known for?**
(A) Education without religion.
(B) **His belief of the importance of school in our lives.**
(C) His concern for social problems.
(D) He wanted education for all.

> スクリプト和訳

　合衆国の教育観が過去200年間でどのように変化したかについて簡潔な概要を述べたいと思います。まず植民地時代には、教育の主要な目的は人々を宗教的、道徳的目的のために訓練すること、良い行いの普及を促進することでした。後になって、ホレイス・マンのような改革者は、全ての人々と教師の職業訓練のための公共教育を求めました。植民地時代の教育者とは対照的に、後の教育者は公共教育を宗教と切り離したいと思っていたのです。
　19世紀になってジョン・デューイは実地訓練という理論を教え始めました。さらに重要なことに、彼は学校を人生の準備をするための期間ではなく、人生そのものであると強調しました。最後に、今世紀になって田舎から都市へ人口が推移したため、学校は社会問題により関心を持つようになりました。お分かりのように、教育観の傾向は200年間で大きく変わったのです。

> 重要単語

- **educational philosophy**：教育観、教育哲学
- **as opposed to ～**：～とは対照的に
- **learning by doing**：実地訓練

> 解答 Questions 186 - 190

186 B　187 A　188 B　189 B　190 D

> スクリプト／解答のポイント

Good morning, class. Instead of my scheduled geology lecture,(186) I wanted to share with you an interesting article I read last night.(187) Scientists made a discovery deep on the ocean floor that greatly increases our knowledge of the sea. What scientists have found is a dynamic system that recycles all the water in the world's oceans.(190) Sea water flows constantly through an underground pressure cooker system that helps maintain the sea's chemical balance. This system is responsible for laying down many of the world's richest mineral deposits and tightly controls the amount of salt in the water. The water is believed to be recycled in this manner every 8 million years. Even though this may seem like a slow process, in the earth's lifetime of about four billion years, it is fast enough to have already recycled the sea water 500 times.

In conclusion, I would urge you to read this article yourselves(189) because it may be the most important discovery of the decade. It will provide us with a new understanding of the oceans, their chemistry, and history.(188) I will hand out copies of the article at the end of the class.

186 Who is the speaker?
(A) A history teacher.
(B) A geology professor.
(C) An explorer.
(D) An astronomer.

187 Why did the speaker change his scheduled lecture?
(A) To report on an article about oceans he had read.
(B) To give a new assignment about mineral deposits.
(C) To discuss pressure cookers.
(D) To review the numerous formulas for salt.

188 What information is provided by this discovery?
(A) The location of large salt deposits.

(B) **A new understanding of the chemistry and history of oceans.**
(C) A new system of manufacturing pressure cookers.
(D) The latest theory about the age of the earth.

189. What does the speaker want his listeners to do?
(A) To attend his next lecture.
(B) **To read the article themselves.**
(C) To take a chemistry course.
(D) To copy the article.

190. Which of the following best describes this new discovery?
(A) A dynamic new system of recycling earth's plant life.
(B) A new understanding of the way the earth is changing.
(C) A different perspective on the history of chemistry.
(D) **A manner in which balance is maintained in our seas.**

スクリプト和訳

みなさん、おはようございます。予定通りの地学の講義をする代わりに、私が昨晩読んだ面白い記事についてお話をしたいと思います。科学者達は深い海の底で海に関する我々の知識を大いに増やしてくれる発見をしました。科学者が発見したものは、世界中の海洋のすべての水を再循環させる動力システムです。海水は、海の化学物質のバランスを維持するのに役立つ地下の圧力釜のようなシステムを通って、絶えず流れています。このシステムが、世界の最も豊富なミネラル堆積物の多くを沈殿させる原因であり、海水中の塩の量をきっちりとコントロールしています。海水はこのようにして800万年ごとに再循環していると信じられています。遅いプロセスのように思うかもしれませんが、約40億年という地球の存続期間において、十分に早く、すでに海水を500回再循環しているのです。

結論として、この記事を自分で読むことをお勧めします。なぜならそれはこの10年で最も重要な発見かもしれないからです。その記事は海について、その化学成分、その歴史に関する新しい理解を与えてくれるでしょう。授業の終わりに、記事のコピーを配ります。

重要単語

- **recycle**：再循環する
- **deposit**：沈殿物、堆積物

解答 Questions 191 - 195

191 D　192 D　193 C　194 C　195 A

スクリプト／解答のポイント

You are about to finish four years of study at college. (191) At last it's time to start looking for a teaching position. If you're like most seniors, your training didn't include a course on finding a job. (193) We're always surprised at the casual way many beginning teachers treat job hunting. After four years of constant writing, reading, and preparing projects and papers, some students seem to think that filling out a form for the placement office and getting a few recommendations will get them a job. It just doesn't happen that way anymore. (192) On the other hand, it's not as hard to find a teaching job as many newspaper articles would have you think. You may be discouraged by hearing (194) that five hundred teachers applied for four openings, or by reading that only 1/3 of last year's graduates found jobs. (195) That may be true for a particular college, but conditions constantly change.

191 To whom is this report directed?

　(A) Newspaper writers.
　(B) Retiring teachers.
　(C) Third-year graduate students.
　(D) Graduating seniors.

192 How is job hunting different today?

　(A) Recommendations aren't necessary.
　(B) Filling out forms is usually adequate.
　(C) Placement offices locate most jobs for you.

(D) A few recommendations won't get you a job.

193. What kind of course would be helpful to college students?
 (A) A letter-writing course.
 (B) A reading course.
 (C) **A course on job hunting.**
 (D) A course on newspapers.

194. How can newspaper reports about job hunting be best described?
 (A) Optimistic.
 (B) Impractical.
 (C) **Discouraging.**
 (D) Helpful.

195. What statistics does the professor give to demonstrate the difficulty in finding a job?
 (A) **500 teachers applied for 4 openings and only 1/3 of new graduates found jobs.**
 (B) 5,000 teachers applied for 400 openings and only 1 in 3 new graduates found jobs.
 (C) 500 teachers applied for 400 openings and only 103 new graduates found jobs.
 (D) 5,000 teachers applied for 40 openings and only 1 in 3 new graduates found jobs.

スクリプト和訳

君たちは大学における4年間の勉強を終えようとしています。ついに、教師の職を探すときが来ました。もし君らがほとんどの4年生と同じならば、みなさんの教育にも仕事を探すコースは含まれていないでしょう。ですが、私たちは、多くの教師の卵が就職活動に気軽な様子を見ていつも驚いております。作文、読解、そして課題やレポートの準備を4年間ずっとこなした後、就職課への申込用紙を書きいくつかの推薦状をもらえば仕事が与えられるだろうと考えている学生がいるのです。こうしたことは今や全くあり得ません。とはいうも

のの、多くの新聞記事から君たちが考えさせられるほど、教師の職を見つけるのは難しくありません。おそらく、500人もの教師がたったの4人の空きを巡って応募したと聞いたり、または去年の卒業生の3分の1だけが仕事にありつけたと読んだりして、がっかりしてしまった人もいるでしょう。このことは、ある特定の大学には当てはまることでしょうが、状況はいつも変化しているのです。

重要単語
- **teaching position**：教職
- **job hunting**：就職活動
- **placement office**：学生就職指導部

解答 Questions 196 - 199

196 D　197 A　198 C　199 C

スクリプト／解答のポイント

　Millions of times a day bits of matter fall from space and enter the earth's atmosphere. Traveling at speeds of seven to nineteen miles per second these pieces of matter are heated up by friction as they pass through the air surrounding the earth. The friction produces heat and light, light that is clearly visible in the night sky. Non-scientists call these streaks of light shooting stars, but astronomers recognize them as meteors. <u>The smallest meteors, the vast majority, melt completely before they reach the earth's surface.</u>(196)　However, a meteor that weighs a gram or more when it enters the atmosphere will probably not burn away entirely and will eventually reach the ground. We call such a meteor a meteorite. Most meteorites are so small that they are nothing more than cosmic dust. However, some weigh as much as several tons. For instance, about twenty thousand years ago, in what is now the state of Arizona, <u>a meteor weighing about one hundred thousand tons landed,</u>(197) and the impact when it hit the earth left a crater one mile wide and six hundred feet deep. Because meteorites were formed during the early life of our solar system, they offer valuable information about the history of the earth.(198)(199)

196 What happens to most meteors?
(A) They are collected by scientists.
(B) They are buried in craters.
(C) They leave the Earth's atmosphere.
(D) They burn up in the air.

197 Why does the speaker mention Arizona?
(A) A very large meteorite struck there.
(B) An important observatory is located there.
(C) Its desert is a good source of cosmic dust.
(D) An unusual number of meteorites land there.

198 What will the speaker probably discuss next?
(A) The effects of friction on satellites.
(B) The inner solar system.
(C) What meteorites reveal about the history of the Earth.
(D) Famous meteorites in recorded history.

199 Why is studying meteorites so important to scientists?
(A) They can learn how to destroy dangerous meteorites.
(B) They can learn more about the Arizona meteorite.
(C) Meteors could contain important evidence about our planet.
(D) They can learn more about shooting stars.

スクリプト和訳

　一日に何百万回も、物質のかけらが宇宙から降ってきて、地球の大気圏に突入します。秒速７マイルから19マイルで進みながら、これらの欠片は地球を取り巻く大気を通り抜けるとき、摩擦によって熱せられます。その摩擦が熱と光を作り、夜空にはっきりと見える光を生み出します。科学者でない人は、その光の筋を流れ星と呼びますが、天文学者はそれらを流星体として認識していま

す。最小単位の流星体は、大多数がそうですが、地表に着く前に完全に溶けてしまいます。しかしながら、大気圏に突入したとき１グラム以上の重さを持つ流星体は、おそらく完全には焼失せずに、ついには地表にたどり着きます。そのような流星体を隕石と呼びます。ほとんどの隕石は非常に小さい宇宙塵に過ぎないものです。しかし、中には、数トンの重さを持つ隕石もあります。例えば、約２万年前、現在のアリゾナ州で約10万トンの重さの隕石が衝突し、地表にぶつかったときの衝撃で、幅１マイル、深さ600フィートのクレーターが出来ました。隕石は、太陽系が出来て間もなく形成されたので、地球の歴史について貴重な情報を与えてくれます。

重要単語

- **friction**：摩擦
- **streak**：筋、線
- **shooting star**：流星、流れ星
- **meteor**：流星体、隕石、流星
- **meteorite**：隕石
- **nothing more than ～**：～以外の何ものでもない、～に過ぎない
- **cosmic dust**：宇宙塵
- **what is now ～**：現在の～

解答 Questions 200 - 205

200 A　201 C　202 A　203 A　204 C　205 B

スクリプト／解答のポイント

Today I'd like to discuss the first sea battle involving iron-plated battleships, or "ironclads." As you know, this battle occurred in the American Civil War.(200)　Both sides, the North and the South, had one such ship. The North constructed its ironclad, the Monitor, in 1861. Hearing the news, the South set about building an ironclad of its own. The engineers of the South used a wooden frigate that had been badly damaged in the war(201) and repaired it by coating it with two inches of metal plating. The ship was rechristened as the Virginia, but was still widely known by its former name, the Merrimack.(202)

　The battle, which took place in March 1862, was indecisive. Both crews lacked training and their shooting was not effective. (205) The Merrimack was much larger (203) and had more guns, but it was heavy and slow. The Monitor was much faster, but was unable to inflict any serious damage to its larger opponent. Finally, it sailed away from the Merrimack, thus ending the battle. In spite of the failure of each boat to destroy its opponent — or perhaps because of it — the battle proved that the era of wooden fighting ships was near an end. (204)

200. When did the first battle of ironclads take place?
    (A) **During the Civil War.**
    (B) In colonial times.
    (C) In the early twentieth century.
    (D) In the 1960s.

201. What did the South use to construct its ironclad?
    (A) The Monitor.
    (B) Metal from many guns.
    (C) **A damaged wooden ship.**
    (D) Pieces of various ships.

202. What was the original name of the ship that the South used for its ironclad?
    (A) **The Merrimack.**
    (B) The Virginia.
    (C) The Monitor.
    (D) The Ironclad.

203. What advantage did the Merrimack enjoy in the battle?
    (A) **Its size.**
    (B) Its speed.
    (C) Its trained crew.
    (D) Its metal plating.

204 According to the speaker, what was proved by the battle?
 (A) Southern engineering was superior.
 (B) Ironclad ships were impractical.
 (C) Wooden ships were out of date.
 (D) Speed is more important than size.

205 Why was the battle indecisive?
 (A) The North's Merrimack ship was slow; the South's Monitor ship was small.
 (B) Both sides needed more preparation, and their ships had weaknesses.
 (C) Wooden ships were out of date.
 (D) Speed is more important than size.

|スクリプト和訳|

　今日は、鉄で被われた戦艦、つまり装甲艦が使われた最初の海戦について論じたいと思います。ご存知のように、この戦いは南北戦争で起こりました。北軍南軍の両方がその装甲艦を一隻持っていました。北軍は、装甲艦モニター号を1861年に造りました。その知らせを聞いて、南軍は独自の装甲艦を造り始めました。南軍の技師は戦争でひどく傷んでいた木製のフリゲート艦を使いました。それを2インチの金属板でコーティングして修理したのです。その船は、ヴァージニア号と再び名付けられましたが、以前の名前メリマク号で当時広く知られていました。

　戦いは1862年3月に起こったのですが、決着がつきませんでした。両方の乗組員とも訓練をしておらず、砲撃も効果的ではありませんでした。メリマク号の方がずっと大型で、大砲もたくさん持っていたのですが、重くて動きが遅かったのです。モニター号の方は、ずっと速かったのですが、そのより大きな敵に重大な損傷を与えられませんでした。とうとうモニター号はメリマク号から逃げてしまい、そうして戦いは終わりました。どちらも敵を倒せなかったにもかかわらず、むしろおそらくはそのために、その戦いは木造戦艦の時代が終わりに近づいたことを証明したのです。

重要単語

- **Iron-plated battleship**：鉄で被われた戦艦
- **ironclad**：装甲艦
- **frigate**：フリゲート艦
- **plating**：メッキ
- **rechristen**：再命名する
- **inflict damage to ～**：～に損害を与える

解答 Questions 206 - 210

206 C 207 A 208 D 209 B 210 B, C

スクリプト／解答のポイント

　Today I would like to talk about the early days of movie making in the late nineteenth and early twentieth centuries. Before the pioneering films of D. W. Griffith, filmmakers were limited by several misguided conventions of the era. According to one, the camera was always fixed at a viewpoint corresponding to that of a spectator in a theater, a position now known as the long shot.(206) It was another convention that the position of the camera never changed in the middle of the scene. In last week's films we saw how Griffith ignored both these limiting conventions and brought the camera closer to the actor. This shot, now known as a full shot, was considered revolutionary at the time. For a Lump of Gold was the name of the film in which we saw the first use of the full shot. After progressing from the long shot to the full shot, the next logical step for Griffith was to bring in the camera still closer, in what is now called the close-up. (210) The close-up had been used before, though only rarely and merely as a visual stunt, as for example in Edwin S. Porter's The Great Train Robbery, which was made in 1903.(207) But not until 1908 in Griffith's movie called *After Many Years*, (208) was the dramatic potential of the close-up first exploited. In the scene from *After Many Years* that we are about to see, pay special attention to the close-up of Annie Lee's worried face as she awaits her husband's return. In 1908 this close-up shocked everyone in the Biograph Studio, but Griffith had no time for argument. He had another surprise even more radical to offer.

Immediately following the close-up of Annie, he inserted a picture of the object of her thoughts, her husband cast away on a desert isle. (209) This cutting from one scene to another without finishing either of them brought a torrent of criticism on the experimenter. (210)

206 What kind of motion picture camera shots were generally used in early films?
   (A) Close-up shots.
   (B) Full shots.
   (C) Long shots.
   (D) Action shots.

207 What occupation did Edwin S. Porter probably have?
   (A) Film producer.
   (B) Movie critic.
   (C) Stuntman.
   (D) Actor.

208 When was *After Many Years* produced?
   (A) 1898.
   (B) 1903.
   (C) 1905.
   (D) 1908.

209 Why was the close-up of Annie Lee followed by a shot of Annie's husband?
   (A) To shock Griffith's contemporaries.
   (B) To show who Annie Lee was thinking about.
   (C) To indicate when Annie Lee's husband would return.
   (D) To avoid criticism of the close-up shot.

210 Which of the following were innovations by Griffith? (Choose 2 answers.)

(A) Slow motion.
(B) Close-up.
(C) Cutting from one scene to another.
(D) Long shot.

> スクリプト和訳

　今日は19世紀終わり、20世紀初めの映画作りの初期について話したいと思います。D.W. グリフィスの先駆的な映画以前、映画製作者は幾つかの誤った慣例によって歯止めをかけられていました。ある慣例によると、カメラはいつも劇場の観客に対応する視点、今ではロングショットとして知られている位置に固定されていました。別の慣例では、場面の途中でカメラの位置を変えることは決して許されていませんでした。先週の映画で、私達は、グリフィスがこれらの慣習を無視し、カメラを俳優に近づけた手法を見ました。この今ではフルショットとして知られるショットは、当時は革命的だと考えられました。我々は『金塊を求めて』という名前の映画において、フルショットが最初に使われたところを見ました。ロングショットからフルショットへ進化した後、グリフィスにとって次の必然的一歩は、カメラをさらに引き寄せる、いわゆるクローズアップにすることでした。クローズアップは以前にも使われたことはありましたが、極まれにしかも単に視覚的に驚かせる手段として使われただけでした。例えば、1903年に作られたエドウィン・S・ポーターの『史上最大の列車強盗』中で使われたように。1908年、グリフィスの映画『時は流れて』の中で初めて、クローズアップの劇的な潜在力が引き出されたのです。我々がこれから見る『時は流れて』からの場面では、夫の帰りを待つアニー・リーの心配そうな顔のクローズアップに特に注意してください。1908年、このクローズアップはバイオグラフスタジオの全員を驚かせましたが、グリフィスには議論する時間がありませんでした。彼は、さらに過激な驚きを用意していたのです。アニーのクローズアップに引き続いて、彼は彼女の心の中にある絵、夫が無人島に漂流した場面を挿入しました。ある場面から別の場面へ、どちらも終わってもいないうちに移り変わるよう編集したことは、その実験者であるグリフィスに対する非難の渦を巻き起こしました。

重要単語

- **correspond to ～**：～に相当する、対応する
- **the next logical step**：次の必然的一歩
- **stunt**：あっと言わせる行為
- **exploit a potential**：潜在力を開発する
- **cast away**：漂流させる
- **desert isle**：無人島
- **cutting**：編集作業
- **a torrent of criticism**：非難の渦

解答 Questions 211 - 215

211 A　212 C　213 D　214 C　215 D

スクリプト／解答のポイント

　Now that you've listened to me talk about all the rewarding aspects of competitive swimming, I'd like to talk to you about some of the sacrifices necessary to become a dedicated swimmer. Competitive swimming is one of the most demanding of all sports. Since all of you today are interested in joining the swim team,(212) you might be wondering where your training here can lead. That's a good question, and not a very easy one to answer. There is a high attrition rate among competitive swimmers.(211) If we compare swimming to a sport like running, you will note that runners will often continue to train and compete in races after the age of thirty.(213) But most swimmers will stop competing after they graduate from college. There are probably two major reasons for this. The first is financial. Unlike runners, tennis players, or golfers, swimmers cannot make much money in their sport. (214) Swimmers compete for the pleasure and the glory of winning, not for the monetary rewards. The athletic scholarships that colleges award to the top swimmers are probably the culminating financial reward that swimmers receive for their swimming ability. The second reason for the high attrition rate is a physical one. Most top competitive swimmers undergo grueling workouts four hours a day, eleven months out of the year. Swimmers pay a heavy price in developing the physical and mental discipline necessary for swimming excellence. For most swimmers, this type of schedule is too demanding in terms of time, and too draining in terms of physical energy. (215) Competitive swimming needs to offer swimmers additional incentives, in order for them to continue beyond college, or to compete in a professional situation. So, knowing all this, if you are still enthusiastic about competitive swimming, I'd like to hand out this schedule of tryouts.

|211| What is the purpose of this talk?
 (A) To explain the high drop-out rate in the sport of competitive swimming.
 (B) To enlist support from parents for scholarship contributions.
 (C) To recruit swimmers from other sports.
 (D) To raise funds for a swimming competition.

|212| What group is the speaker addressing?
 (A) Parents of swimmers.
 (B) Tennis coaches.
 (C) Candidates for the swim team.
 (D) Competitive runners.

|213| The speaker compares competitive swimming with what sport, in terms of the athletes' age?
 (A) Golfing.
 (B) Tennis.
 (C) Football.
 (D) Running.

|214| What does the speaker say about competitive swimming?
 (A) It is a lifelong sport.
 (B) It may interfere with academic studies.
 (C) It does not offer many financial rewards.
 (D) It is less demanding than other sports.

215 **Why do most swimmers stop competing after college?**
(A) There's not much pleasure or glory in winning.
(B) Swimming can be very expensive - they have to pay a heavy price.
(C) There are not enough athletic scholarships these days.
(D) **They have to sacrifice most of their life for winning competition.**

スクリプト和訳

　これまで君たちは、競技水泳の良い側面について私の話を聞いてきましたが、これから水泳に賭ける競技者になるには避けられない犠牲について、いくつか話したいと思います。競技水泳は、すべてのスポーツの中でも最も厳しいものの一つに数えられます。今日ここにいる全員が水泳のチームに入会することに興味を持っているので、おそらくここでのあなたの練習がどこへ導いてくれるのか不思議に思っているでしょう。いい質問です。だが、その答えに答えることは、そんなに単純ではありません。競技水泳の選手は最も辞める率が高いです。仮に水泳を競走と比較しましょう。すぐに気が付くことは、競走選手が30歳を超えた後でも練習を続け競技に参加することはよくあるが、一方、水泳選手はそのほとんどが大学を卒業した後、試合に参加しなくなることです。おそらくこれには二つの大きな理由があります。まず、経済的な問題。競走、テニスそしてゴルフの選手と異なり、水泳選手は水泳でたくさん稼ぐことができません。水泳選手は喜びと勝利の栄光のために戦うのであり、お金のためではないのです。大学が一流の水泳選手に授与するスポーツ奨学金が、たぶん水泳選手が自らの水泳能力によってもらう、最高の報奨金でしょう。選手を辞める割合が高い理由の二つ目は、肉体的なものです。一流の水泳選手のほとんどが、とても厳しい練習を1日4時間、年間11か月行います。水泳選手は最高の泳ぎの為の身体的、精神的自制心を鍛えあげるために、非常にきつい犠牲を払わなければなりません。水泳選手のほぼ全員にとって、こうしたスケジュールは時間的に厳し過ぎ、体力的にもあまりに消耗させられるものです。競技水泳は選手が大学を卒業した後、またはプロという立場で試合を続けるために、さらなる動機となるものを彼らに与えなくてはなりません。以上、今話したすべてのことを理解し、もしまだ競技水泳に情熱を失っていないのならば、入団試験の日程表を渡しましょう。

重要単語

- **rewarding**：やる価値のある
- **competitive swimming**：競泳
- **dedicated**：献身的な、熱心な、ひたむきな
- **demanding**：要求の多い、骨の折れる
- **attrition rate**：減少率
- **athletic scholarship**：体育奨学金
- **culminating**：最高潮に達する
- **grueling workout**：厳しい練習、訓練
- **pay a heavy price**：大きな犠牲を払う
- **draining**：疲れさせる、使い尽くす

解答 Questions 216 - 220

216 A　217 C　218 A　219 D　220 B

スクリプト／解答のポイント

　One of the primary materials used in the construction of buildings and roads is cement, (216) a powder made primarily from limestone and clay. (220) Even though ancient Egyptians and Romans used a kind of cement, it was not until 1824 that an English bricklayer developed (217) a cement strong enough for modern roads and buildings. (218) While experimenting in his kitchen, the bricklayer found that a mixture of limestone and clay that had been heated together formed a hard stone-like chunk as it cooled. When this substance was ground into a fine powder, it could be stored indefinitely. (219)

　When the powder was mixed with water, it made an excellent quality of cement. It quickly hardened in sunlight or even under water. With only a few variations, this is how cement is made today.

216 What is the main topic of the talk?
(A) The development of cement.
(B) The uses for cement.

(C) Various construction materials.
(D) Cement-producing countries.

217 Who developed the kind of cement that is used today?
(A) An Egyptian.
(B) An ancient Roman.
(C) A bricklayer.
(D) An architect.

218 What was significant about the new kind of cement?
(A) It was very strong.
(B) It looked like stone.
(C) It resisted heat.
(D) It cooled quickly.

219 How was cement stored?
(A) As a water-based paste.
(B) As a liquid.
(C) In stone-sized blocks.
(D) In powdered form.

220 Which of the following best describes cement?
(A) Hard, solid stone mixture used for buildings and roads.
(B) A powder comprised mainly of clay and limestone.
(C) A watery, stone-lined chunk of material.
(D) A mixture heated and cooled and often used in kitchen floors.

| スクリプト和訳 |

　建物や道路の建築に使う主要な原料の一つに、石灰石や粘土から主に作られる粉末であるセメントがあります。古代のエジプト人やローマ人がある種のセメントを使っていたのですが、1824年に初めて、イギリスの煉瓦積み職人が、近代の道路や建物に使えるほど強いセメントを作り出しました。台所で実験をしながら、その煉瓦積み職人は、石灰石と粘土を混ぜて一緒に熱すれば、冷え

たときに堅い石のような固まりになることを発見しました。この物質を細かい粉にすると、無期限の貯蔵をすることが可能になったのです。

　その粉を水と混ぜたとき、素晴らしい品質のセメントになりました。日光に当たるとすぐに堅くなり、水中でさえ堅くなりました。ごくわずかな違いはありますが、このようにして今日のセメントは作られています。

重要単語
- **limestone**：石灰石、石灰岩
- **clay**：粘土
- **bricklayer**：煉瓦積み職人

解答 Questions 221 - 225

221 D　222 B　223 C　224 D　225 C

スクリプト／解答のポイント

　It's always a pleasure to show visitors the different parts of our newspaper operation. Please step this way. Here, you see our printing presses, (221) and you probably notice the smell of the printer's ink. This is where the paper is printed. Printing is a really messy process, because of the black, oil-based ink we use. You've read newspapers, and come away with the black ink all over your hands, and then probably gotten it on your clothes, or on the woodwork at home. That may change soon, with the use of a different type of ink. Several major daily newspapers are now trying out a new printing process called "flexography". (222) This process produces smear-free pages, that are remarkably clean, and do not smudge. (224) "Flexography" is often referred to as "flexo". Flexo presses use water-based inks that dry quickly, unlike the standard news press oil-based inks that take much longer to dry. (223)

　The new flexograph inking process is also simpler and faster than the standard method, but there is one major problem. The ink may dry too quickly, and thereby gum up the machines. (225) It may, literally, obstruct the presses, so that they won't work right. Or, it might cause them to break down altogether. If the machines clog too easily, the process will have to be changed and retested. There's a possibility our newspaper will convert to the flexograph process sometime in the future. In any case, our readers have already expressed a definite preference for the new smudgeless papers, and clean hands. I see we are running out of time and so I'd like to thank you for your interest in our printing operation. Goodbye.

221 Where does this talk take place?

(A) In a department store.
(B) In a mechanic's workshop.
(C) At a newsstand.
(D) In a newspaper pressroom.

222 What is the main topic of the talk?

(A) Recent developments in news photography.
(B) A new process to print newspaper.
(C) The advisability of frequent changes in dry-cleaning methods.
(D) Experimental printing with oil-based inks.

223 In what way is the "flexo" process considered better than standard printing?

(A) The newspapers remain thin and flexible.
(B) The presses can print larger sheets of paper.
(C) The ink is fast-drying and clean.
(D) The ink can be changed and retested.

224 According to the speaker, what advantage is there for people who read newspapers printed by flexography?

(A) Large print.
(B) Smooth pages.
(C) Pleasant smell.
(D) Clean hands.

225 **What is a possible negative point of "flexography"?**
(A) It can be quite expensive.
(B) It can only be used with special paper.
(C) **The ink may dry too rapidly.**
(D) They might have to change and retest the machines.

スクリプト和訳

　新聞作りのいろいろな行程を見学者にお見せすることができるのを、いつも嬉しく思っております。こちらへお進み下さい。ここに我々の印刷機があります。皆さんおそらくインクの匂いに気付かれたでしょう。ここで、新聞が印刷されます。印刷は、黒い油性のインクを使っているため非常に汚い作業です。皆さんも新聞を読んで黒インクが手の至るところにつき、それからおそらく服や家の木製品にもついた経験がおありでしょう。それも、違う種類のインクを使うことですぐに変わるかもしれません。数社の有名な日刊紙は今、フレキソ印刷という新しい印刷工程を試しています。この工程のおかげで、非常に鮮明で滲まず汚れないページを作ることが出来ます。フレキソ印刷は、よく「フレキソ」と呼ばれます。フレキソの印刷機には、乾くのに長時間かかる油性の新聞印刷用の標準インクと違って、早く乾く水性のインクを使います。

　新しいフレキソ印刷のインクを付ける工程もまた、標準的な方法より簡単で早いですが、大きな問題が一つあります。インクが早く乾きすぎて、機械の動きを悪くすることがあるのです。文字通り、印刷機を詰まらせてしまい、その結果正常に作動しなくなります。もしくは、完全に壊れてしまうこともあり得ます。もし機械があまりにも簡単に詰まってしまう場合は、その工程を変えて、再試験をする必要があります。我々の新聞は将来いつか、フレキソ工程に変わるかもしれません。とにかく、我々の読者は、すでに新しい滲まない新聞、つまりきれいな手のままでいられるほうが絶対に好ましいと仰っています。時間が無くなりつつありますね、我々の印刷工程に興味を示していただいたことを感謝致します。それではさようなら。

重要単語

- **oil-based**：油性の
- **flexography**：フレキソ印刷（ゴム版またはプラスチック版に顔料インクを使って印刷する方法）

- **smear**：汚れる
- **smudge**：滲む
- **water-based**：水性の
- **gum up**：動きを悪くする
- **obstruct**：塞ぐ、詰まらせる
- **clog**：詰まる

解答 Questions 226 - 230

226 B　227 D　228 B　229 C　230 A

スクリプト／解答のポイント

　Last week we were discussing the way weather conditions wear away rock. (227) At that time, in talking about how rainwater affects rock, we concentrated on what happens to the rock. Today we'll talk about what happens to the water. You know that rainwater usually alters rock and soil chemically as it filters into the ground. (226) This process results in ground water that contains dissolved ions and other materials from the plant and animal life on and in the soil. We use the terms "soft-water" and "hard-water" to indicate the extent to which water has minerals dissolved in it. Soft-water has few impurities or none at all. (230) Hard-water contains calcium plus certain other dissolved minerals. (228) Hard-water is normally drinkable but it may have a slight taste because of the various ions in the solution. When soap is added to hard water the minerals prevent lathery soap suds from forming. One place where hard ground water can be found is below the water table in a soil covered terrain with an underlying calcium base of limestone and shale. Rainwater dissolves materials as it filters down and these contribute to the ground water's taste and hardness. We can sometimes find ground water that is almost as soft as rainwater under a bare sandy hill or sand dune that is made of pure quartz sand. Analyses of such ground water show that it has about the same amount of carbon dioxide dissolved in it as rainwater does and little else. This is because quartz is so insoluble that for practical purposes it is inert and adds no dissolved substances to the water as it seeps into the ground. (229) Now in view of the geological make-up of our region, would you expect our ground water to be primarily hard or soft?

226 What is the main topic of the talk?
(A) How quartz sand is formed.
(B) How underground waters differ.
(C) How rain is formed.
(D) How water tables change over time.

227 What was discussed in class last week?
(A) The formation of sand dunes.
(B) The purification of water.
(C) The formation of limestone.
(D) The weathering of rocks.

228 What characteristic of hard-water does the speaker mention?
(A) It is undrinkable.
(B) It has minerals in it.
(C) It is slightly colored.
(D) It feels slightly oily.

229 What does the speaker say about quartz?
(A) It usually absorbs mineral impurities.
(B) It is rarely found in sand dunes.
(C) It does not dissolve in water.
(D) It wears away other rocks.

230 What characteristic of soft water does the speaker mention?
(A) It contains a few impurities.
(B) A lot of minerals are dissolved in it.
(C) It contains few impurities.
(D) It contains many dissolved ions and other materials.

スクリプト和訳

　先週は、天候状況がどのようにして岩石をすり減らすのか、議論いたしました。そのとき、雨水が岩石に与える影響がどのようなものかお話しするなかで、岩石に何が生じているのかについて集中的に論じたと思います。それで今日は、水がどのようになっているのか、お話しいたしましょう。お分かりのように、雨水が地面に浸透する際、ふつう雨水は岩石や土壌に化学的な変化を生じさせます。この過程により、地表上もしくは地中に生息している動植物から溶け出すイオンやその他の物質が地下水に含まれるのです。我々は水にどの程度のミネラルが溶け込んでいるかを示す為に「軟水」と「硬水」の用語を使います。軟水にはほとんど、または完全に不純物が含まれておりません。硬水にはカルシウムとその他の溶解したミネラル分が含まれています。普通の場合、硬水も飲むことは出来ますが、溶液中に含まれる様々なイオンにより、わずかに味がするかもしれません。石鹸を硬水に入れると、ミネラル分が石鹸の泡の泡立てを阻んでしまいます。硬水を見つけることのできる一つの場所は、カルシウムがベースとなっている石灰岩や頁岩（けつがん）を底に敷く、土に覆われた地形の中にある地下水の下部であります。雨水は地下へと浸透するにつれ、ミネラル分を溶解し、こうして溶解されたミネラル分がこの地下水の味や硬さの一因となっているのです。しかしときたま、純粋な石英を成分とする珪砂（けいさ）で構成される草木のない砂の丘や砂丘の下では、雨水とほとんど同じくらい軟らかい地下水に出会うこともあります。この種類の地下水を調べてみると、そこに溶解している二酸化炭素の量は、雨水に含まれるものとほぼ同じであり、それ以外のものは含まれていないことが分かります。この理由は、石英がかなりの不溶性を持ち、そのために事実上不活性であり、水が地下に浸透する際に溶解した物質が混ざることもないからです。それでは、我々の今いる場所の地質学的な構成要素を考えてみると、この地下水は主として硬いか軟らかいか、予想できるでしょうか。

重要単語

- **wear away**：すり減らす、摩滅させる
- **impurity**：不純物
- **lathery soap suds**：泡だらけの石鹸水
- **water table**：地下水面
- **terrain**：地形
- **limestone**：石灰岩
- **shale**：頁岩
- **sand dune**：砂丘

- **quartz**：石英
- **for practical purposes**：実際上は、事実上
- **insoluble**：不溶性の
- **inert**：不活性の、不活発な
- **in view of 〜**：〜を考えると、考慮すると

解答 Questions 231 - 235

231 A　232 A　233 C　234 A　235 C

スクリプト／解答のポイント

　　May I have your attention please? On our tour this morning, you just may be lucky enough to get a glimpse of some long necked white birds. If not, you may hear their loud trumpeting calls. Keep your eyes and ears open. The only natural wild flock of whooping cranes — about 76 birds in all (235) — arrives here every fall around this time. It's a 2,500 mile journey from their Canadian nesting region, (235) to where we are on the Texas coast of the Gulf of Mexico. (231) I said that this flock is the only natural one. Attempts to establish another flock are now being made by wildlife scientists in the U.S. and Canada. We're doing everything we can to prevent the small population of whooping cranes (233) from becoming still smaller. For some reason, although whooping cranes ordinarily lay two eggs every season, (232) they raise only one chick. Scientists have been collecting the extra eggs and placing them in the nests of other cranes. (234) The smaller, more common sand-hill cranes hatch the eggs and care for the young whooping cranes. We hope that the adopted whooping cranes, when they mature, will eventually mate with each other and establish second wild flocks with a different migratory route. The whooping cranes that come to this refuge are a rare sight. They are still on the endangered species list, but the chances that these birds will survive are getting better. If there aren't any questions, why don't we start out now? Please watch your step.

231. Where is the talk taking place?
    (A) In Texas.
    (B) In Idaho.
    (C) In Mexico.
    (D) In Canada.

232. What does the speaker say is true of whooping cranes?
    (A) They usually lay two eggs every season.
    (B) They seldom lay more than one egg every two years.
    (C) They have often been known to hide their eggs.
    (D) They have recently increased their rate of egg production.

233. Why has research on whooping cranes been done recently?
    (A) They protect smaller birds.
    (B) They will soon be exported to other countries.
    (C) They are in danger of dying out.
    (D) They have been laying extra eggs.

234. What have scientists done to help improve the survival rate of whooping cranes?
    (A) Placed their eggs in the care of other types of cranes.
    (B) Cross-bred the cranes with stronger varieties of birds.
    (C) Combined several small flocks into one large flock.
    (D) Encouraged the cranes to nest in warmer regions.

235. How many birds that the speaker mentioned arrive early and how long is their journey?
    (A) 760 birds; 25 miles.
    (B) 1,706 birds; 25,000 miles.
    (C) 76 birds; 2,500 miles.
    (D) 706 birds; 205 miles.

> スクリプト和訳

　ちょっとお耳を拝借します。今朝のツアーでは、皆様方は何羽かの首の長い白い鳥を見ることができるほどの幸運をお持ちかもしれません。もし見ることがかなわなくても、彼らの大きな鳴き声を耳にすることはできるのではないでしょうか。目を見開き耳をそばだてていてください。アメリカシロヅルの唯一の野生の群れが、およそ全部で76羽を伴って秋には毎年この時間帯にここにやってくるのです。巣を作るためのカナダの営巣地から、我々のいるメキシコ湾に面するテキサス州の沿岸地域まで2500マイルもの長旅です。先ほど私は、この群れは唯一の野生のものだと言いましたね。もう一つの群れを作ろうとする試みが、現在アメリカ合衆国とカナダの野生生物の研究者達の手により実施されております。私たちはできることのすべてを行い、今でも少ないアメリカシロヅルの生体数がさらに減少することのないようにしています。各季節にアメリカシロヅルは通常二つの卵を生みますが、しかし幾つかの理由により彼らは一つの卵しか孵しません。そこで研究者達はもう一つの卵を集め、他のツルの巣に移しているのです。比較的小型のよく知られているカナダヅルがこうした卵を孵化させ、幼いアメリカシロヅルの世話をするのです。このように養子に出されたアメリカシロヅル達が大きく成長したとき、それぞれがつがいとなって異なる移動経路を持つもう一つの野生の群れを作ることを望んでおります。この保護地帯にこの鳥が渡って来ることは珍しい光景です。彼らはまだ絶滅危惧種一覧表に記載されてしまっておりますが、この鳥が生き残る可能性はより高くなってきているのです。もし質問をされる方がおられないのなら今から出発いたします。足元に気を付けてくださいね。

> 重要単語

- **get a glimpse of ～**：～を一目見る、垣間見る
- **flock**：群れ、一群、一団、群衆
- **refuge**：避難所、鳥獣保護区域
- **endangered species**：絶滅危惧種

> 解答 Questions 236 - 240

236 B　237 C　238 D　239 D　240 A

> スクリプト／解答のポイント

　In yet another effort to find new sources of food,(236) to help alleviate world hunger, researchers are studying a species of South American palm tree.(237) Again, they considered these three main criteria for a new food source: the ease of producing the crop, its protein content, and its caloric density. So far, the palm tree seems to meet all three criteria. Its food products are easy to cultivate, harvest, and process. The oil of the tree's purplish-black fruit is remarkably similar in chemical composition to olive oil. And the fruit's biological protein value is equivalent to that of the best animal proteins. In addition, the milk produced from the fruit pulp is almost exactly the same as a human mother's milk(239) in terms of fat, protein, and carbohydrate composition. This high caloric density, along with its protein content and ease of cultivation, would make the palm an attractive addition to the food supply(238) in areas where grains are now the principle source of food. (240)

236 What is the main topic of this talk?
  (A) Hungry people of the world.
  (B) A good source of food.
  (C) New varieties of fruits.
  (D) The processing of food.

237 According to the speaker, what new food source are scientists studying now?
  (A) Olive oil.
  (B) Human mothers' milk.
  (C) A kind of palm tree.
  (D) A rare type of grain.

238 What is an essential quality of a good food source?
  (A) Attractive foliage and fruit.
  (B) The ability to yield oil.

(C) A similarity to mothers' milk.
(D) **A high caloric content.**

239 What can be inferred about a human mother's milk?
(A) Nothing equivalent to it occurs elsewhere in nature.
(B) It is relatively low in calories, but high in protein.
(C) Only babies can benefit from it.
(D) **It is considered a high-quality food.**

240 What areas would benefit most from the new tree?
(A) **Regions which grow products such as wheat and barley.**
(B) South America.
(C) Southern U.S.
(D) Regions which produce olive oil.

> スクリプト和訳

　世界の飢餓を軽減するための、新しい食糧源を見出すための努力として、研究者達は南アメリカ産のヤシの木の一種を研究しています。もう一度言いますが、彼らはこれら三つの主要な基準を、新しい食糧源に当てはめます。まず作物の生産の容易さ。次にタンパク質含有量。そしてカロリー密度です。今のところ、このヤシの木はこの三つの基準のすべてを満たしているように思えます。この木から作られる食料品は、簡単に栽培、収穫、加工をすることができます。この木の暗い紫色をした果実から抽出される油は、驚くほどオリーブ油の化学成分に近いのです。更に、この果実の生体タンパク質は、最高の動物性タンパク質と同じ価値を持ちます。加えると、この果肉から取り出せるミルクは、人間の母乳と脂肪、タンパク質、炭水化物の量がほとんど同じです。こうした高いカロリー密度は、そのタンパク質含有量や簡単に栽培できることと相まって、現在穀物が中心的な食糧源である地域の食糧供給に、このヤシを魅力的な供給源として加える原因となっております。

> 重要単語

- **alleviate**：軽減する、緩和する
- **criteria**：基準
- **biological value**：生物学的栄養価

- **be equivalent to ～**：～に相当する、～と同価値の
- **fruit pulp**：果肉
- **carbohydrate**：炭水化物、糖質

解答 Questions 241 - 245

241 C 242 C 243 D 244 B 245 B

スクリプト／解答のポイント

　The last time we met I told you about the problems we had in harvesting our farm's fruit. Now comes the shipping aspect of the business. A problem we had experienced in shipping our fruit to various markets is how to delay its ripening and spoiling.(244) Scientists are now testing a new product that may help us solve this problem. As you know, newly harvested fruit is alive, breathing, and producing heat. If we slow down the respiration, (241) and thereby reduce the fruit's oxygen intake, the fruit will ripen more slowly and less spoilage will occur. This new product is first mixed with water, and then the freshly picked fruit is dipped into the solution.(242) The tasteless nontoxic solution(243) then partially blocks the tiny openings in the fruit's skin. This blockage reduces the flow of oxygen in and out, and thus slows the ripening process. This means that as soon as the product is available on the market, we're going to be able to pick our fruit when it's nearly ripe and ship it to more distant markets.(245)

241 **What is the intended purpose of the new product?**
- (A) To stop air from drying out the fruit.
- (B) To keep the fruit's skin clean.
- **(C) To slow down the fruit's breathing.**
- (D) To prevent the fruit from being bruised.

242 **How is the new product applied?**
- (A) By spraying it on the trees.
- (B) By putting it into the soil.

（C）**By dipping the fruit into it.**
　　（D）By wrapping it around the fruit.

243 From the talk, what can be inferred about the use of the new product?
　　（A）It's difficult to apply.
　　（B）It's only for certain types of fruit.
　　（C）It won't be effective in warm climates.
　　（D）**It won't change the taste of the fruit.**

244 According to the talk, what often happens when fruit is shipped?
　　（A）It's badly damaged.
　　（B）**It ripens too quickly.**
　　（C）It acquires a new flavor.
　　（D）It turns an unusual color.

245 What is one of the benefits of the new process from a business point of view?
　　（A）It will decrease the number and length of delays in shipping.
　　（B）**It will allow the company to send the fruit to places farther away.**
　　（C）It will help to decrease the fruit's price on the commodities market.
　　（D）It will help scientists to focus on testing other products.

> スクリプト和訳

　最後に私たちが会合をした際、皆様に我々の農園の果物の収穫における問題についてお話しました。今回は、ビジネスをする際の輸送についての側面におけるものです。私たちの果物を様々な市場へと輸送する際に直面する問題の一つに、どのようにすると果物が熟し腐ってしまうことを遅らせることができるのか、があります。科学者は今、ある新しい製品の試験をしております。これが我々の問題解決に一役買ってくれるかもしれません。お分かりのように、新しく収穫された果物は生きており、呼吸をして熱を生み出します。もし、この呼吸作用を低下させ、それにより果物が吸収する酸素量を減らすことができるのならば、果物はよりゆっくりと熟し腐敗も少なくなるでしょう。まず、この新しい製品を水と混ぜ、その後新しく摘み取った果物をこの溶液に浸すのです。

そして、この味が無く無毒な溶液が、果物の表皮にある小さな穴を部分的に塞ぐのです。こうして塞ぐことが、酸素の流入、流出を抑え、熟する過程を遅らせます。このことは、この製品が市場に出回るとすぐに、我々が熟しかけている果物を収穫し、より遠くにある市場へと輸送できるようになることを意味しています。

重要単語

- **aspect**：側面、状況、見地
- **respiration**：呼吸
- **intake**：吸い込み、摂取量
- **spoilage**：駄目にする(なる)こと、損傷
- **available**：利用できる、使用できる、入手できる

解答 Questions 246 - 250

246 D 247 B 248 A 249 A 250 B

スクリプト／解答のポイント

Have you ever noticed that swallows and other insect eating birds generally fly quite high (246) in the air, but that they fly considerably lower just before a storm or other changes in the weather? Animals are, of course, more sensitive to changes in weather than humans, but why do you suppose they are affected in this way? I think that storms and other changes in the weather are often preceded by increases in the atmospheric pressure and/or the humidity. There is probably some effect directly on the birds themselves, but it's my theory that the effect is much greater on the insects that are their food supply. Increased atmospheric pressure and humidity make the insects fly more slowly and closer to the ground, (247) and the birds are forced to fly where their food supply is. (250) In clear fair weather, (248) the insects fly further from the ground, and therefore the insect eating birds fly higher. (249)

246 According to the speaker, where do insect eating birds usually fly?

(A) Above the clouds.
(B) Below the insects.
(C) Near the ground.
(D) **Quite high in the air.**

247 What does increased atmospheric pressure and humidity cause insects to do?
(A) Cease flying.
(B) **Fly lower.**
(C) Fly faster.
(D) Fly higher.

248 What weather conditions would cause swallows to fly the highest?
(A) **Dry and clear.**
(B) Cool and damp.
(C) Heavy rain.
(D) Fog.

249 What can be inferred from the speaker's comments about the flight of swallows in clear, fair weather?
(A) **They probably fly high in the air.**
(B) They probably fly in small groups.
(C) They probably fly quite slowly.
(D) They fly faster than other birds.

250 What can be inferred about the professor's explanation that insects are more affected by this phenomenon than the actual birds themselves?
(A) Increased atmospheric pressure and humidity make the insects fly more slowly and closer to the ground.
(B) **The insects are part of the birds' food supply and the birds are forced to fly at the same altitude as the insects.**
(C) In clear fair weather, the insects fly further from the ground.

(D) They fly considerably lower just before a storm or other changes in the weather.

> スクリプト和訳

　ツバメやその他の虫を食べる鳥が、普段はとても高い所を飛んでいますが、嵐やそれ以外の天候の変化が生じる直前には、とても低い所を飛んでいることにこれまでに気が付いたことはありますか？　動物は、当たり前ですが、天候の変化に対し人間よりも影響を受けやすいのです。しかし、どうして彼らはこのように影響を受けてしまうのでしょうか。私は嵐を始めとする天候の変化は、気圧が大きくなったり、湿気が多くなったりすることが生じてから起こると思います。おそらく、幾分の影響が鳥にも直接的にあるのでしょう。ですが私の考えでは、鳥のエサとなる昆虫類に対する影響の方がより大きいのです。気圧が大きくなったり、湿気が増えたりすることで、昆虫は飛ぶ速度を落とし、地面により近い所を飛ぶことを余儀なくされます。そして鳥も彼らの食糧がいる場所を飛ばなくてはならないのです。快晴のときは、地面から遠く離れた場所を昆虫は飛んでいます。だから虫を食べる鳥は高く飛ぶのです。

> 重要単語

- **precede**：先行する、先に起こる

解答 Questions 251 - 255

251 A　252 C　253 D　254 D　255 D

> スクリプト／解答のポイント

　Good morning everyone. Today, I'd like to discuss the demographic transition model.(251)　The demographic transition model was put forth by the American demographer Frank Notstein in 1945. Notstein based his model on the effect of economic and social development on population growth. This model classifies all societies into one of three stages. If you take a look at the board, you'll see that I've drawn the model in graph(252) form to help you understand it visually. During the first stage of the transition, both birth and death rates are high, and as a result of this, population grows slowly. Please note the line on the graph representing the first stage. In the second stage, living conditions improve because of such things as better public health measures and increased food production. With improved living conditions, the population grows more rapidly. (255) In the third stage, social and economic development reduces the people's desire to have large families. So, birthrates are low. Also in the third stage, the birthrate and the death rate are in equilibrium. Thus population in the third stage grows slowly, just as it does in the first stage, though for a different reason. (253) Now I think this is fairly straightforward as a model, but it doesn't account for everything, and it does have its critics. Part of the problem is that Notstein's model has relied heavily on western European experiences. (254) The model was useful for countries such as those in western Europe that experienced rapid industrialization. Unfortunately, the model cannot satisfactorily account for many other countries.

251 What does the speaker mainly discuss?
(A) **A theory of population growth.**
(B) The latest theory of social development.
(C) Results of global economic progress.
(D) The importance of demography.

252 What does the speaker use to help the students understand?
(A) A three-dimensional model.
(B) An illustration in the textbook.
(C) **A graph on the board.**
(D) A large cardboard poster.

253 According to the speaker, what do the first and third stages have in common?
(A) High death rates.
(B) Food production difficulties.
(C) Rapid economic development.

(D) Slow population growth.

254 What problem concerning Notstein's model does the speaker mention?

(A) Accurate statistics are lacking.
(B) The model is too complex to be applied in practice.
(C) It fails to account for wars and natural disasters.
(D) **It does not weigh equally the experiences of all countries.**

255 What does the professor mention about the second stage?

(A) Social and economic development reduces the people's desire to have large families.
(B) Both birth and death rates are high, and as a result of this, population grows slowly.
(C) The birthrate and the death rate are in equilibrium.
(D) **The population grows more rapidly because of improved living conditions through public health measures and increased food production.**

スクリプト和訳

みなさんおはようございます。本日は人口転換モデルについての議論を行いたいと思っております。人口転換モデルは、1945年アメリカの人口統計学者であるフランク・ノットシュタイン（Frank Notstein）によって提唱されました。ノットシュタインは、彼のモデルを人口成長における経済および社会発展に基づいて作りました。このモデルでは、すべての社会を三つの段階に分類します。黒板を見ると、皆様が視覚的に理解する助けとなるように、このモデルをグラフとして書いた図があります。最初の転換の段階では、出生率と死亡率の両方が共に高く、そのため人口がゆっくりと増加しています。この最初の段階を示すグラフ上の線に注目してください。二番目の段階では、より良い公衆衛生の対策や食糧供給の増加といった理由で、生活環境が改善していきます。生活環境の進歩に伴い、急速に人口も増加します。三番目の段階では、社会的、経済的な発展により、大きな家族を持ちたいという欲求が抑制されます。その結果、出生率は低い。同じくこの三番目の段階では、出生率と死亡率がつり合います。

そのため、この三番目の段階における人口の緩慢な増加は、一番初めの段階とちょうど同じですが、しかし理由は異なるのです。確かに、これは一つのモデルとして、非常に明快なものであると思います。しかし、これですべてを説明できるわけではなく、批判をする人もいます。ノットシュタインのモデルが持つ問題の一つは、西ヨーロッパ的な体験に過度に依存している点です。このモデルが有効なのは、西ヨーロッパのように急速な工業化を体験した国です。ですが残念なことに、このモデルでは他の多くの国々に関して十分な説明をすることができません。

> **重要単語**
> - **demographic transition**：人口転換
> - **in equilibrium**：つり合って
> - **put forth**：進める、提案する、提起する
> - **straightforward**：分かりやすい
> - **classify**：分類する、類別する
> - **public health measure**：公衆衛生の施策

解答 Questions 256 - 260

256 C　257 B　258 D　259 D　260 D

スクリプト／解答のポイント

　I thought jewelry might be an interesting topic to talk about today, since it has been a part of our culture throughout recorded history. People have always been interested in objects of adornment, whether they were simple stone charms or gem-encrusted tiaras. Jewelry was first worn because it was thought to hold some magical power, such as increasing the wearer's material or physical well-being.(256) It was believed to protect one from injury, and often served as a sign of office or of wealth. It was also used to adorn statues of the gods, and as a means of exchange. A man who had a great interest in the many aspects of jewelry was the railroad magnate, Henry Walters.(257) He collected hundreds of pieces of jewelry(258) during the late 19th and early 20th centuries. These objects of adornment spanned five thousand years of history, and represented much of the evolution of jewelry-making. Over two hundred of them were included in a traveling exhibit and displayed at museums in ten cities throughout the country. (260) Did anyone in this class happen to see the exhibit? (259)

256 Why did people first wear objects of adornment?
  (A) To keep themselves warm.
  (B) To become magicians.
  (C) To protect themselves.
  (D) To fasten their clothing.

257 Who was Henry Walters?
  (A) A medical doctor.
  (B) A railroad owner.
  (C) A history professor.
  (D) A clothing manufacturer.

258 What did Henry Walters collect?
  (A) Coins.
  (B) Magnets.
  (C) Badges.
  (D) Jewelry.

259 Where is this talk probably being given?
  (A) In a temple.
  (B) In a jewelry store.
  (C) In a bank.
  (D) In a classroom.

260 According to the professor, how many pieces of jewelry were involved in traveling exhibits, and in how many cities were they displayed at museums?
  (A) Less than 200 pieces in more than 10 cities.

（B） Around 200 pieces in approximately 10 cities.
（C） 200 pieces in 10 cities.
（D） **More than 200 pieces in 10 cities.**

> スクリプト和訳

　今日の話題として、宝石について話すのが面白いのではないかと考えておりました。なぜなら、宝石は私達の文化の一部として、有史以来ずっと存在しているからです。単純な石のお守りであれ、貴石のちりばめられたティアラであれ、人々はいつも装飾品について興味を持っております。宝石を身に着ける最初の理由は、宝石が何かしらの魔力を持っていると考えられていたからです。例えば、それを身に着けている人の物質的、身体的幸福が大きくなるといったようなものです。また、宝石は人を怪我から守ると信じられ、さらに要職についていることや、裕福であることのしるしとしても役立っていました。加えて、神々の像を飾るためや、交換手段としても利用されていました。宝石の持つ非常に多くの性質にとても興味を持ったのが、鉄道王のヘンリー・ウォルターズ（Henry Walters）という人物です。彼は19世紀の終わりから20世紀の初めの間に、数百という宝石を収集しました。これらの装飾品は5000年の歴史を跨ぎ、宝石制作の進化の多くの部分を提示していました。その中の200点以上が移動展示物の中に入れられ、この国を横断して10の町の博物館に展示されました。この教室の中で、偶然にも、この展示をご覧になった方はいらっしゃいますか？

> 重要単語

- **recorded history**：有史
- **material well-being**：物質的幸福
- **physical well-being**：肉体的健康
- **adornment**：装飾
- **statue**：彫像
- **charm**：お守り
- **magnate**：大立て者、業界の有力者
- **encrusted**：覆われた、びっしりついた
- **span**：〜に及ぶ、亘る、〜の橋渡しをする

> 解答 Questions 261 - 265

261 B　262 A　263 D　264 A　265 A

> スクリプト／解答のポイント

　As a follow-up to our discussion last week on the early political activists in this country, today I want to talk about a very interesting woman, Clara Barton, one of the most determined 19th century political activists in the United States. (261) She founded the American Red Cross, but, strangely enough, she was originally a school teacher and a writer, (262) not a hospital nurse like her famous contemporary, Florence Nightingale. During the Civil War, Clara Barton turned to nursing in order to help the thousands of wounded soldiers receiving little or no medical care in the understaffed army hospitals. She openly defied military authorities who did not allow female nurses on the battlefield, maintaining that wounded soldiers often died because of lack of food, clothing, or simple medication and bandages, not just from medical problems that required doctors' expertise. (265) Even though it was against orders, (263) she followed the troops and helped medical personnel with vital supplies that she gathered herself. She became a living legend, and the soldiers called her the "Angel of the Battlefield." After the war, she worked for the ratification by the United States of the Geneva Treaty, which officially established the International Red Cross. (264) She also served as the first president of the American Red Cross for over twenty years, and it was she who convinced that organization to extend relief efforts to victims of natural disasters as well as to victims of war. To this day, the activities of the American Red Cross are highly valued, both here and abroad. Therefore, our next class will be devoted to a discussion of the work done on behalf of victims of such disasters.

261　What is the main subject of the talk?
　(A) Nineteenth-century political activists.
　(B) The work of Clara Barton.
　(C) A comparison of Clara Barton and Florence Nightingale.
　(D) The ratification of the Geneva Treaty.

262　What was Clara Barton's original profession?

(A) School teacher.
(B) Hospital nurse.
(C) Military advisor.
(D) Zoologist.

263 How did military authorities react to Clara Barton's work on the battlefields?
(A) They recognized her medical expertise.
(B) They proclaimed her a heroine.
(C) They gave her administrative tasks.
(D) They opposed her presence there.

264 What does the speaker mean by referring to Clara Barton as a "living legend"?
(A) She became famous in her own lifetime.
(B) She lived according to her beliefs.
(C) She was a talented storyteller.
(D) She was a fictional character.

265 Why did Clara Barton feel that it was important for female nurses to serve on the battlefield regardless of their gender?
(A) Because the injured soldiers needed food, clothing and bandages to stay alive.
(B) Because nurses were vital to help maintain a positive morale in combat.
(C) Because that nurses provided a different perspective than regular doctors.
(D) Because that she was convinced they needed an organization to extend relief efforts.

スクリプト和訳

この国における初期の政治活動家を論じた先週の議論の補足として、今日はクララ・バートン (Clara Barton) という非常に面白い女性についてお話しし

たいです。彼女はアメリカ合衆国における19世紀の政治活動家の中で、最も意志の固い人物の１人に数えられるでしょう。彼女はアメリカ赤十字社を設立しましたが、奇妙なことに、彼女はもともと学校の教師と文筆家をしており、彼女と同時代を生きた有名なフローレンス・ナイチンゲール（Florence Nightingale）とは異なり、看護師ではなかったのです。南北戦争の際にクララ・バートンが看護師になったのは、人員不足の野戦病院ではほとんど、ときには全く医療を受けることのできなかった何千もの負傷兵を助けるためでした。彼女は怪我を負った兵隊は食糧、衣類、そして単純な薬物治療と処置を受けられないから、多くの場合死に至るのであって、医者の専門知識が必要な医学的の問題からではないと主張し、女性の看護師が戦場に来ることを許さなかった軍の権力者に明確に反抗しました。規則に反することではあったのですが、彼女は軍隊に付き従い、医療関係者を自前で集めた必需品によって助けました。彼女は生きる伝説となり、兵隊達は「戦場の天使」と彼女を呼びました。戦後、彼女はアメリカ合衆国がジュネーブ条約を批准するために働きました。この条約は公的に国際赤十字社の設立を行うものでした。彼女はまた、アメリカ赤十字社の初代会長として20年間も働き、まさに彼女こそが、この組織の救助活動の幅を戦争の被害者と同じく、自然災害の被害者までに広げるべきだと説得した人物でした。今日まで、アメリカ赤十字社の活動は国内外問わず高く評価されています。それではこうした災害による被害者のために行われた活動について、次の授業では論じることにしましょう。

重要単語

- **follow-up**：続行、追加、再調査
- **expertise**：専門知識
- **determined**：決然とした、意を決した
- **troop**：軍隊
- **contemporary**：同時期の人、同年齢の人
- **medical personnel**：医療団
- **defy**：無視する、ものともしない
- **ratification**：批准、承認
- **military authorities**：軍当局
- **relief effort**：救援活動
- **medication**：投薬、薬物、医薬品

解答 Questions 266 - 270

266 D　267 D　268 C　269 B　270 A

> スクリプト／解答のポイント

   About one-third (1/3) of the energy consumed in the United States is used inside buildings. Now that the age of cheap fuel has ended, many architects are becoming concerned because as much as half of that energy is being carelessly wasted.(266)(267) The most visible symbol of this waste is the glass-box office building. These buildings have many large windows that don't open. They must be constantly heated in the winter and cooled in the summer, even when outdoor temperatures are quite comfortable. These buildings were once considered artistic triumphs, but they are now recognized as ecological disasters. The glass-box type building can be built from low-cost materials, and, when fuel for energy was inexpensive, people wanted buildings that could be made as cheaply as possible.(270) They ignored the operating costs that would continue for the life of the building.

   Now the situation has been reversed. Higher-priced energy will encourage planning on the basis of what it will cost to operate a building over a period of 25 or 50 years. For instance, north-facing walls should be quite thick, with heavy insulation and dark coloring so as to conserve heat during the winter. (268) And heated air, which is often blown outside and wasted, can be stored in tanks under buildings. The same is true for cooled air in the summer. The waste of energy for lighting can also be cut. Though bright lights may be needed in specific working areas(269), lobbies and halls can have dimmer lights with plenty of switches so that lights can be turned off when they aren't needed. Use of elevators and escalators can be limited to certain hours or certain locations. Setting thermostats higher in summer and lower in winter can result in substantial savings. Many architects are quite positive about the future. They see past energy waste as a mistake that can be corrected with care and planning.

266 What is the speaker's main topic?

　　(A) How changes in architectural styles can make peoples' lives easier.
　　(B) What kinds of heating systems are least wasteful of energy.
　　(C) What homeowners can do to prevent energy waste.

(D) How energy used inside buildings can be cut down.

267 According to the speaker, what is true concerning the energy used in buildings?

(A) The sources of the energy used will disappear.
(B) The kinds of energy used can be changed.
(C) The cost of energy used must remain unchanged.
(D) The amount of energy used can be cut.

268 What energy-saving procedure does the speaker suggest for buildings in cool climates?

(A) Blow the cold air outside.
(B) Increase the amount of glass on the south side.
(C) Make the north-facing walls thick and dark.
(D) Use low-cost materials in their construction.

269 According to the speaker, where are the brightest lights needed in office buildings?

(A) In stairwells.
(B) In working areas.
(C) In elevators.
(D) In halls and lobbies.

270 According to the speaker, why were ecologically-inefficient architectural styles used in the past?

(A) The most important thing to focus on was cheap material to build.
(B) They ignored the operating costs for the life of the building.
(C) They wanted to use heat in the winter and cool air in the summer.
(D) The glass-box office building was so popular.

スクリプト和訳

アメリカ合衆国内で消費されているエネルギーの約3分の1は、建物の内部

で使用されています。安価な燃料の時代が終わった今、多くの建築家が興味を持っているのは、このエネルギーの半分が不注意に無駄に使われている事実です。最も明白にこうした無駄を象徴するシンボルが、ガラスの箱のようなオフィスビルです。そこにはたくさんの大きな窓がありますが、それは開きません。このような建物は、たとえ、外の気温がとても心地よいものであったとしても冬期にはずっと温め続けなくてはならず、夏期には冷やし続けなくてはなりません。こうした建物はかつて芸術上の偉業として考えられていましたが、今となっては環境的な惨事として認識されています。このガラスの箱のような建物は、コストの低い材料から作ることができ、エネルギーのための燃料が安価だったときには、できるだけ安く建設できる建物が人々から望まれました。彼らは維持費という、建物の生涯に渡って必要なものについて、考えていなかったのです。

　しかし、状況は反転しました。高コストのエネルギーは25年もしくは50年といった期間、建物を維持し続けるコストを元に設計を考えることを促すことでしょう。例えば、冬期に熱を保つために、北向きの壁は非常に分厚くし、そこに重層な断熱材と暗い色の塗装が必要です。温められた空気はよく外に吹き出され無駄遣いされていますが、建物の下のタンクに貯めておくことができるのです。同じことが、夏期における冷やされた空気について言えます。また、照明のためのエネルギーの無駄も無くすことができます。明るい照明は、ある特定の職場では必要になるでしょうが、ロビーやホールには薄暗い照明を置きます。そこにはたくさんのスイッチをつけ、不必要なときには消すことができるようにします。エレベーターやエスカレーターの使用を、ある特定の時間帯や場所に制限することもできるでしょう。夏にはサーモスタットの温度調節を高くし、冬には低くするようにすれば、相当な節約になります。多くの建築家は未来にとても前向きです。彼らは過去のエネルギーの無駄は慎重になり計画性を持つことで修正できる誤りであると考えています。

> **重要単語**
> - **Now that 〜**：〜した以上、今や〜したので
> - **triumph**：大勝利、大成功
> - **ecological disaster**：環境的な惨事
> - **on the basis of 〜**：〜に基づいて、〜の視点から
> - **north-facing**：北向きの
> - **insulation**：断熱材、防熱材、絶縁、防音

- **be true for ~**：~にもあてはまる
- **lobby**：ロビー、大廊下
- **hall**：玄関、廊下
- **dim**：薄暗い
- **thermostat**：温度自動調節器
- **substantial**：かなりの
- **be positive about ~**：~について積極的である、前向きである

解答 Questions 271 - 275

271 B　272 D　273 A　274 D　275 C

スクリプト／解答のポイント

　Good evening. Welcome to our regular Sunday night edition of Consumer Line. Tonight's program is for all you would-be campers(272) wondering how to buy the necessary equipment for outdoor vacationing. Here are a few tips to make your first trip a safe and enjoyable one. When it comes to camping gear, don't skimp on quality.(273) Buy the best equipment you can afford.(271) Not only does it feel lighter to carry and take up less room in your car, but the rewards in terms of comfort and convenience are immeasurable.(275) And, most important, good equipment will perform more reliably and safely for you in the long run. Topping your shopping list should be a nylon tent with an exterior frame. Once you've got a tent over your head, don't dismiss the importance of a well-insulated sleeping bag, also nylon, to keep you warm and dry, as well as a sleeping pad. Many novice campers forget about the sleeping pad, only to find that the sleeping bag alone doesn't cushion them against the rocks under the tent floor. Avoid air mattresses, they leak. No experienced camper would ever head for the trails without a well-stocked backpack. In your backpack, be sure to include anything you could possibly need in an emergency.(274) The final word tonight on safe camping is to pay attention to where you're going and observe the rules of the campgrounds. That's all for now. Next week's program, we'll show you how to set up a campsite. See you next time.

271 What is the purpose of the talk?

(A) To tell campers where to buy inexpensive equipment.
(B) **To discuss necessary camping supplies.**
(C) To tell campers about new products on the market.
(D) To warn campers about dangerous campsites.

272 What audience is the speaker addressing?

(A) Veteran campers.
(B) Sales representatives.
(C) Students in summer camp.
(D) **First-time campers.**

273 What comment does the speaker make regarding the price of equipment?

(A) **Quality is worth the extra cost.**
(B) A good bargain is easy to find.
(C) Money can't buy safety.
(D) Lighter equipment is generally cheaper.

274 What does the speaker imply that campers should have in their backpacks?

(A) A guide to campgrounds.
(B) A tent frame.
(C) A folding chair.
(D) **A first-aid kit.**

275 **According to the speaker, what are some of the features of the best equipment?**

(A) Cool, stylish, fashionable, trendy.
(B) Practical, rugged, strong, waterproof.
(C) Lightweight, comfortable, convenient.
(D) Colorful, good design, long-lasting.

スクリプト和訳

　こんばんは。日曜夜のレギュラー番組、「コンシューマー・ライン」にようこそ。今日のプログラムは、アウトドアで休日を過ごすために、どのように必要なものを買えばいいのか迷っている、キャンプにこれから挑戦する皆様のためのものとなります。初めての旅行が安全で充実したものとなるための、いくつかのヒントがありますよ。キャンプ一式を揃えようとするときには、質の面でお金を惜しんではいけませんよ。買うことのできる一番良いものを選ぶべきです。なぜなら、持ち運びをするときにより軽く、車の中で場所をとらないというだけでなく、快適さや便利さという観点からも、かけがいがないからです。そして最も重要なことは、良質の装備は長期的により高い信頼と安全性を達成します。買い物のリストの一番上に書くべきものは、外枠のついたナイロン製のテントです。そして頭の上にくるテントを手に入れた後、体を温め乾燥させるため、断熱性の良い寝袋とナイロンと敷布団の重要性を排除してはなりません。多くのキャンプ初心者は、マットレスについて忘れてしまって、寝袋だけではテントの下にある岩のクッションにはならないことに、気が付くばかりなのです。ただし、エア・マットレスは避けてください。空気がもれます。キャンプの経験がある人は、決してリュックの中身を十分備えず、山道へと進んで行かないです。リュックには緊急事態のとき必要となるであろうすべてのものを入れるように、注意してください。安全なキャンプのために最後に一言。あなたはどこへ向かっているのか、しっかりと意識してください。また、キャンプ場のルールを遵守するようにしてください。今日はこれでおしまいです。来週の番組では、どのようにキャンプを設営するのかお話しいたします。それではまた次回、お会いしましょう。

> 重要単語

- **edition**：版
- **would-be**：～になるつもりの、～志望の
- **tip**：ヒント、情報、助言、忠告
- **when it comes to ～**：～については、～の話になると
- **camping gear**：キャンプ用具
- **skimp on ～**：～を節約する、けちる、～の手を抜く
- **novice**：初心者、未熟者、新米
- **leak**：漏れる
- **head for ～**：～に向かう、～の方に進む

解答 Questions 276 - 280

276 C　277 B　278 A　279 A　280 B

スクリプト／解答のポイント

For the past few weeks, we have been discussing national energy conservation alternatives for the future. Today, I'm going to talk about <u>what one community is presently doing to conserve energy.</u>(276) The people of Davis, California have succeeded in cutting their energy consumption by one-third since 1973. <u>The first energy-saving action that was taken in the early 70s was the legislation of strict building codes.</u>(280) <u>All new houses in Davis must have the proper insulation, so that heat will not escape unnecessarily during the winter.</u>(277) New houses must also face north or south, <u>so that they will not be overheated by the sun in summer.</u>(278) The laws have had a definite effect. Since 1976, there has been a 50-percent saving in the amount of natural gas and electricity used in heating and air conditioning. There are other energy-saving features about Davis. Buses, partially supported by the city, transport university students throughout the area. There are 24 miles of bicycle paths, and today, <u>there are twice as many bicycles as cars in the city.</u>(279)

By reducing the available parking spaces, the city council has succeeded in reducing the number of cars in the city every day. Another benefit of the reduced parking is the greater number of small cars. People are saving gas because they are choosing not to drive, or because they are driving fuel-economic cars. Davis, California has become an energy-saving model for other cities. Time is up for today. Next week, we'll return to our regular topic of national energy alternatives.

276 What is the main topic of this lecture?
 (A) Bicycles and cars.
 (B) Building codes.
 (C) Energy conservation.
 (D) New housing construction.

277 Why is insulation required in new houses?
 (A) To limit discussion on heating bills.
 (B) To prevent heat loss.
 (C) To determine the temperature in homes.
 (D) To convert homes to electric heat.

278 What is the purpose of building new houses facing north or south?
 (A) To avoid direct sunlight.
 (B) To limit space used.
 (C) To keep out the cold.
 (D) To conform to other houses.

279 What has the city of Davis provided for bicycle riders?
 (A) Special paths.
 (B) Resurfaced highways.
 (C) More parking space.
 (D) Better street lighting.

280 What was the first energy-saving action taken by the city of Davis?
 (A) Banning large, inefficient automobiles.
 (B) Enacting more energy-conserving construction laws.
 (C) Utilizing more fuel-efficient public transportation.
 (D) Reducing the number of parking spaces.

> スクリプト和訳

　これまでの数週間、私たちは未来のために国の省エネルギーへの代替案について議論をしています。しかし今日私がお話しするのは、省エネルギーを現在行っている、とある地域についてです。カリフォルニア州のデイビスの住民は1973年以来、エネルギー消費量を3分の1節約することに成功しています。70年代前半に行われた最初の省エネ運動は、厳格な建築基準法の制定でした。デイビスに新しく建設される家には、例外なく適切な断熱材を入れなくてはならないというものです。それは冬の間、熱が無駄に逃げることのないようにするためです。また、新たに建設される家は、北向きか南向きでなくてはなりません。それは夏の間、熱くなりすぎないようにするためです。この法律は、目に見えて結果を出しています。1976年以来、天然ガスの消費量と暖房やエアコンで消費される電力を、50パーセントも節約しているのです。デイビスについては、その他にも省エネについての特徴があります。市から部分的な支援を受けているバスは、この地域中の大学生の交通手段です。また、自転車のための道路が24マイルあり、今日この市においては、車の2倍の数の自転車があります。市議会は、駐車できる場所を減らすことで、市内を毎日走る車の台数を減らすことにも成功しています。駐車場を減らすことのもう一つの利点は、小型車の数が多くなることです。人々は車を運転しないようにすることや、また燃費の良い車を運転することにより、ガソリンの節約をしています。カリフォルニア州デイビスはエネルギー節約の他州の為のモデルになりました。今日はここまでにしましょう。来週は、いつものトピックである、国の省エネルギーの代替案に戻ります。

> 重要単語

- **alternative**：代替案、選択肢、別の手段
- **legislation**：律法行為、法律制定
- **building code**：建築基準法、建築規制条例
- **city council**：市議会

解答 Questions 281 - 285

281 C　282 A　283 C　284 B　285 C

> スクリプト／解答のポイント

　　Today, it's my turn to give the weekly oral report, (281) and the topic that Professor May has assigned me is the life of the poet Emily Dickinson. (282) Compared to Walt Whitman, whom we discussed last week, I found Emily Dickinson strikingly different. She seems, in fact, to be the complete opposite of Whitman in her life and in her work. I would like to share briefly with the class some of the essential facts of her biography. Emily Dickinson was born in 1830, in Amherst, Massachusetts, barely a decade after Whitman. In her early 20s, for reasons which still remain a mystery, she began to withdraw from ordinary contact with the world. (285) For the remaining 30 years of her life, she was seldom seen outside her home. In this respect, she was quite unlike Whitman, who loved the great outdoors. Emily Dickinson spent her solitary days corresponding with friends, and writing hundreds of remarkable poems, notably, "I Heard a Fly Buzz", and the poem we read for today, "I'm Nobody". Although she showed some of her poems to her family and sent some in letters to friends, only four were published in her lifetime. Most of them, almost 1,200 poems, were discovered in her room after she died in 1886 at the age of 56. (283) These poems established her as a major poet, and several modern critics consider her the greatest woman poet in the English language. Uh, that's about all I have. Are there any questions? If not, we should probably begin talking about Dickinson's "I'm Nobody", the poem Professor May assigned for this week's class discussion. (284)

281 **Who is the speaker?**
　(A) A poet.
　(B) A teacher.
　(C) A student.
　(D) An artist.

282 **What is the main topic?**
　(A) The life of Emily Dickinson.
　(B) The poetry of Walt Whitman.

(C) The poem "I Heard a Fly Buzz."
(D) The poem "I'm Nobody."

283 Approximately how old was Emily Dickinson when she died?

(A) In her twenties.
(B) In her thirties.
(C) In her fifties.
(D) In her eighties.

284 What will the class do now?

(A) Hear another report.
(B) Discuss one of Emily Dickinson's poems.
(C) Hear a lecture by the teacher.
(D) Discuss poems they have written themselves.

285 What happened to Emily Dickinson starting in her 20s?

(A) She began to write her most famous poetry.
(B) She began to write many mystery poems.
(C) She became a very unsociable isolated person.
(D) She began to love the great outdoors.

> スクリプト和訳

　本日は、毎週行われる口頭発表の私の順番です。トピックは私にメイ先生が渡した課題で、エミリ・ディキンソン（Emily Dickinson）という詩人の生涯についてです。先週議論をしたウォルト・ホイットマン（Walt Whitman）と比較すると、エミリ・ディキンソンは全く異なる人物だと思いました。実際、生き方と作品において、彼女はホイットマンと全く正反対の人のように見えるのです。彼女の伝記で本質的な事実について、みなさんと簡単にお話ししたいと思います。エミリ・ディキンソンは、マサチューセッツ州アマーストで1830年に生まれました。ホイットマンの生まれた年から、ほぼ10年後です。20代のとき、理由はいまだわかっておりませんが、彼女は世界との日常的な接触から身を引いてしまいます。残りの人生の30年間、家の外で彼女を見かけられることはほとんどなかったのです。この点で、彼女はすばらしい野外を好んだホイッ

トマンと完全に異なります。エミリ・ディキンソンは友達との文通や数百もの素晴らしい詩を書くことで、一人の時間を過ごしていました。例えば彼女の有名な詩は、"I Heard a Fly Buzz" や今日のためにわたしたちが読んできた "I'm Nobody" という詩です。確かに彼女は自分が書いた詩のいくつかを家族に見せたり、友人に送る手紙に同封したりしていましたが、彼女が生きている間たった4本しか出版されなかったのです。彼女の書いた詩のほとんどすべては、1200本に及びますが、1886年に56歳でこの世を去った後に彼女の部屋で発見されました。これらの詩が、彼女のメジャーな詩人としての地位を築きました。英語圏における最も偉大な女性詩人だと、彼女を評価する批評家もいます。これが調べてきたすべてです。質問はありますか。もし無いのなら、メイ先生が今週の授業の議論の課題に出したディキンソンの "I'm Nobody" についての議論に取り掛かりましょう。

重要単語

- **the opposite of 〜**：〜の反対
- **biography**：伝記、経歴、略歴
- **great outdoors**：野外、大自然
- **solitary**：孤独な、ひとりぼっちの

解答 Questions 286 - 290

286 C　287 D　288 C　289 C　290 D

スクリプト／解答のポイント

I'd like to tell you about a series of lectures that are going to be presented on campus. Guest lecturers will speak on the political changes sweeping across Europe.(286) The lecturers are professors at universities in the countries where those changes are taking place.(289) Their views are current, and their presentations are sure to be fascinating. (287) Political science majors are required to attend all the lectures,(290) but I highly recommend them to anyone with the slightest interest in international politics.(288)

286 **What will be the subject of the lectures to be presented on campus?**

(A) Police departments.
(B) European universities.
(C) **Political changes in Europe.**
(D) A new system of economics.

287 What is the purpose of the lectures?

(A) To raise money for a new political movement.
(B) To explain why change occurs slowly in Europe.
(C) To increase aid to needy nations.
(D) **To explain what is currently happening in Europe.**

288 Why does the man recommend the lectures?

(A) Because they are required for all majors.
(B) Because they were very expensive to fund.
(C) **Because they are a good opportunity to get the most recent information.**
(D) Because all of the lecturers are famous.

289 Why should the lectures be interesting?

(A) Because they are sweeping across Europe.
(B) Because the speakers are all well-known.
(C) **Because the speakers are all experts in their field.**
(D) Because the man highly recommends them.

290 Who is required to go to all of the lectures?

(A) Science majors.
(B) Physical Science majors.
(C) International Politics majors.
(D) **Political Science majors.**

スクリプト和訳

皆さんに、学内で行われる予定の連続講義についてお話ししたいと思います。ゲスト講師陣は、ヨーロッパ中を激しく吹き荒れている政治上の変化について

話します。講師陣は、このような変化が実際に起こっている国々の大学教授たちです。彼らの意見は最新のものであり、その発表はきっと興味をそそるものでしょう。政治学を専攻する人は、これらすべての講義に出席する必要がありますが、私は国際政治に少しでも興味のある人であれば誰でも講義にでることをお勧めします。

重要単語

- **sweep across 〜**：〜中を激しく吹き荒れる
- **political science major**：政治学を専攻する人

解答 Questions 291 - 295

291 B　292 D　293 A　294 B　295 A

スクリプト／解答のポイント

Not until relatively recently have courses, such as this survey of American Art History, included Folk Art. Since the 1930s, however, there has been increasing interest in the beauty and historic significance of such art. Today we will consider a form of Folk Sculpture, the figureheads carved for American ships. Figureheads are certainly not unique to America. From the earliest times, people have decorated the front of boats with human or animal figures. Throughout the colonial period, American figureheads closely followed English models.(295)　Soon after the American revolution,(291) however, a national style began to emerge. And, by the mid-19th Century, American figureheads were unique in their elaborate variety.

Different types of sailing ships had different types of figureheads.(292) The practical whaler, a boat used for hunting whales, often had a simple, brightly-colored portrait of the Captain's wife or daughter.(293) The swift and elegant Clipper Ships had more elaborate figures, often painted in white and gold. The figureheads on military ships generally portrayed national heroes. When steamships replaced sailing ships in the 1870s and 1880s, the age of the figurehead was over,(294) and the carvers turned to making trade signs, and fanciful circus wagons.

291. When did American figureheads start to have a distinct national style?
 (A) In the Colonial period.
 (B) Soon after the American Revolution.
 (C) Around 1880.
 (D) Around 1930.

292. According to the speaker, what determined the type of figurehead used on a ship?
 (A) The kind of wood it was carved from.
 (B) The kinds of models the carver used.
 (C) The kinds of tools that were available.
 (D) The kind of ship it was made for.

293. What did the figurehead on a whaling boat most often portray?
 (A) A woman.
 (B) An animal.
 (C) A national hero.
 (D) A captain.

294. What caused the disappearance of figureheads?
 (A) The deaths of the leading carvers.
 (B) Changes in the types of ships used.
 (C) Lack of interest in folk art.
 (D) The decline of the whaling industry.

295. Which models did American figureheads originally follow?
 (A) British models.
 (B) American Revolution models.
 (C) Folk Sculpture models.
 (D) Folk Art models.

スクリプト和訳

　比較的最近になって、アメリカ美術史調査のようなコースが民芸品を含むようになりました。しかしながら、1930年代以降、このような芸術の持つ美しさや歴史的な価値について、関心がますます高くなってきています。本日、私たちが考察するのは、民芸彫刻の様式で、船首につけられる木彫りの彫刻、フィギュアヘッドについてです。フィギュアヘッドは決してアメリカ固有のものではありません。昔から、人々は船の先頭部を人間や動物の像で飾っています。植民地時代を通して、アメリカのフィギュアヘッドは、イギリスのモデルにとても沿ったものでした。しかしアメリカ独立戦争が終わるとすぐに、この国独自のスタイルが開花し始めます。そして19世紀の半ばに至るまでには、アメリカのフィギュアヘッドは手の込んだ様々なスタイルで、他に類を見ないものになりました。

　それぞれの異なる帆船にあわせて異なるフィギュアヘッドがあったのです。クジラ漁に使われる実用の捕鯨船は、単純でありますが美しい色に塗られた船長の妻や娘の肖像を飾っていました。速度の速い豪華なクリッパーは、もっと手の込んだ像で飾り付けられており、白と金で着色されていることがよくありました。軍用船のフィギュアヘッドには、だいたい国民的な英雄の肖像が彫られていました。しかし、1870年代と1880年代にかけて蒸気船が帆船に取って代わると、フィギュアヘッドの時代は終わりました。その職人たちは看板を作ったり、おしゃれなサーカスの荷馬車を作ったりするようになったのです。

重要単語

- **figurehead**：船首像
- **elaborate**：複雑な
- **carver**：彫刻家

解答 Questions 296 - 300

296 B　297 A　298 C　299 B　300 D

スクリプト／解答のポイント

　Today, let's turn to the economic turmoil that gripped the United States in the early to mid 1980s. (296) One of the harsh realities of the economic policies (297) of those years was the closing of factories, or the severe cutback in their operations. The mass layoffs caused a huge increase in unemployment. Many of these newly unemployed people were dedicated workers who had job skills, but no place to use them. (298) In total, about 10.8 million American workers lost their jobs during this period. Nearly half of them, about 5.1 million, had at least three years of experience at their jobs. The problems faced by these displaced workers have been the subject of several studies. Almost all of the workers continued to look for new jobs, but fewer than half were able to find a new job within two years of their layoff. (300) And many of those who found new jobs had to settle for part-time jobs, or jobs that paid a substantially lower wage than they had received in their earlier job. Two out of three of the displaced workers were men, (299) and the hardest-hit region was the North Central states.

296 What period of time is discussed in the lecture?
(A) 1970-1980.
(B) 1980-1985.
(C) 1985-1990.
(D) 1985-the present.

297 How does the speaker describe the economic conditions of that period?
(A) They were dreary.
(B) They were mixed.
(C) They were upbeat.
(D) They were hopeful.

298 According to the speaker, what caused the rise in unemployment?
(A) The lack of dedication among workers.
(B) The workers' desire to move to other regions.
(C) The closing of work places.
(D) The increase in the population.

299 **What can be said about the majority of the displaced workers?**
(A) They soon went on to other jobs.
(B) **They were male.**
(C) They had a great deal of working experience.
(D) They lived in the North Central states.

300 **When they looked for new jobs, how many workers found a new job and in how long of a time period did it take them to do so?**
(A) More than half found a new job within two years.
(B) A few more than half found a job after two years.
(C) About half found a job in under two years.
(D) **Less than half found a job in two years or less.**

スクリプト和訳

　本日は、1980年代前半から半ばまでにアメリカ合衆国を襲った経済危機に目を向けましょう。これらの年代に実行された経済政策の最も厳しい現実の一つに、工場の閉鎖や工場の稼働率の縮小があります。莫大な一時解雇により、失業率が大きく跳ね上がったのです。新たに解雇となった多くの人々が、仕事の技術はあるがそれを活かす場のない、熱心な労働者でした。全体で、およそ1080万人ものアメリカ人労働者がこの時期に失業しました。その中の約半数に至る510万人の人は少なくとも3年以上の職務経験を持つ人たちでした。こうした働く場所を失った労働者が直面した問題は、いくつかの研究の主題となっています。ほとんどの労働者は、新しい仕事を探し続けていましたが、一時解雇の後の2年の内に新しい仕事に在りつける人は半数にも満たなかったのです。仕事を見つけることのできた人の多くも、パートタイムや、以前の仕事で得ていた給料に比べると相当低い賃金しかもらえない仕事で我慢をしていました。職業を失った労働者の3分の2が男性で、最も厳しい打撃を受けた地域が中北部の州でした。

重要単語

- **economic turmoil**：経済混乱
- **mass layoff**：大量解雇
- **displaced worker**：離職者
- **settle for ～**：～に甘んじる
- **hardest-hit region**：一番被害を受けた地域

TOEFL® TEST
模擬試験＆
「レクチャー問題」
リスニング徹底練習
300問

別冊解答集